Counseling for the Growing Years: 65 and Over

Edited by

Charles J. Pulvino
University of Wisconsin-Madison

Nicholas Colangelo
University of Iowa

i

Copyright ©1980

EDUCATIONAL MEDIA CORPORATION
P.O. Box 21311
Minneapolis, Minnesota 55421

Library of Congress Catalog Card No. 80-65516

ISBN 0-932976-06-0

Production editor—

Don L. Sorenson

Graphic design—

Earl Sorenson

jwe

ii

3-15-84

DEDICATION

For both of us this book has special significance because of our love for the following family members:

Lena E. Pulvino
who began growing on November 22, 1910.

John Colangelo
who began growing on October 24, 1904.

Effie Johnson Ogburn
who began growing on August 12, 1892.

Grazia Contella Squillante
who began growing on May 12, 1890.

Anna Molisani
who began growing on August 31, 1894.

CJP
NC

Preface

The man in this photograph is involved in the process of living. He is thinking about what must be done. He is needed. The picture does not show several young people waiting for his instructions. He knows what needs to be done next on a brick patio they are building. It is incidental that this man is 76 years of age—it is fundamental that he is vibrantly using his knowledge and skills. Perhaps this photograph best captures the spirit of this book—that older persons are actively involved in growing. Also, they have much to share with others who have not been growing as long. This is not a book about stability—but about growth.

Photograph of John Colangelo taken by Kay Colangelo.

TABLE OF CONTENTS

Acknowledgments

We wish to thank individuals that have contributed to this book. Each has added a dimension to the final product that demonstrates sensitivity to the elderly. Practicing counselors should benefit from their efforts.

We also wish to thank our publisher, Don Sorenson, for his enthusiastic support.

Special thanks to our secretaries, Ruth Lytton, Reta Litton, and Ginny Volk for their work on this manuscript.

Guest Foreword

I shall always remember the first time I was called a senior citizen. At age 63 I was flying home from a speaking engagement and had just got belted in and my newspaper open when a spry young man sat down beside me. "Hello," he said, "This is just great. I've wanted to have a talk with a senior citizen." "Me! A senior citizen?" Then the thought, "Yes you, and you'd better start thinking about what that means and what it implies."

After I'd had some time to think about such matters, I began to realize that the classification of senior citizen meant that I, like others so classified, would need to give careful consideration to five main aspects of the final developmental process, so I made up the word *FAIDS* to remind me of them. (*FAIDS* can also be thought of as fades since, whether we acknowledge it or not, a fading process has been in operation.)

The first letters of the words indicate in turn the need to establish *f*inancial security for self and family; *a*daptability to a regime which is not likely to include a full-time job; *i*nevitability (of death) within a relatively short period; acceptance of *d*ispensibility (no one is ever indispensable); and of course, the likelihood of some *s*ickness as the physical machine starts to wear out. These *FAIDS* seem to summarize the most common areas of concern for those who reach senior citizen status. Long before I received the request to write this foreword, I wondered how counselors could help in their solution or mitigation. The contributors to this volume present many suggestions, but some of my own reactions follow.

Financial matters must concern all senior citizens regardless of their monetary status when they retire from regular employment. Savings, pensions, and social security benefits, which seemed adequate, are deflated by inflation. Substitute sources of support are hard to come by despite the efforts to eliminate discrimination by employers on the basis of age. Such conditions can lead to deep feelings of despair that are difficult to appreciate by counselors who get, and can anticipate getting, a regular and adequate monthly income.

Few counselors will be capable of giving sound information about expenditures, investments, savings, wills, and other financial arrangements and they must defer to specialists in such matters. They may, however, be helpful in referring their elderly counselees to dependable sources, in avoiding pitfalls caused by those who would exploit them, in developing budgets that make sense, in applying to proper authorities for assistance when it is needed, in avoiding waste, and in consideration of life-long habits of saving for a rainy day which they may never live to see.

Despite the fact that monetary matters raise serious problems for many of the elderly, the literature contains little unbiased (the junk mail one gets as a senior citizen seems *so* biased) information about the ways in which they can best manage their financial affairs. Until such information is made available, counselors will have to supplement their counseling based upon the common sense they have developed in attending to their own financial arrangements by referring their counselees to dependable sources.

Although some of the twenty-two million senior citizens choose to continue in employment, most do not. For those who don't, the selection of activities from the countless numbers available may be a difficult task in which counselors can be truly helpful. The offerings of senior citizen centers are impressive in their quantity and variety and for some of the elderly they are sufficient. Many, however, want to choose their own pastimes. Some want to carry on variations of their previous work such as the accountant who volunteers income tax assistance. Others want to try something new such as my own attempts to make the desert bloom with cacti (a non-profit but finger sticking enterprise) after fifty years of non-agricultural educational activities. Still others will choose purely physical pastimes such as golf every day ("Is golf purely physical?" some duffer asks), while others select more mentally demanding tasks. And some mey eschew any routines and enjoy what they call "goofing off."

The non-judgmental counselor will, of course, avoid any condemnation of that choice. It is in the consideration with the counselee of the choice from among the many activities open to senior citizens that the counselor may be most helpful. In doing so, the counselor will be aware that what is one person's meat may be another's poison. The contributors to this volume present many suggestions for the counselor who will help in decision-making in the activity area.

The acceptance of dispensability will need much counselor attention. The change from full-time employment to retiree may seem, because it is usually abrupt, more of a break than just one natural aspect of development. For some of the elderly, it is so hard to take counseling that is badly needed. I meet many who just can't believe that the large industrial organization, the local machine tool company, the church, university, accounting firm or, the family farm can carry on without them. In such disbelief, they cannot enjoy the freedom from responsibility that retirement brings. If counselors can help such persons to recognize that there has always been someone who can take the place of those who have gone before, they may resolve a serious problem. Some of the elderly do recognize their dispensability and counselors may reinforce that recognition. Some may choose to work well beyond usual retirement years. Counselors who sense the importance of work to those persons can give them needed support. All work and little play can be, for some, an excellent senior citizen diet.

Much (I want to say) drivel has been written about the need for empathy between counselor and counselee. Most of that writing has implied that a high level of empathy can be established between persons of vastly different ages. Those who believe that can be done are deluding themselves. Carl Rogers, at an advanced age, suggests that he can develop empathy with (always highly vocal) teen-agers and young adults of both sexes. Middle-aged counselors think they can empathize with elementary and secondary school students.

There is something to be said for such claims, but development of real empathy with the elderly who are faced with the certainty of death within a relatively short period (relatively short when compared with a whole life span) verges on the impossible.

Empathy is essential when options are to be considered, but in this matter of finality there are no options. Perhaps with the realization that young to middle-age counselors cannot really know what it feels like to meet a situation where there are no options, and therefore cannot fully empathize with the elderly, there will be a more sensible approach to the matter of empathy than has been apparent so far in the counseling movement. The literature will not, hopefully, be cluttered with the preposterous statements expounded and exploited by those who write and talk about the processes of empathy, but are strangely silent when asked about evidence of its effectiveness. Certainly, good counselors of the elderly will try to be empathic, but they will never recognize the limitations imposed by the counselees' awareness of the inevitable, final outcome of advanced age.

Health records indicate that the elderly suffer more sickness than the young since many years of living take their toll. Few senior citizens can avoid illness, reduction of physical and sexual vitality and the resultant fears, concerns, and worries that such conditions bring. When such problems arise, counselors must defer to specialists in medicine for diagnoses and treatment. When medical experts have finished their job (or concurrently and in cooperation with the doctors), counselors can help their counselees with knowledge that physical factors, in the last analysis, are embedded in the total life of a person and that the particular motivation pattern of the individual is the principal factor.

Persons usually respond to their health difficulties in ways consistent with their prevailing modes of adjustment. Their health cannot be considered apart from their motivational structures. A health problem for one person may provide an alibi while for another it presents a challenge. A physical condition is so deeply embedded in the total person that its significance may not always be obvious, but good counselors of the elderly will search thoroughly for it. Then they will do what they can to help their counselees compensate for physical conditions that cannot be remedied, or assist them in the mitigation of their disturbing effects. The counselor who is not a specialist in medicine and fully acknowledges that fact can still be a potent force in health matters which are of such vital importance to senior citizens.

There has been in the past an unfortunate tendency for counselors to delve into fields such as clinical psychology and even psychiatry for which they are not prepared. They will be tempted to go too far into physical and medical domains when they see that illness is a major area of concern for senior citizens, and that those concerns are not always alleviated. The temptation must be steadfastly rejected.

The authors of this book discuss at greater length many more of the challenges that counselors of the elderly will meet but the five noted above seem most demanding to this writer who is now a senior citizen but was a counselor. They will also discuss some of the matters considered in the following paragraphs, but I need to express my thoughts on some of them.

The tools of the trade, what shall they be? It is hoped that counselors of senior citizens will find, while working in this relatively new field, a chance to move away from such ridiculous instruments as interest and values inventories, absurd personality tests and silly rating scales. No doubt as the field becomes more popular, some persons will develop such instruments for use with the elderly and hucksters will promote them at conventions and workshops. Certainly there will be articles about them that purport to report experiments, but will actually be advertisements. Surely counselors must now realize how ineffective such instruments have been in counseling and will relegate the new ones to use as fuel for the faculty picnic. Hopefully, they will realize that most of their counselees (I hope they won't call them clients as prostitutes and other sales persons do) have had enough experience with various forms and questionnaires to have doubts about their validity.

The most effective tool in counseling the elderly, as it has been with others, will be the interview in which counselees can tell what is significant to them in their own words and in the length and detail of their own view of the limitations noted above. The counselor will listen and, not stopping there, will assist in making choices that may be satisfying and productive.

None of the problems of the final developmental stages of life will be completely new to the individual since each is a common part of a process that began in early infancy. There is, however, a marked tendency to think that a person *is* of a certain fixed nature, and that each individual *has* permanent characteristics. (This tendency is too often reinforced by measurement enthusiasts and too many career counselors who are still trying to plug square pegs into square holes.) This way of thinking ignores the fact that change is characteristic of a healthy human being.

The reaching of senior citizen status is just one more aspect of a developmental process. There seems to be little hope that counselors can be effective if they don't recognize that they are dealing with moving pictures rather than snapshots. Maybe as counselors enter into this relatively new field of gerontological counseling (new to them but "counseling" of the elderly has been done from time immemorial), we will see the longitudinal approach come into the counseling field as it has seldom done in the past.

Perhaps the study of this volume will encourage readers to do something that counselors have seldom done in the past. Maybe, and I say maybe because I'm not very sanguine about it happening in view of the past record, counselors of the elderly will state their objectives in terms that permit evaluation and then evaluate their work in terms of those stated objectives. Despite the efforts of a few of us to get counselors to evaluate their work, and the examples some of us have provided in our follow-up studies, most do not do so. Counseling has been offered for many decades on the bases of boldness and faith — boldness in undertaking such a difficult task as counseling a complex person and faith that doing so will produce worthwhile results.

Discussions of counseling usually concentrate only on practices. If by chance the matter of follow-up evaluation is given any consideration, it is commonly of the "quickie" (two weeks after counseling I felt better) variety. The short -term evaluation reports imply that counseling can be productive, but if counselors work only for the immediate future that fact should be announced to counselees and to the public. The length of time for follow-up has been difficult to determine for young subjects. In counseling the elderly there is an inevitable end that can define the evaluation period. In light of the failure to evaluate counseling over the last six decades, one cannot be optimistic about it happening now. One can only hope.

Even at this early stage of emphasis on gerontological counseling, the usual periphrastic simplistic sentimental articles (how to help the little old lady across the street type) are appearing. There is no mention of evaluation in such epistles and one must wonder if counselors will ever learn that they must justify their existence to those who pay the freight. But this time maybe it will be done. Hope springs eternal.

Somewhere, I can't remember where (memory lapses are not unusual for the elderly), I found the following little statement which makes a good point. "Old age," it says, "is a matter of the mind. If you don't mind it doesn't matter." Two elderly friends of mine illustrated the point. The first who had many infirmities said, "They call them the golden years. What the hell is golden about them?" The second with no other problems than high scores, exclaimed on the golf course, "How wonderful it is to be alive on a day like this!" To both, old age mattered, but in vastly different ways. Neither had any DESIRE to see a counselor and neither would have appreciated any attempts to counsel them.

Gerontological counselors must realize that there are times when they are dispensable, when what matters is in the senior citizen's mind and that it is something to be left alone. Any interference is likely to be resented, rejected, or refused. For many years I, like others, advocated counseling for all persons, but I realize now that we were mistaken because we had not given consideration to the special case of the elderly. It is to be hoped that counselors will not in the future be what the English call "so bloody wholesale."

Why, one wonders, must the literature about the elderly be so sad, gloomy—even morbid? When senior citizens' hair and teeth want to go out but the whole person doesn't want to do so, there can still be lots of circumstances which produce bellylaughs, chuckles, and grins. There is no evidence that one's sense of humor degenerates with age. In all the discussions I have read about the elderly, I have not found reports about the possible positive effects of using humor-arousing procedures as a counseling technique. Laughing together can be as effective a device as the commonly suggested techniques of field trips, album study, prayer sessions, joint reading of poetry, listening to music together and sundry other activities. Getting old is no joke, but old people can enjoy jokes. Readers of the literature might be better served if the all too prevalent morbidity were replaced, or at least modified, by a touch of humor.

The authors of this volume suggested that in their foreward I should, "as a counselor and an elder, reflect your own *personal* thoughts on the subject of counseling the elderly." My own thoughts after seven years of retirement would fill a volume, but I have no intention of writing one. A few years ago, in response to a question on how I felt about retirement and why I felt that way, I wrote the following statement: "I can't recall a day in which I didn't want to go to work. Now I enjoy every day of *not* going to work. Why? I never thought anyone was indispensable and was quite confident that my colleagues could do fine things without me. Change of behavior was, to me, just part of the life process—something to be appreciated rather than regretted. I really enjoy being outdoors almost all day every day, and there's a new kind of satisfaction. When I see trees that I planted years ago growing where none grew before, I *know* that I've accomplished something." (I could never be *sure* in fifty years of teaching, writing, researching, and counseling that I had fostered growth that continued for many years.) Perhaps the readers of this book will help to bring similar satisfactions to their senior citizen counselees and satisfaction to themselves by procuring irrefutable evidence that they have done so.

John W. M. Rothney
Wisconsin Emeritus Professor of Counseling and Guidance
Roswell, New Mexico
March 17, 1979

Contributors

Donald R. Atkinson, Associate Professor, Graduate School of Education, University of California, Santa Barbara, California 93106.

William M. Clements, Assistant Professor and Pastoral Counselor, Department of Family Practice, University of Iowa, Oakdale, Iowa 52319.

Herbert A. Exum, Assistant Professor, Division of Counselor Education, University of Iowa, Iowa City, Iowa 52242.

Gail F. Farwell, Professor, Department of Counseling and Guidance, University of Wisconsin-Madison, Madison, Wisconsin 53706.

Judy H. Katz, Assistant Professor, Human Relations and Education, University of Oklahoma, Norman, Oklahoma 73019.

Steven W. LeClair, Assistant Professor, Counseling Psychology, The Ohio State University, Columbus, Ohio 43210.

Kristan Sheridan Libbee, Doctoral Student, Guidance and Counseling Department, Norman, Oklahoma 73019.

Peter E. Maynard, Associate Professor, Human Development, Counseling and Family Studies, University of Rhode Island, Kingston, Rhode Island 02881.

Leonard A. Miller, Professor, Division of Counselor Education, University of Iowa, Iowa City, Iowa 52240.

Helen S. Panje, Language Arts Teacher, Helen C. Lemme School, Iowa City, Iowa 52240.

Steve Peltier, Doctoral Student, Department of Counseling and Guidance, University of Wisconsin, Madison, Wisconsin 53706.

Phillip A. Perrone, Professor, Department of Counseling and Guidance, University of Wisconsin, Madison, Wisconsin 53706.

Lauralee Rockwell, Assistant Professor, Division of Counselor Education, University of Iowa, Iowa City, Iowa 52242.

David M. Rosenthal, Assistant Professor, Division of Counselor Education, University of Iowa, Iowa City, Iowa 52242.

John W. M. Rothney, Emeritus Professor, Department of Counseling and Guidance, University of Wisconsin, Madison. Presently residing in Roswell, New Mexico 88201.

Nikki Smith, Doctoral Candidate, Department of Counseling Psychology, Northwestern University, Evanston, Illinois 60201.

Robert M. Soldofsky, Professor, College of Business Administration, University of Iowa, Iowa City, Iowa 52242.

Donald Steele, Instructor in Counseling and Guidance, University of Wisconsin, Platteville, Wisconsin 53818.

Katherine Perry Supiano, Masters Student, Department of Counseling and Guidance, University of Wisconsin, Madison, Wisconsin 53706.

Glenys O. Williams, Assistant Professor, Department of Family Practice, Director of Division of Geriatrics, University of Iowa, Oakdale, Iowa 52319.

Patricia L. Wolleat, Associate Professor, Department of Counseling and Guidance, University of Wisconsin, Madison, Wisconsin 53706.

Editors

Charles J. Pulvino, Ph.D.

As a professor in the Department of Counseling and Guidance at the University of Wisconsin, Madison, Dr. Pulvino has developed expertise in creativity, counselor burn-out and financial counseling.

Nicholas Colangelo, Ph.D.

An assistant professor in the division of Counselor Education at the University of Iowa, Iowa City. Dr. Colangelo has developed a professional reputation for his knowledge of gifted and talented education, program evaluation, and educational applications of the group process.

Both authors have shown an interest in development of Counseling strategies and programs for the elderly. In addition to the present book they have edited two special issues of *Counseling and Values* which focus on counseling the elderly. Also, they have presented on this topic at the local and national level.

Section 1

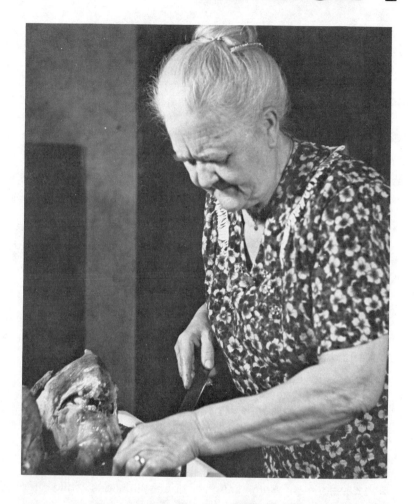

Conceptualization

OVERVIEW

The needs of older persons in our society have generally been ignored. The reasons for this range from subtle neglect to overt forms of agism. The elderly are unique in that they represent all races, religions, both sexes, and reflect every other distinction recognized in society.

Potentially all of us are members of this group. Understanding and meeting the needs of the elderly are not simply attending to the needs of a "special population." Rather, our reaction to this population attests to the value we, as a society, place on human life and dignity.

The special focus in this book is on identifying and providing for the *counseling* needs of the elderly. To date, counselors have not addressed these needs. In the "INTRODUCTION," we address basic attitudes about older persons and suggest reasons why counselors have not worked with these individuals. We also include a conceptualization of this volume and a discussion of how various sections are related to each other and to the central theme of the book.

In the chapter titled "A DEVELOPMENTAL PERSPECTIVE," we set forth a theoretical base for understanding older age. The rest of the book is founded on this perspective which holds that the elderly are very much involved in the growing process. Also, older age needs to be viewed as a stage of growth with unique tasks and characteristics. From this perspective, counselors are encouraged to offer services that promote growth and development. Remediation of crises situations, while often necessary, is viewed as insufficient.

Introduction and Perspective

Introduction

The percentage of elderly persons in the United States population has risen sharply this century. It is projected that by the year 2000, 11.2% of the population will be over 65 compared to 4.0% in 1900 (Atchley, 1977). There are presently about 24,000,-000 persons over 65 and by the year 2000 this figure will rise to over 30,000,000 (Blake & Peterson, 1979). The interest in older persons historically has been expressed in the form of statistics, graphs, and taxonomies. While such information has provided the impetus to further interest and investigation in the area, it misses the human experience. Statistics alone offer very little to counselors in terms of understanding the individual needs of elderly persons.

Another caution that needs to be made about statistics and other forms of group data is that they can be used to oppress a group. Relying on group data can lead to an undifferentiated view of persons within the group. The thinking is in terms of "group" rather than about the individual. When persons are primarily referred to as Blacks, immigrants, Indians, women, handicapped, and so forth, there is little attempt to understand the variation in individuals subsumed by these titles. This makes it rather easy to stereotype and generalize. One of the most destructive features of agism (prejudice based on age) is the belief that aged individuals are all alike. One of the purposes of this book is to provide counselors with insight into the individual concerns of elderly persons.

Counselors have long neglected the process of aging. A 1975 national survey revealed that only 18 out of 304 (about 6%) counselor education programs even offered elective courses in counseling the elderly (Salisbury, 1975). Also, Ganikos (1979) reports , "Older people historically have not received their fair share of counseling, mental health, and social services. For example, only 4% of people seen in mental health clinics are 65 and over" (p. vii). The reasons for this lack of involvement are varied and range from "benign neglect" to blatant agism. Reasons for this neglect are discussed by several of the contributors to this volume.

This book appears at a significant time since the counseling profession has recently begun an effort to recognize and provide for counseling needs of the elderly. This trend is evidenced by an increase in the number of presentations at the American Personnal and Guidance Association (APGA) National Conventions in 1978 and 1979, the recent publication of *Counseling the aged: A training syllabus for educators* by APGA (1979), and two special issues of counseling the elderly in *Counseling and Values* (1980).

The fact that counselors are making deliberate efforts to extend services to the elderly is no guarantee that these services will be effective and meaningful. Agist attitudes have effectively contributed to society disenfranchising, oppressing, and often simply ignoring older persons. Agist attitudes and other obstacles that have prevented counselors from providing needed services in the past must be clearly understood and confronted so as not to be repeated. The contributors to this volume present specific information on the physical, psychological, and social aspects of aging necessary for counselors to develop sound programs and therapeutic services for the elderly.

DEVELOPMENTAL PERSPECTIVE

This book reflects a unique perspective for understanding and counseling the elderly. It is the belief of the editors that a developmental perspective offers counselors the most useful model. Many of the problems, prejudices, and misunderstandings about elderly are due to the fact that they are viewed as being out of the mainstream or "post productivity." From a developmental perspective, older age is viewed as an integral part of natural life-span development. Elderly individuals are involved in a dialogue with their environment.

While older age is viewed as part of the life-span development, there are unique characteristics and challenges that the elderly face at this stage of development that must be understood by counselors. Older age is certainly accompanied by diminishing physical and mental functioning. While the rate of diminishing functioning varies considerably among individuals, and the rate and amount is *less* than generally believed (Usdin & Hofling, 1978), the process is happening nevertheless. The last stage of development is typically characterized by multiple losses—including loss of physical mobility, mental abilities, job, spouse, friends, and independence. In-depth understanding of these issues, and how they affect an aged individual, are areas for counselor involvement. Another unique feature of the late stages of development is that unresolved issues and problems from prior stages are brought into the elderly years. Some people view the "golden years" as a reprieve from the problems of life—that somehow now everything will be "behind us." There is no evidence to indicate this. It seems that a healthy and successful past are good predictors of adjustments in older age (Smith, 1979). It is imperative that counselors recognize that many elderly continue with life struggles from the past and that these struggles are no less painful nor less important because a person is considerably older.

OBSTACLES TO COUNSELOR INVOLVEMENT WITH THE ELDERLY

There are several reasons why counselors (and other professionals) have not been more actively involved in providing services needed by aged individuals. While many of these are addressed by the contributors to this book, there are three themes that we would like to address.

Counselors usually perceive themselves as providing a humanistic service—typically promoting respect and growth for all people. Yet, as previously stated, counselors do not typically counsel nor are they trained to work with the elderly. Children (including pre-schoolers), adolescents, and adults (under the age of 65) are given primary counseling attention. In part this reflects society's "investment syndrome" which is the attitude that we ought to invest our time and resources into those areas that have potential long-term payoff. Working with younger people may bring a payoff of later contributions to society—hence a wise investment. The belief is that the elderly are neither interested in change or growth nor capable of it and that further development of their lives and talents is not really important to the welfare of society—hence a poor investment. With this attitude, the value of individual growth and fulfillment is secondary to a person's perceived market worth.

Second, various writers have indicated that professionals (including counselors and physicians) have not worked extensively with the elderly because they may be uncomfortably reminded of their own aging and eventual death (Ganikos, 1979; Schlossberg, et al, 1978; Usdin & Hofling, 1978). This point needs to be examined. It is our contention that the elderly do not typically trigger unconscious fears of aging and death so much as *immediate* reaction based on agist attitudes. We think that professionals become *impatient* with people that are not perceived as significant. Also, it can be seen as a waste of time to work with people who are viewed as nearing senility and death. It would be more fruitful for counselors and other professionals to identify and confront their agist attitudes rather than get sidetracked by trying to come to terms with their unconscious fears about aging.

Third, counselors must not be fooled that certain overt programs for the elderly are adequate and comprehensive for the needs of the elderly. It has been our observation that society's response to the elderly tends to be in the form of overt programs. Programs such as Medicaid, Medicare, tax breaks, nursing homes, and senior citizen centers are certainly important social provisions. However, they can seduce the general public into believing that the elderly are adequately cared for. This seduction also leads to what can be called "elderly guilt"—the feeling among the elderly that given these social programs, how could they demand more? What is missing from these programs is the personal experience—the need to feel a sense of dignity and emotional fulfillment. In this light it is understandable why so many of the elderly feel a "burden" to others or feel that they are "in the way." These feelings stem from perceptions of individual non-importance. Counselors are in the position to enhance individual respect and to complement "impersonal" social programs.

THE MYTH OF AGING

Agist attitudes have helped to relegate the elderly to a world defined by constricting parameters. The myth of aging is that many of the behaviors and attitudes of the elderly are natural consequences of the aging process rather than the consequences of social learning. With age comes inevitable decline in mental and physical functions, although not as uniform nor extensive as most people believe (Kalish, 1977; Usdin &

Hoflind, 1978). Many behaviors of older persons can be viewed as conformity to what the elderly have learned society expects of them. Society expects elderly persons to be passive, forgetful, nurturant, dependent, and "retired." In a 1975 survey by the National Council on Aging (Report of the Special Committee on Aging, 1975), it was found that "for too long the people of this country have accepted without question all of the stereotypes and cliches about growing old." This finding was true not only with younger populations, but with elderly as well.

We know from behavioral science that people do respond to environmental expectations. Society has set up an environment for the elderly where they are expected to be "slower," less active, forgetful, and so forth. Robert Kastenbaum (1968), in an address to the American Psychological Association, argued that young adults immersed in a prepared environment that is faster than their normal tempo will develop agedness behavior. In addition, Kastenbaum states, "They behave less—which is another characteristic of the aged. They are less receptive to novelties and opportunities, which are further descriptive characteristics of the aged. They begin to develop a negative self image, to seek external sources of support, and so forth." Birren (1965) and Zinberg (1965) have also argued that the elderly are put in a situation where the environment is outside their control and thus "aged" behaviors become evident.

Older age is unique from previous ages in another significant way. Expectations of other (younger) ages are that as a person gets older, one can anticipate more autonomy, responsibility, and personal control. Thus the child anticipated the teens with the prospect for more decision making responsibility and personal control. Teens look to young adulthood as increased personal responsibility and autonomy. When a person enters the 65 years and over category, there is a rapid removal (especially after retirement) of responsibilities, personal control, and independence. In place of these , the individual is offered dependency, passivity, and impotence. The older an elderly person gets, the more that person is likely to lose that once held autonomy.

In 1958 R. W. White wrote an excellent expose on the concept of competence. White (1958) defined competence as the "organism's capacity to interact effectively with its environment." This sense of competence is critical to mental health and adjustment. The elderly (especially the "old-old"—75 and over) find themselves in a predicament where the environment assumes increasing control of their lives. While the feelings of helplessness among the elderly have received considerable attention in the literature, they have often been associated with diminishing physical and mental functions. We would argue that helplessness is primarily a result of the systematic withdrawal by society of the opportunity for an elderly person to be competent. Atkinson (this volume), in his chapter on the elderly as victims of oppression, vociferously supports this idea and makes a compelling argument for changing the oppressive social system that engulfs the elderly.

THE FUTURE

Perhaps the best indicator that the elderly will receive more attention in the future comes from the political arena. The presidential election of 1976 was the first overt sign of courting the "elderly vote." It is our prediction that the elderly vote will be a more significant issue in the election of 1980 and afterwards. With the help of such consciousness raising groups as the Gray Panthers, Senior Advocates International, and the National Caucus on the Aged, the elderly will politicize to achieve positive results.

Given these trends, counselors are faced with an important challenge—providing needed services for the continued development of older persons. To do this effectively we must understand the realities of aging. When a group has been long neglected and then "discovered," there is a tendency to glamorize it. It is possible that in time the elderly may be subject to more "help" and services than they desire. The charge of counselors is to provide *appropriate* counseling opportunities.

In learning about the issues of aging and the aged, we learn about ourselves. As Maggie Kuhn, Convenor of the Gray Panthers, stated, "Old age is an accomplishment." Understanding and providing for elderly can be a part of our own preparation towards this accomplishment. Respect and care for aged individuals can be a unifying bond since aging cuts across race, sex, culture, creed, and all other vistiges of separateness.

That counselors will be more involved with the elderly is imminent— that they will make a significant contribution remains to
be seen. The spirit and content of this book is to help counselors make that significant contribution. The elderly are not a
"special" population—they are potentially all of us. The value
that a society places on the dignity of the individual can be best
witnessed by how that society deals with its aged members.

OVERVIEW OF THE BOOK

The purpose of this book is to provide insight and current information on the counseling needs of elderly. Basic assumptions
in this volume are that elderly have counseling needs that have
not been met. If counselors are to make a significant contribution, there is a need to address the:

1. Conceptualization of a theoretical basis for providing
   effective counseling to the elderly;

2. Specific and current information on the various counseling needs of the elderly;

3. Adequate training of counselors to work with the elderly;
   and

4. Development of effective techniques in counseling with
   elderly.

The book has been organized from a developmental perspective of human growth. The belief of the editors is that the most
promising understanding of older age is in terms of viewing it
as a phase (stage) of universal human development. This phase
has some challenges and characteristics in common with previous stages. However, there are developmental challenges
and characteristics unique only to this stage. These unique
considerations are expanded upon by the various contributors.

Specific information on the elderly has been divided into two
sections—"Basic Concerns" and "Special Issues." Basic concerns are those most likely to affect all elderly persons. Special
issues are concerns which affect a particular group within the
population of the elderly.

A third section of the book addresses issues in counselor
education and therapeutic practice in working with the elderly.
Figure 1 illustrates the conceptualization of this volume.

Figure 1

CONCEPTUALIZATION OF THIS BOOK

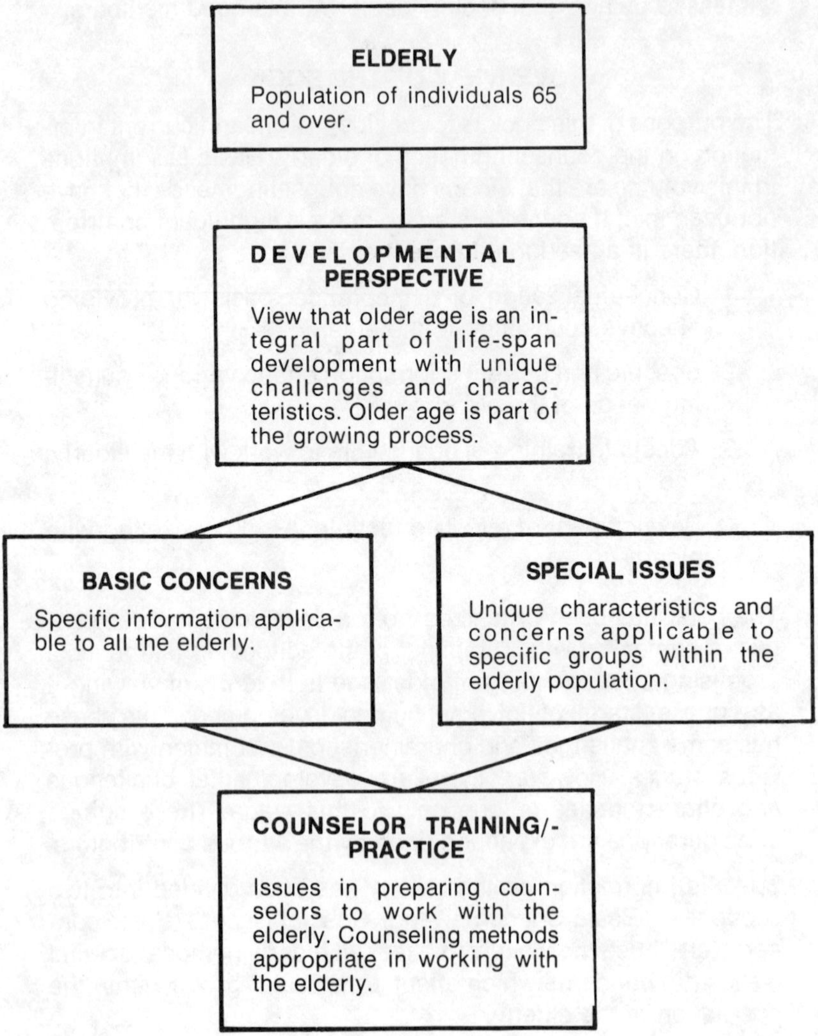

ELDERLY

Population of individuals 65 and over.

DEVELOPMENTAL PERSPECTIVE

View that older age is an integral part of life-span development with unique challenges and characteristics. Older age is part of the growing process.

BASIC CONCERNS

Specific information applicable to all the elderly.

SPECIAL ISSUES

Unique characteristics and concerns applicable to specific groups within the elderly population.

COUNSELOR TRAINING/PRACTICE

Issues in preparing counselors to work with the elderly. Counseling methods appropriate in working with the elderly.

WHO ARE THE ELDERLY?

There has been considerable controversy among gerontologists and other specialists in aging about defining what
constitutes being elderly. Presently there is no consensus
definition. The spirit of this book has been that older age can
best be understood in a developmental context. Obviously, no
single chronological age can be given to correspond with a
phase of development. With all the limitations of chronological
age, the information in this book is essentially aimed at the
developmental and typical every day life concerns of people 65
years and over.

USES OF THIS BOOK

This book is intended for use in college courses on counseling
the elderly or for courses where providing services to the
elderly is a concern. This book is also intended for all people interested in a better understanding of elderly people. It is everyone's loss when an elderly individual is deprived of the opportunity to grow or maintain respect for one's personhood. We
hope that elderly individuals reading this book would feel that
the editors and contributors were not simply making a case for
improved counseling services for the elderly, but were also advocating a society that promotes dignity for all individuals.

REFERENCES

Atchley, R.C. *The social forces of later life.* Belmont, California: Wadsworth Publishing Co., 1977.

Birren, J. Reactions to loss and the process of aging: Interrelations of environmental changes, psychological status. In M.A. Berezin & S.H. Cath (Eds.), *Geriatric psychiatry.* New York: International Universities Press Inc., 1965.

Blake, R., & Peterson, D. Demographic aspects of aging: Implications for counseling. In M. Ganikos & K. Grady (Eds.), *Counseling the aged: A training syllabus for educators.* Washington, D.C.: APGA, 1979.

Developments in aging: 1974 and January-April 1975. Report of the special commission on aging, United States Senate. Washington, D.C.: U.S. Government Printing Office, 1975.

Ganikos, M., & Grady, K. (Eds.). *Counseling the aged: A training syllabus for educators.* Washington, D.C.: APGA, 1979.

Kalish, R.A. *The later years: Social applications of gerontology.* Belmont, California: Wadsworth Publishing Co., 1977.

Kastenbaum, R. *Perspectives on the development and modification of behavior in the aged.: A developmental field perspective.* Paper presented to the 76th Annual Convention of the American Psychological Association, San Francisco, California, August 30, 1968.

Salisbury, H. Counseling the elderly: A neglected area in counselor education. *Counselor Education and Supervision,* 1975, *14,* 237-238.

Schlossberg, N.K.; Troll, E.L.; & Leibowitz, Z. *Perspective on counseling adults: Issues and skills.* Monterey, California: Brooks/Cole, 1978.

Smith, N. *Psychological profile of the aged. A review of the literature.* Unpublished paper, 1979.

Usdin, G., & Hofling, C.J. *Aging: The process and the people.* New York: Brunner/Mazel, 1978.

White, R.W. Motivation reconsidered: The concept of competence. *Psychological Review,* 1958, *66,* 297-333.

Zinberg, N.E. Introduction and special problems of gerontological psychiatry. In M.A. Berezin & S.H. Cath (Eds.), *Geriatric psychiatry.* New York: International Universities Press Inc., 1965.

A Developmental Perspective

INTRODUCTION

> In considering the needs of older people, it is well, first, to remember that older people have the needs that are common to all people, and second, that they have special needs due to the fact that they are old people (Havighurst, 1959, p. 439).

The purpose of this chapter is to present an overview of the developmental needs of older people and to outline counseling strategies which meet these needs. In order to accomplish this task, the chapter is divided into three major sections. The first of these emphasizes characteristics of development commonly associated with older people, the second highlights developmental counseling conceptualizations that have been forwarded for a general population of counseling clients, and the third specifically points to application of developmental counseling with older clients.

WHO IS THE OLDER CLIENT?

In order to appreciate the unique characteristics of the older client, it is necessary to understand the developmental scheme for all individuals and how, specifically, an older person fits into this scheme. Eric Erikson (1963) postulated a theory of ego development which addresses life stages individuals pass through. Erikson formulated eight stages of ego development that extend from infancy to old age. Each of the eight stages represents a choice for the individual's expanding ego. This conceptualization accounts for effects of maturation, experience, and social institutions on the developing individual. The resolutions of ego choices are foundational for the individual's development of personality, success adapting to both inner- and outer-world demands, and eventual self evaluation.

In Erikson's theory, basic psychological issues are confronted by individuals at all stages of development. The manner in which individuals resolve these issues at one level has an impact on how they will resolve issues at all subsequent stages. In addition, for psychological development to occur, issues at one level must be adequately resolved before individuals can reach resolution of issues at higher levels (Neugarten, 1968). Erikson's eight stages of development are:

1. *Early infancy*: A sense of basic trust versus a sense of mistrust.
2. *Later infancy*: A sense of autonomy versus a sense of shame.
3. *Early childhood*: A sense of initiative versus a sense of guilt.
4. *Middle childhood*: A sense of industry versus a sense of inferiority.
5. *Adolescence*: A sense of ego identity versus a sense of role diffusion.
6. *Early adulthood*: Development of intimacy versus a sense of ego isolation.
7. *Middle Adulthood*: Development of generativity versus a sense of ego stagnation.
8. *Late Adulthood*: A sense of ego identity versus a sense of despair (Erikson, 1963).

In Erikson's theory of ego development, growth is seen as a continuous process, one that is never completely stablilized nor completed. Individuals are always in the process of resolution. For our purposes the last two stages (seven and eight) have the most import and of these, eight has the most significance. Erikson views the process of generativity (stage seven) as being that time in life when an individual is primarily concerned with "establishing and guiding the next generation" (Erikson 1963, p. 267). He views this stage as being essential in the psychosexual and psychosocial development of the individual.

Peck (1968) suggests that during this developmental stage individuals evidence a change in the ways they view and respond to their worlds. These new ways of experiencing are chacterized by:

1. Valuing wisdom to a higher degree while devaluating physical powers;
2. Placing increased emphasis on socializing while decreasing emphasis on sexuality in human relationships;
3. Increasing emotional flexibility while reducing emotional impoverishment; and
4. Developing mental flexibility with a consequent decline in mental rigidity (p. 88-90).

Progressing along the developmental ladder, the individual is faced by new role expectations which can result in role uncertainty, changing internal drives which lead to new perceptions of the world and relationships, new points of view which represent the individual's developing sense of self and the world, and some awareness that one can never return to what one was. This process is continuous in that it persists as the individual moves from stage seven (generativity) into stage eight (ego integrity).

Ego integrity implies "an emotional integration which permits participation by followership as well as acceptance of the responsibility of leadership" (Erikson, 1963, p. 269). Individuals pass from stage seven to stage eight at different chronological ages. They appear ready to make this transition, not when the "right" age has been reached, but when certain psychological characteristics are manifested.

Peck (1968) suggests that this transition occurs when individuals are more concerned with "ego differentiation" than "work-role preoccupation," when they move toward body transcendence instead of body preoccupation, and when they become concerned with ego transcendence, not ego preoccupation. To expect older people to reach this transitional stage at, or near the same age, is not realistic. Rather, Peck (1968) offers that ". . . there is far greater variability in the chronological age at which a given psychic crisis arises in later life, than is true of the crisis-points of youth" (p. 92).

Erikson's stages of ego development are helpful in understanding the older person. However, unlike youth, older persons seem to pass through stages with a much wider gradient. Therefore, Erikson's stages of generativity (seven) and ego integrity (eight) can be viewed only as a rough approximation of what occurs with older people and must be used in conjunction with varying aspects of time and aging. Neugarten and Datan (1973) shed some light on this consideration when they depict time in three interrelated, yet distinct ways; chronological time, social time, and historical time. They suggest that people traditionally have viewed "the life cycle as a series of orderly changes, from infancy through childhood, adoloscence, maturity, and old age with the biological timetable governing the sequence of changes in the process of growing up and growing old" (p. 56). This manner of viewing individuals is frought with difficulties because all people do not progress at the same rate or in the same manner through lifes' stages.

The impact of time is better understood when chronological time is examined in conjunction with social time which underlies the age-status system of a society. Examination of other cultures clearly indicates that age expectations and age status varies from culture to culture. Whereas Oriental elders are revered, frequently Occidental elders are not. It is apparent that social time differences have an impact on chronological time expectations. In like manner, historical time influences both chronological and social time. Historical time shapes the social system, the social system creates a changing set of age norms and a changing age-grade system which shapes the individual life-cycle (Neugarten & Datan, 1973). All three dimensions of time must be taken into account when considering developmental life stages. This is especially true when older persons are considered.

Very closely tied to this conceptualization of time is the concept of aging. Like time, aging must be viewed in a number of ways. Birren (1964) suggests that aging must be viewed from biological, psychological, and social perspectives. Biological aging, or gradual diminishing of bodily functions, is what most conceive to be the aging process. Although this form of aging is important, the psychological aging process, or developmental adaptive capacities of the individual, are equally meaningful to the total human organism. An individual that is able to maintain an open, adaptive psychological capability can do much to overcome the difficulties of biological aging.

The concepts of biological and psychological aging are closely tied to social aging—social roles and habits learned by individuals relative to group expectations. All three forms of aging are interrelated and have direct implications on the total aging process *and*, when coupled with time considerations, help determine how and when an individual will pass through Erikson's ego developmental stages. A closer look at stage eight follows.

As individuals develop from birth to death, they will face a number of developmental tasks. Havighurst (1959) defines these as tasks which arise at or about a certain period in the life of an individual, successful achievement of which leads to happiness and to success with later tasks, while failure leads to unhappiness in the individual, disapproval by the society, and difficulty with later tasks (p. 2).

During the later years of life (Erikson's eighth stage), individuals are faced with tasks which are unique to their developmental stage. Havighurst (1959) states that this time in life is " . . . a period of learning, rather than a period when learning is past. It is a period of facing new and unresolved problems rather than a period of floating gently on the surface of familiar solutions to familiar problems" (p. 442). In addition to continuing human *needs* such as the need for emotional security and affection, the need for social recognition and status, the need for maintenance of worth and self respect, and the need for adequate food, clothing, and shelter (Havighurst, 1959), older people must learn to *cope* with a number of developmental concerns. Specifically, they must learn to cope with:

1. Death of spouse and friends;
2. Retirement and a reduced income;
3. Reduced physical vigor;
4. Changed living arrangements;
5. Singular affiliation within an age group of elders;
6. Development of new leisure time so that it will be constructive and satisfying;
7. Caring for an aged body;
8. The need to develop new social roles that can result in recognition and respect;
9. Making satisfactory living arrangements;
10. Making new friends; and
11. Treating grown children as adults.

Also, the older person frequently fears becoming physically or mentally helpless, becoming economically insecure, being rejected by society and suffers particular insults of the aging process such as loss of physical attractiveness, lessoning of physical health, and loss of social status (Havighurst, 1959).

All of the above demand that the older person be an efficient learner. With the exception of early childhood, demands for development of coping skills are greater on the older person than during any other period of life. The only conclusion that can be drawn is that if older persons wish to live out their last years with any semblance of respect, they must continue to learn, to grow, to cope, and to become.

WHAT ARE THE SIGNIFICANT DEVELOPMENTAL COUNSELING COMPONENTS?

Developmental counseling is based upon the concept of change— change which individuals experience as a result of internal growth and social interaction. The internal growth that occurs is dependent upon psychological maturation which, in turn, is influenced by psychological changes which result from sociological involvement. As individuals experience the inevitable process of internal growth and subsequent change, they perceive themselves in differing roles, each of which influences the individual's psychological makeup. Personality development occurs within the context of this schema. In fact, Perlman (1968) suggests that "... personality can only be perceived and assessed within the context of a social situation where the individual is oneself, yes, but oneself in some role" (p. 41). In addition, it is pointed out that "... no roles are carried solo; all are carried in transaction with one or more persons. Therein lies the greater part of their meaningfulness" (p. 42).

Blocher (1966a), a leading proponent of developmental counseling, proposes that human effectiveness is highly dependent upon the manner in which individuals interpret and accept expectations inherent in social roles, develop coping behaviors for functioning in role situations, and how they respond to psychological-sociological developmental tasks.

Counseling, from a developmental perspective, is founded on this dynamic interaction between the maturing individual and the social system. This approach to counseling is relatively recent. Hummel (1962), in an article titled "Ego-Counseling in Guidance: Concept and Method," is credited with providing a working foundation for the developmental counselor. Hummel outlined five key variables which serve as models for the process:

1. *Setting*: Counselors are expected to be aware of the opportunities and limits inherent in their function. Counselees clarify for themselves these opportunities and limits as part of the treatment process. Both counselor and counselee are involved in a dynamic interchange and both have responsibility for changing in a way which will produce the greatest counselee growth. The setting provides a model for the developmental life process.

2. *Relationship*: Counselors must communicate understanding to the counselees in a non-conditional manner. Counselors must function as genuine collaborators, working toward growth and development of the counselee.

3. *Analysis*: The counselor's task is to conduct a "systematic appraisal of self and of external circumstances" (p. 478) to determine characteristics of the counselee's present situation to uncover significant elements which could be meaningful in the future, to identify potential obstacles to growth, and to understand the connectedness between the counselee's qualities and aspects of the counselee's problems.

4. *Reorganization and Synthesis*: This step flows from step three and is aimed at helping "the counselee to attain a revised set of intentions, of 'concepts,' of 'personal constructs' with reference to a defined sector" (p. 479). In this step, change and growth are paramount, the counselee demonstrating an emerging quality which can lead to new, or different, response modes.

5. *Actions*: The purpose of this final stage is to prepare counselees, through the counseling relationship, for action that will occur outside the relationship. "The counselor attempts to help the counselees envision how they he will act—how they might plan—how they might respond—or how they might obtain certain information critical to their plans" (p. 480).

Elements of Hummel's work can be found in most recent conceptualizations of developmental counseling. The reader is encouraged to keep his five step process in mind. The relevance of these steps will become increasingly apparent.

Byrne (1963), in discussing developmental counseling applications in school settings, suggested that the counseling process should use the counselor client relationship as a means for evaluating the status and trends of clients' development, to help clients work through obstacles to development and to work through situationally caused dissatisfactions, and to facilitate clients as they "make and implement decisions about and plans for their life courses" (p. 39). This approach to counseling reflects Hummel's suggestions and sets the stage for later developmental theorists. Like Hummel, Byrne has emphasized (1) use of the counseling relationship to (2) analyze the counselee's situation so that (3) action can occur that will facilitate counselee development.

A number of theorists have approached developmental counseling from a similar perspective. The most noteworthy are Blocher (1966), Peters (1970), Peters and Farwell (1967), and Farwell (1979). A brief overview of their positions follows.

Hopefully, this overview can provide a basis for viewing and working with older clients. Peters and Farwell (1967) worked together to produce a text entitled *Guidance: A developmental approach*. In developing their position, four key assumptions were forwarded:

1. Individuals have a basic predisposition toward growth;
2. Individuals integrate their experiences into recognizable patterns;
3. "There is a place for positive interaction on the part of the professional counselor in the life of the individual" (p. 226); and
4. "The counselee is invariably an individual-in situation" (p. 227).

Their assumptions set the stage for Peters' and Farwells' developmental perspective which emphasizes the individuals' integration of learning experiences which result from the individuals' "chronological stage and the institutional and interpersonal involvements nurturing one's growth" (p. 223). Counseling, in this model, is geared toward facilitating learning so that the counselee increasingly becomes capable of functioning more productively in changing environment. Emergence of "more expression," "more appreciation," and "more functional use of inner resources" (p.224) are primary goals of this approach.

Peters (1970), in his book, *The guiance process: A perspective*, maintained the major focus of this work and added a number of significant variables which he felt were inherent in the process of developmental counseling.

The first of these variables was referred to as *dimensionality* , defined as being the client's level of concern. This variable has significance at five levels of client development, i.e., directional level, encouragement level, reinforcement level, attitudinal level, and reorganizational level. At the directional level, the counselor is responsible for making informational inputs and in helping the client develop decision-making processes. At this level, it is important that the counselor maintain active involvement with the client.

At the second level, encouragement, through discussion and action, the counselor serves to motivate client growth, whereas at the level of reinforcement, the counselor must help clients define their problem, make sure that they take appropriate action, and follow through to reinforce and guide subsequent behaviors. Level four, the attitudinal level, focuses on the individual's developing insight and requires that the counselor be an active participant in the client's developmental process. The final level of dimensionality is that of reorganization. This level suggests that clients be able to sufficiently reconceptualize their life so that they might obtain optimal living by moving in a totally new direction.

In conclusion, dimensionality refers to the depth of client concern and the intensity of counselor involvement. Both play a significant role in the client's development.

In Peters' (1970) model, the second significant variable revolves around *mutuality of participation*. Counseling is viewed as a process in which the developmental process is shared by the counselor and client. Like the earlier work of Peters and Farwell (1967), the client is viewed-in-situation, or more specifically the client and counselor are viewed-in-interaction.

Movement is the third variable of significance and refers to "movement toward new behavior" (p. 51). It also implies development of feelings of personal fulfillment. This variable emphasizes the "growth" aspects of dimensional counseling.

Searching, the fourth variable, emphasizes an individual's movement within one's life space and involves knowing oneself, intimacy in living, and freedoms and responsibilities which accrue as one encounters others.

Peters' (1970) final variable is *follow-through* which suggests that the counselor/client interaction exists beyond the "time and place of the counseling experience" (p. 52). Counseling is viewed as a longitudinal process, one which surpasses counselor/client interactional contact time. The individuals's life space is the natural extention for continued development of behaviors and attitudes.

Finally, Peters (1970) offers fourteen keys to his "dimensional counseling." These keys are listed below:

1. Individuals may need co-participants in their lives.
2. Counseling is learning oriented but is activated by a feeling-orientation.
3. Relationship is important. Mutuality of involvement is essential.
4. The counselor is an active participant in the counseling process.
5. The level of counseling dictates the level of voluntarism mandated.
6. Analysis focuses on clarity of cognitions and input of feelings.

7. "Dependency is used to facilitate rather than limit" (p. 54).
8. "Although the environment may need to be changed, effort is made to participate with the counselee in maximum use of one's environment" (p. 54).
9. Sensibility is not confused with sentimentality.
10. Caring participation shows more concern than encouragement.
11. The counselor frequently has a teaching or briefing job.
12. Subjectivity is important in counseling.
13. Trust results from participation.
14. "Counseling is focused on developing" (p. 54).

The five variables and fourteen keys presented above are intended to summarize the significant aspects of Peters' (1970) work. The reader is referred to the original source for elaboration of the basic points that have been presented.

Blocher (1966a, 1966b), like Peters and Farwell, has posited a developmental approach to counseling. At the core of his approach is the belief that individuals should maximize human "freedom" and "effectiveness" (pp. 5-6). These goals can be achieved if counseling is educational in orientation and is designed to facilitate learning of a deeply personal nature" (p. 12). The developmental counselor, in Blocher's model, must understand complex processes which influence development of human behaviors and be knowledgeable about ways in which behaviors can be modified. At a primary level, the counselor must appreciate the client's need for *homeostasis*, that comfortable level of equilbrium between inner needs and outer forces and one's need for *differentiation*, that need of the organism to grow in selfactualizing ways. For Blocher, healthy development is a dynamic balance between these two forces (p. 45).

The developmental counselor, sensitive to these contrasting forces, must use counseling interventions that can assume a dynamic growth producing balance. Frequently, this intervention is needed when social or physiological discontinuities occur and the balance between *homeostasis* and *differentiation* is dramatically effected.

Superimposed on this overriding theory are Blocher's five major stages of development: organization (from birth to age 14); exploration (from ages 15 to age 30); realization (from age 30 to age 50); stabilization (from age 50 to age 65); and examination (age 65 and beyond). For purposes of this text, his final stage, examination, is most important. Blocher states that examination is "characterized by reflection, active disengagement from events, and playing roles of observer and mentor rather than participant and actor" (p. 66). He concludes by stating that the "danger in this stage is *isolation* and *detachment*, which will deprive life of its sense of meaning and reality" (p. 66).

A developmental counselor working with older clients is cautioned to keep Blocher's statements about the examination stage in mind. Counseling complications can result if disengagement, isolation, and detachment occur and affect the balance between homeostasis and differentiation. To prevent this from occurring, the counselor must prepare older clients for this eventuality and teach them ways for maintaining their freedom and effectiveness. One of the purposes of this text is to show ways that this can be accomplished.

Farwell (1979), like Blocher and Peters, has continued to refine his model of developmental counseling. His most current statement suggests that "the ultimate goal to be achieved by the counselor is self-competency for each individual" (p. 3). He defines self-competency as being a composite, a gestalt, a becoming, and a phenomenon of development that includes personal awareness of what one is, what one stands for, and what one is becoming (p. 3). This concept includes recognition, development, and use of seven intertwined processes: assimilation, reporting, demonstration, integration, decision-making, accommodating, and new organization or re-structuring.

Farwell places no age restrictions on any of these variables and, in fact, does not offer developmental stages. Rather, each of these processes is viewed as being viable and applicable to any individual at any developmental stage. Therein lies their utility. Both young and old can assimilate new material, report on their experiences, demonstrate their reactions to stimuli, integrate new information into their personality, arrive at appropriate decisions, accommodate disparate environmental inputs, form new ways of responding, and move to a higher planes of existential existence. Age is not the primary factor. The major consideration is the individual's ability to employ these seven processes as they move toward self-competency. Because Farwell's theory is *not* age bound, it has high relevance for the present text.

WHAT ARE THE IMPLICATIONS OF DEVELOPMENTAL COUNSELING FOR OLDER CLIENTS?

"All things are in a state of flux."

Heraclitus

To believe that older persons have ceased growing is detrimental to their well being and societally shortsighted. Their self-worth is depricated and their value to society diminished. A more beneficial viewpoint is to understand the older person's pattern of growth. If Havighurst (1959) is correct that older persons must adjust to a number of developmental tasks and if Erikson (1963) is accurate in his belief that older persons must come to grips with ego identity and a sense of despair, then it is important that counselors understand older persons' particular concerns and develop strategies to deal with existing developmental issues.

As with youth, older persons are moving toward self-competency (Farwell, 1979). The counselor's task is to facilitate this movement. To do so, the counselor must understand characteristics of older persons, be cognizant of the myriad of intervention strategies available for clients of all ages, and be able to select and utilize procedures that are most appropriate for specific older clients. As an aid for doing this, counselors are advised to keep the following questions in mind:

1. What personal limitations hinder older clients from obtaining their goals?

2. What environmental factors affect older clients' goal achievement?

3. How can personal or environmental obstacles to goal achievement be altered or circumvented?

4. What skills can older clients develop which will help them to move toward self-competence?

5. Can development of client skills be fostered through practice within the counseling relationship?

6. Can older clients be taught self-education and selfsupervision systems which will lead to increased personal responsibility and diminished dependence on others?

As a basis for answering these questions, counselors must keep in mind that developmental tasks resulting from psychological environmental, and sociological change will exist and that obstacles are not within these tasks but within the older person's ability to handle the tasks. Difficulties that arise for individuals can be physical, psychological, or social and may result from lack of awareness of self or environment, insufficient skill development, diminished opportunity for practicing adaptive behaviors, insufficient social reinforcement, inadequate incentive, or a low motivational level.

Counselors must also be aware of the dynamic quality of older persons, helping them to assess their competencies and limitations while assisting them in the development of decision-making and coping skills which are consistent with their capabilities.

To be of greatest assistance, counselors must understand older clients and be aware of the mental set from which they function. For the most part, older clients want to view themselves as being strong and independent, not weak and dependent. Self-sufficiency is an important societal value, one which is inculcated in the psyche of most people.

Older persons are frequently caught in a paradoxical situation of having experientially learned behavior patterns which cry for indepentent choice and action while being faced with declining physical ability which may foster dependence on others. Empathic understanding by the counselor can help older clients deal with the apparent paradox of being dependent in an independent society.

Counselor understanding also can help older clients overcome feelings of anomie or aloneness. These feelings frequently occur as individuals make significant changes in life style which separate them from more youthful populations. Retirement from age integrated jobs, living in retirement homes or communities, and separation from family members can lead older persons to feel socially isolated.

Counselor empathic understanding can help reduce this feeling. Finally, as clients age they frequently are more comfortable with counselors that are approximately their age (Pressey & Pressey, 1972). Counselor empathic understanding can help overcome the older client's preference by revealing to their clients that despite an age difference they do understand the thoughts and feelings which are being communicated to them.

In summary, it is important that counselors understand older clients and that they empathically communicate this understanding. Client growth will occur when older clients believe that counselors care for them as growing individuals.

In addition to understanding and caring, counselors must demonstrate knowledge about older clients. This knowledge appears in two general categories. First, counselors must be aware of the following:

1. Older clients are constantly growing, changing, and developing. Older clients are continuously facing developmental tasks, adjusting to changing physical and psychological characteristics, and learning new coping skills which use their life experiences in new or different ways.

2. Older clients have changing physical characteristics which may alter their mental processes. As an example, an older client may have difficulty in remembering specific facts about a situation but be able to deal with a particular dilemma by drawing on previous experiences in new ways. In many situations, experience and general knowledge has greater value than recall of specific facts.

3. Older clients must be treated as individuals. Older clients are not identical in physical or psychological makeup. Consequently, counselors must be aware of developmental tasks and stages of development *but* guard against categorization of individual older clients.

4. Older clients frequently move away from external dependence toward internal reliance. As individuals age, they separate themselves from dependent liasons with institutions and make more individual, idiosyncratic choices. As one retired banker said, "I always wore conservative clothes, but now I wear what I damn will please!" This characteristic is evident in many aspects of behavior of older persons.

5. Older clients frequently value different things than they did in their youth. As an example, an individual may value money, power, or status during youth and middle age and be more concerned with social issues as an older person. In most cases, the change that occurs is movement away from concern for self toward concern for others.

The second category of knowledge which should concern counselors is directly related to the counseling enterprise. This knowledge is about counseling process and outcome.

1. Counselors should establish a productive attitude by:

   a. Treating older clients with respect, emphasizing their strengths and not deploring their weaknesses;

   b. Developing older clients' interdependence while diminishing their dependence;

   c. Developing skills and attitudes for effective problem solving; and

   d. Developing attitudes of decision making and action taking (Manion, 1976).

2. Counselors must build on their understanding of the older clients' internal characteristics and knowledge about the older clients' environmental conditions. In addition to being aware of environmental elements, counselors must help older clients to understand their environments and to productively deal with them. *The counselor has to be able to help older clients utilize their personal strengths to positively affect the environment.*

3. Counselors must be able to use remedial, preventive, and productive counseling with older clients (Lombana, 1976; Pulvino & Lee, 1979).

From a remedial perspective, older clients need personal counseling when there are serious mental health concerns, supportive counseling when there are physical health problems, motivation and adjustment counseling for clients residing in residential institutions, financial counseling when fiscal difficulties are encountered, and avocational counseling and retraining when this is appropriate.

Preventive counseling is highly educational in nature and includes preretirement counseling, life-long health education, information sharing about avocational opportunities and leisure activities, programs regarding available community services, information about educational and recreational opportunities, counseling opportunities for families of older clients, information dissemination to the general public about the many aspects of older clients, and preparation and employment of professional and paraprofessional counselors to work with older clients (Lombana, 1976, p. 143-144).

Productive counseling should be employed to help older clients utilize their resources to their best advantage. Based upon client goals and objectives, counselors should help older clients to use their material and personal assets in ways which will maximize client independence and self-sufficiency.

All three of these approaches are geared toward helping older clients to become self-competent. As they approach this elusive, yet meaningful state, they should be leading a richer, fuller, existence.

The remainder of this book will deal with ways that counselors can identify major elements of concern in older person's lives and how, as counselors, they can facilitate client growth. The areas presented are not intended to be all inclusive. Rather, issues addressed are intended to be representative of concerns facing older persons as they continue to grow.

REFERENCES

Birren, J.E. *The psychology of aging*. Englewood Cliffs, New Jersey: Prentice-Hall, Incorporated, 1964.

Blocher, D. *Developmental counseling*. New York: Ronald Press Company, 1966a.

Blocher, D. Wanted: A science of human effectiveness. *Personnel and Guidance Journal*, March, 1966b, *44*, 729-733.

Byrne, R.H. *The school counselor*. Boston: Houghton Mifflin Company, 1963.

Erikson, E.H. *Childhood and society* (2nd edition). New York: W.W. Norton and Company, Incorporated, 1963.

Farwell, G.F. *The counselor as model: His relevancy and his outcomes*. (Unpublished manuscript.) University of Wisconsin, 1979.

Gowen, W. Adult personality: An empirical study of Erikson's theory of ego development. In B. Neugarten (Ed.), *Personality in middle and late life*. New York: Altherton Press, 1964, 1-14.

Havighurst, R.J. Social and psychological needs of the aging. In L. Gorlow & W. Katkovsky (Eds.), *Readings in the psychology of adjustment*. New York: McGraw Hill Book Company, 1959, 443-447.

Hummel, R.C. Ego-counseling in guidance: Concept and method. *Harvard Educational Review*, Fall, 1962, 32, 463-482.

Lombana, J.H. Counseling the elderly: Remediation plus prevention. *Personnel and Guidance Journal*, November, 1976, 55, 143-144.

Manion, V. Preretirement counseling: The need for a new approach. *Personnel and Guidance Journal*, November, 1976, 55, 119-121.

Neugarten, B.L. *Middle age and aging: A reader in social psychology*. Chicago: The University of Chicago Press, 1968.

Neugarten, B.L., & Datan, N. Sociological perspectives on the life cycle. In P.B. Baltes & K.W. Schaie (Eds.), *Life-span developmental psychology*. New York: Academic Press, 1973, 53-69.

Peck, R.C. Psychological development in the second half of life. In B.L. Neugarten (Ed.), *Middle age and aging*. Chicago: University of Chicago Press, 1968, 88-92.

Perlman, H.H. *Persona: social role and personality*. Chicago: University of Chicago Press, 1968.

Peters, H.J. *The guidance process: A perspective*. Itasca, Illinois: F.E. Peacock Publishers, Incorporated, 1970.

Peters, H.J., & Farwell, G.F. *Guidance: A developmental approach*. Chicago: Rand McNally Company, 1967.

Pressey, S., & Pressey, A. Major neglected need-opportunity: Old-age counseling. *Journal of Counseling Psychology*, September, 1972, 19, 362-366.

Pulvino, C.J., & Lee, J.L. *Financial counseling: Interviewing skills*. Dubuque, Iowa: Kendall/Hunt Publishing Company, 1979.

Section II

Basic Concerns

Gainsville Sun photo by Tom Kennedy

Counseling for the Growing Years

OVERVIEW

The elderly face certain developmental tasks. Counselors of the elderly must be aware of these tasks, be sensitive to the needs of individual elderly persons, and be skilled in effectively helping the elderly to deal with these issues.

This section of the book has been designed with these issues in mind and is specifically intended to (1) provide foundational information that is central to all (or most) of the elderly and (2) to provide counselors suggestions on how to incorporate presented informaton into their practice. Each chapter is geared toward a specific topic of concern, one that all of the elderly will recognize as they continue to grow. Atkinson addresses the issue of the elderly as victims of oppression. He clearly establishes how society responds to the elderly, documents the negative impact societal attitudes and behaviors have on the elderly and outlines six functions available to those counselors desirous of becoming actively involved in the lives of their elderly counselees.

Williams provides counselors with a wealth of information relative to medical aspects of aging. First, she outlines basic physiological characteristics of growing older. Second, she addresses societal attitudes toward aging and disease clearly noting specific concerns relative to illness in the aged. Finally, Williams discusses common medical problems that affect elderly persons. Although some of the material presented is quite technical, all of the information provided is useful in expanding one's awareness.

Rockwell addresses myths which influence the sexual identity and behavior of the elderly. Particular attention is paid to misconceptions about sexual patterns, customs, desires, and capabilities. Suggestions are offered for ways counselors can help the elderly to understand and appreciate their sexuality and to enjoy sexual activity more fully. Sexual issues with the elderly are clearly examined from a counseling perspective.

Perrone and Supiano have cogently argued for retirement as a developmental transition rather than as a point in time. They suggest that counselors must build intervention strategies on a functional knowledge of clientele personality types. Also, counselors need to assess client attitudes and values and provide clients meaningful feedback so that integration and adjustment can occur. One of the major values of this chapter is that it provides counselors a reasonable goal for many elderly clients and offers specific ideas on how the goal can be achieved.

Steele addresses the negatively ladened issues of death and bereavement. He contends that for counselors to be effective with elderly and their families in issues of death and bereavement, they must confront their own attitudes about these issues. Steele places these issues in a developmental perspective, arguing that death and bereavement are natural parts of the life-cycle. He also brings to the fore difficulties clients and counselors have in dealing with the certainty of death.

Peltier examines the role of family counseling as it applies to the elderly. He looks at the family from a systems perspective, specifically noting the impact an elderly member can have. Family counseling interventions are presented which utilize the systems perspective. Specific family problems situations are discussed and appropriate family counseling approaches are offered. The elderly are viewed in context of the family structure and not as isolated individuals. Their influence on the family is discussed as is family influence on them.

Finally, Soldofsky provides needed technical information on financial concerns facing the elderly. This chapter addresses a number of significant financial issues, e.g., taxes, cash-flow data, cost-of-living considerations, inflation effects, income additions, insurance concerns, and wills and estates. In these and other topics, documentation is offered and counseling implications are outlined. A significant body of information is provided. In addition, Soldofsky lists numerous resources that counselors can use to obtain additional financial information in their work with the elderly.

The Elderly Client as a Victim of Opression

Donald R. Atkinson

ABSTRACT

Elderly people in the United States experience economic and social oppression analogous to that experienced by Third World people, women, and other minority groups. Perhaps the most insidious form this oppression takes is the attitude of benign neglect with which society confronts the needs of the aged. Self-fulfilling stereotypes, based in small part on truth and in large part on fiction, also reinforce an oppressive atmosphere in which the elderly are viewed as "subhumans." The traditional behavior-change approach to counseling in which most counselors were trained fails to recognize the external sources of many problems encountered by the aged. The "oppressed minority" view of the elderly suggests the need for a social-activist approach that operates to change environmental determinants rather than to change behavior. This chapter outlines six functions of a social-activist counseling role for counselors who work with elderly clients.

INTRODUCTION

> Tis well for old age that it is always accompanied with want of perception, ignorance, and a facility of being deceived. For should we see how we are used and would not acquiesce, what would become of us? (Montaigne in "Of the affections of fathers to their children" from *Essays*, 1580-1588).

> People who manage to survive to old age know that the present system is destroying them. They experience discrimination, intolerance, and isolation based on the sole fact that they are old. Their oppression stems from an irreversible biological conditon, as surely as a black person faces oppression because of color and a woman experiences oppression based on sex (Sharon Curtin in *Nobody ever died of old age*, 1972.

> The time has come for the aged to . . . learn to manipulate the system that holds them down, joining with Blacks, browns, women, and other oppressed minorities in acting for social change (Paul Kleyman in *Senior power: Growing old rebelliously*, 1974).

Though largely ignored in the past by social scientists as well as society in general, the aged and the "problems" associated with the increasing proportion of elderly in the general population have been the focus of considerable attention in recent years. With the rising interest in social gerontology has come an increased awareness that the elderly, subject to social and institutional oppression analagous to that experienced by Third World people, women, gays, the underclass, and others, constitute a large though relatively unorganized and passive minority group (Barron, 1953; Butler, 1969; Palmore & Manton, 1973; Rose, 1965). It is the thesis of this chapter that the elderly (with the exception of a small percentage who retain power and affluence through public office and/or lucrative family investments) are indeed the victims of oppression and as such have unique counseling needs necessitating a departure by counselors form their traditional modus operandi.

ECONOMIC OPRESSION

The aged are clearly among the most economically oppressed groups in the United States by all the usual criteria of discrimination. One of the most widely recognized forms of discrimination due to age is forced (or coerced) retirement. Although some gains have been made through federal legislation aimed at delaying forced retirement until the age of 70 (for most federal employees all upper age limits have been abolished), the net effect may be to only temporarily stay the trend toward an increase in forced retirement. (Schulz, 1974). Frequently promoted as a desire on the part of the employer to provide a leisurely later life for employees, the elderly are all too aware that employer retirement policies actually reflect the expendability of the older worker and that these policies are designed to provide employment opportunities for younger, potentially more "durable," and "cheaper" workers.

Like other minorities, the elderly are frequently the first fired and last hired. Once an elderly person loses a job, age discrimination, although forbidden by law, makes it all but impossible to find a new one. Stereotypes of elderly workers as less productive than younger workers persist despite convincing evidence that, even when level of experience is controlled for, older employees tend to be as productive as their younger counterparts (Schwab & Heneman, 1977).

Nor is age discrimination, presumably due to such stereotypes, restricted to prospective employers:

> Unemployed older workers, as a group, invariably experience longer periods of unemployment than younger workers and the E. S. (U.S. Employment Service) could be a vital resource in the search for employment. Over a fourth of older job seekers attempt to use the E. S. Services, but the agency's overall response to older worker's needs has been disappointing. Only a small proportion receive attention beyond the filing of a standard application. . . . Among many issues that have emerged from the research, the most important appears to be the recurrent observation that an inverse relationship exists between the applicant's age and services received (McConnel, 1977, p. 167).

Forced or coerced retirement and employment discrimination are often only the first of a long series of oppressive forces experienced by the elderly. As might be assumed, income for most individuals following retirement is usually one-half or less what it was prior to retirement (Atchley, 1977). Recent evidence of income inequality can be found in the 1978 U.S. Bureau of Census report on income. According to this report, 14.1 percent of the population over the age 65 existed on incomes below the poverty level of 1977. This compared to percentage figures of 8.5, 7.2, 8.6, and 10.0 for the age ranges of 22-44 years, 45-54

years, 55-59 years, and 60-64 years, respectively. A more alarm-
ing statistic involves the level of income established by the
federal government as necessary to provide a bare minimum
healthful level of living.

According to figures compiled for 1973, over 20 percent of all
elderly couples and nearly 70 percent of all elderly individuals
existed on incomes below this level (Atchley, 1977). A recent
survey in a Florida county revealed that 85.1% of the elderly
surveyed could not keep on their medically-prescribed special
diets, often due to the limited financial resources they had
available for maintaining high cost diets (Hayes, Wahl, Bedard,
Boyd, & Hagen, 1975).

Even when compared to other oppressed groups, the elderly
fare poorly by traditional measures of discrimination. In a study
which compares the relative inequality between age, race, and
sex groups using the Equality Index (EI) and 1950-70 census
data, Palmore and Manton (1973) found that age inequality is
strongest in education and weeks worked per year and second
strongest in terms of actual income (sex inequality was first in
income). Furthermore, their analysis revealed an unfortunate
trend for the elderly across the twenty years of the study. While
inequalities due to race showed modest but clear trends toward
greater equality and sex comparisons indicated little or no
change, inequality due to age appeared, ". . . to be getting substantially worse, with the income EI registering a drop over 7
points and the education EI showing a drop of over 16 points. .
." (p. 367).

By far the most oppressed elderly populations are those who
experience income inequality due to age in combination with
discrimination resulting from their membership in other
minority groups.

> Four factors—old age, inadequate income, minority status,
> and female gender—build on each other to create life situa-
> tions with increasing possibilities for loss and injury. To be
> old puts a person in jeopardy in our society; to be old and
> poor equals double jeopardy; to be old, poor, minority, and
> female equals quadruple jeopardy (Perry, 1978, p. 178).

According to the 1978 U.S. Census Bureau Report on Income,
21.9 percent of the Hispanic elderly and 36.3 percent of the
Black elderly in 1977 existed on incomes below the poverty

level. The objects of triple oppression, an incredible 41.2 percent of the elderly Black women in 1977 live on incomes below the poverty level. With a life expectancy eight years less than the average White person, few Blacks live to enjoy the full benefits of a social security program they have helped to fund. The likelihood of an American Indian ever drawing a social security check or enjoying other programs for the elderly, with a life expectancy of 47 years, is tragically remote (Fields, 1973).

Being aged, female and single results in a particularly devastating combination of oppressive forces. More than half of the single elderly women in 1975 existed on incomes at or below the poverty level. Less than five percent of the single women in 1975 had annual incomes of more than $5,000 (Kreps & Clark, 1975). These figures take on added meaning with the knowledge that women have a greater life expectancy than men and aged women are expected to outnumber aged men 2 to 1 by the year 2000 (Atchley, 1977).

OPPRESSION BY BENIGN NEGLECT

The discussion thus far has focused on the income inequality experienced by the elderly. Unfortunately, the loss of income that confronts most retirees and their elderly spouses is followed in relatively quick succession by the loss of health, mobility, social contact, and freedom (institutionalization). To some degree the loss of health and mobility are a part of a natural aging process. There is little doubt, however, that technology exists at present to substantially reduce the impact of these losses so that later life can be an active, satisfying, growth-enhancing stage of development. Indeed, Alex Comfort (1974), the noted biologist, suggests that the technology even exists to delay the biological aging process for several decades if we are willing to establish this goal as a societal priority.

Like lemmings seemingly unconscious of where our own life experiences will lead us, we have tended to ignore many problems of the elderly and have offered only token efforts for dealing with those problems we acknowledge exist. Attempts to improve the plight of the elderly by local, state and federal agencies have resulted in token programs—surface-level improvements that appease the conscience of younger, middle-class onlookers but which do little to correct (and indeed, may aggre-

vate) conditions for the elderly. It is society's willingness to ignore the losses of the elderly or to offer token programs to appease the public's conscience, despite the existence of the
technology and resources to resolve these problems, that
represents perhaps the most severe form of oppression of the
elderly.

A graphic analysis of oppression by benign neglect and tokenism is offered by Henry (1963) in his description of three
"homes" for the elderly:

> Public institutions for sick "social security paupers"— those
> who have no income but their social security checks— are
> ruled by the social conscience; that is to say, obvious things
> that readily excite conventional feelings of right and wrong
> are taken account of within the limits of miserly budgets, but
> everything else is slighted (p. 392).

> The social conscience is affected by things having "high
> visibility" like clean floors, freshly painted walls, and plenty
> of medical supplies, rather than those having "low visibility,"
> like personal involvement. . . . Routinization, inattention,
> carelessness, and the deprivation of communication—the
> chance to talk, to respond, to read, to see pictures on the
> wall, to be called by one's name rather that "you" or no name
> at all—are ways in which millions of once useful but now ob-
> solete human beings are detached from their selves long
> before they are lowered into the grave (p. 393).

Like retirement, nursing home placement is often pressed upon
elderly persons under the guise of being for their own good.
While some nursing homes make an earnest effort to keep their
residents socially active, many attend to only those "high
visibility" care needs described by Henry above. The tragedy of
social isolation experienced by most elderly residents of nursing homes is particularly devastating for the Third World
elderly, especially those of Hispanic or Asian descent. With
only a few rare exceptions, these individuals are confined to
nursing homes that lack bilingual staff members and that pay
little attention to the unique dietary and other cultural
preferences of their charges.

Society's reponse to other losses suffered by the elderly, while
less dramatic than those associated with institutionalization,
also reflects a posture of benign neglect and tokenism. Despite
the existence of Medicare and Medicaid, poor elderly people
are unable to increase the level of medical attention they re-

ceive to compensate for their declining health as they grow older (Atchley, 1977). In some of our larger cities, the elderly are given reduced fares or even free transportation on the public owned or subsidized municipal transportation system, but then no provision is made for the special needs they may have as users. Many elderly citizens are physically unable to negotiate the steps down to a subway or up into a bus and others are afraid to use public transportation for fear of physical assault. Even with regard to community-centered social programs for the elderly, many of the activities provided only lend a surface appearance of social involvement and do not give the elderly the social contact *they* desire.

STEREOTYPES OF THE ELDERLY

The Self-Fulfilling Prophecy Effect

Like Third World people, women, and other minorities, the elderly are the victims of stereotyping by the majority population. The most unfortunate aspect of olderage stereotyping is that many elderly persons begin to accept and conform to the generalizations made about them. Stereotypes of the elderly are often based on a small measure of truth and a large measure of myth, but are always applied without recognition of individual uniqueness and without a concern for the source of the generalized characteristic. Examples of several generalizations about the elderly are offered to emphasize the point that the same social structure that applies stereotypic labels to aging behavior is responsible in part for engineering the behavior in question.

Senility is a Natural Accompaniment of Aging

Most authorities now agree that a major part of what is labeled senility is a state of mind rather than a form of mental illness due to organic deterioration (Atchley, 1977; Freese, 1978; Looney, 1973). It is also generally acknowledged now that many infirmities formerly thought to be associated with aging are actually symptoms of specific, often treatable, disorders. Furthermore, it is commonly recognized among medical experts that the greatest cause of "senile-like behavior" is "senility anxiety" and the "self-fulfilling prophecy" effect. Those elderly persons who remain socially active and involved throughout their life span seldom show significant signs of bizarre behavior. Those elderly who are isolated from social interaction or constantly reminded of approaching senility are likely to display "senile behavior."

"You Can't Teach an Old Dog New Tricks"

Although aging undoubtedly influences intellectual functioning, there is general agreement among gerontological psychologists that age changes are much smaller than is suggested by many of the earlier cross-generational studies of intelligence and aging. There is, for instance, evidence that most people retain the ". . . essential plasticity of intellectual ontogeny during late adulthood and old age" (Baltes & Labouvie, 1973, p. 202). Dennis (1966) found that creativity declined scarcely at all through age 70.

One of the most commonly accepted stereotypes in this area is the view that elderly people have poor memories.

> It is commonly believed that all kinds of memory show a decline with advancing age. However, studies do not overwhelmingly support this idea. . . . Bright people are less susceptible to memory loss with increasing age than are their less intelligent counterparts, and some people escape memory loss altogether. People who exercise their memories tend to maintain both remote and recent memory well into old age (Atchley, 1977, p. 54).

In studies where evidence of mental deterioration has been found, little attention has been paid to the effect of the environment on this process. When one considers the social and intellectual "deep freeze" our elderly citizens are often placed in, it is little wonder that they show signs of reduced intellectual functioning. While spending billions of dollars on educating the young, our society virtually ignores the educational needs of its senior citizens.

Disengagement is an Inevitable Part of the Aging Process

Disengagement has been defined as a process by which, ". . . the individual responds to aging by gradually and inevitably withdrawing from the various roles he or she occupied in middle age toward ever-increasing concern with self and decreasing involvement with others" (Atchley, 1977, p. 209). Although it is clear that some people do become more inwardly oriented in old age, there is evidence that people are as apt to increase engagement following retirement as to decrease it (Cottrell &

Atchley, 1969; Streib & Schneider, 1971). Furthermore, Rose (1965) found that the most frequent reason elderly persons in his sample gave for disaffiliation from an organization was that they were forced out (mandatory age for disaffiliation).

These are three of the most widely accepted stereotypes of the elderly. There are also stereotypes that the elderly are sedentary by choice, that they prefer to limit their social contact to other elderly, that they are less receptive to new ideas as they grow older, that they can't cope with change, that the majority are disabled, that they are all alike, that old age is a disease, and still others that are discussed in the final section of this book.

Most of these stereotypes about the elderly are negative. Some also are based in part on fact. For instance, a greater proportion of the elderly do display "senile behavior" than occurs in any other age group. The aged are also less sexually active, less educated, and less active in social roles than are members of other age groups. These and other stereotypes can be observed to hold true for the aged population on the average. None of these stereotypes is true for all elderly people, however.

Furthermore, research evidence is beginning to accumulate that social attitudes toward aging and limitations placed on the aged by society contribute more to the observed stereotypic behavior than does the aging process per se (Percy, 1974). This suggests the same paradoxial situation that many other minorities experience. On the one hand, the elderly are viewed as inferior because of observed negative stereotypic behavior. On the other hand, social restrictions and self-fulfilling prophecies insure that the elderly are unlikely to engage in alternative behaviors.

GROWING RECOGNITION OF MINORITY STATUS

According to Wirth's (1945) definition, a group of people constitute a minority if, ". . . because of physical or cultural characteristics, (they) are singled out from the others in the society in which they live for differential and unequal treatment, and who therefore regard themselves as the objects of collective discrimination" (p. 347). The divergence of cultural backgrounds and socio-economic levels among the elderly and their apparent lack of unified political causes have been cited as justification for questioning a minority group designation for the elderly at the present time (Atchley, 1977). Yet, the increased interaction among the elderly and reduced interaction with other age groups, as well as a growing awareness that they constitute a social group, can be viewed as proof that the aged do have a psuedo-culture of their own (Rose, 1965). Furthermore, there is evidence that the elderly themselves are beginning to perceive themselves as the objects of collective discrimination and that they are beginning to recognize their collective needs (Kuhn, 1975).

Although a movement for social insurance and pensions attracted national attention as early as 1922, the advocacy for old age benefits and a heightened awareness of collective needs among the elderly did not crystallize until after the 1950 National Conference on Aging (Pratt, 1976). The recent emergence of the Gray Panthers, Senior Advocates International, the National Caucus on the Aged, California Council for Older Citizens, Massachusetts Legislative Council for Older Citizens, and Action Coalition to Create Opportunities for Retirement with Dignity, as well as the swelling memberships of established organizations like the American Association of Retired Persons, the National Retired Teachers Association, the National Council of Senior Citizens, and the National Association of Retired Federal Employees, testify to the growing group consciousness and political activity of the elderly.

Kleyman (1974) suggests that we have just begun to see the tip of the age-equality iceberg and that, "Students and Third World protestors of the 1960's may be shocked to find that their valuable work may eventually be recorded as a prelude to more sweeping changes fostered by the age-equality movement" (p. 10). Wheeler (1978) has concluded that this revolutionary "rise of the elders" is just beginning to emerge as a social force in the United States.

Despite the impressive potential power and growing awareness of the elderly, it must be acknowledged that most elderly people bear the burdens of institutional and social oppression without public protest. Many elderly persons are reluctant to discuss their living conditions as a matter of pride, having been socialized to a view that, as adults, they should take care of their own needs. Thus, many elderly persons endure incredible conditions of poverty and depriviation without complaint, accepting sole responsibility for their intolerable situation and refusing to transfer the burden to society at large. It is the combination of this attitude of self-blame by the aged and the traditional counseling value that clients must own their problems that threatens to render counseling a repressive influence in the lives of the elderly.

NEEDED: BEHAVIOR AND SOCIAL CHANGE COUNSELING

The counseling profession, with its psychotherapeutic roots embedded in the middle-age, middle-class culture and its developmental roots embedded in youth-oriented public education, has tended to neglect the counseling-related needs of the elderly. This posture of benign neglect by counselors may also reflect the socio-economic structure of the United States. With extremely limited financial resources, many elderly persons simply cannot afford private counseling services. While children, adolescents, and young adults are provided free counseling services through public-supported education, cost-free counseling services for the elderly are nonexistent in many communities and are limited to whatever counseling activities are provided by charitable organizations (frequently staffed by non-professional counselors) and public mental health facilities in others. Whatever the reason for past neglect, the counseling profession has recently begun to acknowledge that people continue to have emotional, social, and psychological difficulties after age 65 and that counseling may enhance the life experiences of elderly persons as well as those of more youthful clientele. Some of the counseling-related needs of the elderly are similar to those confronted by counselors working with younger people (e.g., interpersonal conflict, indecision, existential anxiety). Others are somewhat unique to the change in life experiences concommitant with retirement and the aging process (e.g., adjustment to increased leisure time, shift from occupational to social activities as sources of self-esteem, accepting limitations to physical activity due to declining health).

Many of these problems can be dealt with using the behavior-change counseling strategies traditionally employed by counselors if the counselor is knowledgeable of and sensitive to the unique experiences of the elderly counselee. A major portion of this book is devoted to enhancing the counselor's awareness of the elderly's unique experiences and to a discussion of how behavior-change counseling strategies can be adapted to this particular clientele.

Many of the emotional, social, and psychological problems of the elderly, however, cannot be resolved using traditional, behavior-change counseling methods since these problems have their genesis in the external environment rather than in the counselee. For example, aged counselees who express fear bordering on paranoia because they can only afford apartments in high crime areas may question the usefulness of systematic desensitization to fear of assault as a solution to their problem. Nor are elderly counselees who express feelings of depression and loneliness because their mobility is restricted likely to respond favorably to the counselor's efforts at social-skills training.

Although these examples of mismatched counseling problems and interventions are offered with tongue-in-cheek, the point to be made is an important one. Counseling approaches that culminate in counselee attitude and behavior change are based on philosophical and theoretical concepts that assume the locus of counselee problems is internal. This view of counselee problems is reflected not only in the strategies employed by counselors, but also in their goals for the counseling process (i.e. the client must own the problem; the counselee needs to control irrational self-statements; the counselee needs to learn more adaptive behaviors). When the locus of the counselee's problem can be accurately attributed to an external source, as is often the case with oppressed elders, behavior-change approaches to counseling are rendered ineffective at best and serve to perpetuate the problem at worst.

Recognizing how inappropriate a behavior-change approach to counseling is for externally-imposed counselee problems, a number of earlier authors have proposed the implementation of a social-activist approach to counseling (Adams, 1973; Baker & Cramer, 1972; Banks & Martens, 1973; Ciavarella & Doolittle, 1970; Cook, 1972; Drew, 1973; Dustin, 1973; Dworkin & Dworkin, 1971; Menacker, 1976; Pine, 1976; Warnath, 1973). The major thrust of the social-activist approach to counseling is that counselors should focus their efforts on changing the institutions that oppress their counselees rather than helping conform their counselees to the demands of the institutions.

Counseling for the Growing Years

Although the concept of counselors as social-activists has gained a measure of respectability in the profession in recent years, it remains largely an idea and not a reality (Lewis & Lewis, 1977).

A unique opportunity is afforded to define professional goals, roles, and functions as the counseling profession begins for the first time to serve the elderly on a broad scale. Counselors can be a part of the social movement that helps eliminate the oppression of the elderly or they can continue to support the status quo by restricting their counseling activities to behavior-change strategies only.

A SOCIAL ACTIVIST APPROACH TO COUNSELING THE ELDERLY

Michael and Judith Lewis (1977) have proposed a tentative model for practice designed to move the counselor's role as environmental change agent from the level of theory to the level of practice. As part of their model, the Lewises identify four functions of the counselor/social activist: assessment of community needs, coordinating, skill building, and advocacy. In adapting their model to the special needs of the elderly, the functions of consciousness-raising and organizing are added to the four counseling activities identified by the Lewises.

Consciousness-Raising

Social-activist counseling with the elderly requires consciousness-raising at three levels. First, counselors must begin by raising their own level of awareness of the social/-environmental conditions affecting the aged. It is difficult to determine just how the seed of conciousness-raising is first planted, but it certainly requires an initial concern for the plight of the elderly, perhaps aroused by the problems confronted by one's own parents or grandparents. Given this initial concern, consciousness-raising can be enhanced by such activities as visiting a nursing home for the elderly, listening (for a change) to an elderly relative forced to exist on social security, and reading cold hard statistics like those provided by the U. S. Census Bureau and Bureau of Labor Statistics.

A second level of consciousness-raising involves the non-aged population. Margaret (Maggie) Kuhn (1974), National Convenor of the Gray Panthers, has said that the United States needs ". . . an aroused public awareness of the forces and institutional policies which demean and diminish old people. . ." (p. 4). Many younger people are simply not aware of the conditions of poverty and oppression that the majority of elderly individuals deal with daily. Every counselor, not just those who work directly with the elderly, can help raise the awareness of the non-aged by becoming informed and sharing any insight gained as a result.

School and agency counselors, for instance, are often asked to speak at church club meetings, civic organizations, and PTA's on topics of their own choosing. A most effective means of communicating the needs of the elderly is to take an elderly spokesperson along to these meetings. In addition to invited presentations, the concerned counselor can encourage elementary schools, secondary schools, and colleges to provide a forum for issues related to aging. Actively involving groups of non-aged with the elderly through volunteer programs can be an effective consciousness-raising activity. Consciousness-raising among the non-aged, however, does not mean organizing a once-a-year Christmas caroling tour of a nursing home for the elderly. It means directly acquainting the non-aged with the predjucies and inequalities experienced by the elderly, so that, hopefully, the non-aged participants can become advocates for changing these oppressive conditions.

> Finally, consciousness-raising among groups of us oldsters is basic to our own image and self-esteem. It is also basis to societal change and redirection. A technological society is basically wasteful—wasteful of human resources. . . . Consciuosness-raising is also an important element in building the new supportive caring community essential to maintaining life at any age, but absolutely essential to selfhood in old age (Kuhn, 1974, p. 4).

Armed with data acquired during their own consciousness-raising process, counselors can help the aged become aware of the environmental forces that shape their lives. Sharing with the elderly the knowledge that they are not alone in their experiences of poverty and oppression can be a first step in helping them realize the true causes of their problems. As suggested earlier, many elderly refuse to acknowledge their condition of poverty or forced isolation or mistreatment because they have been socialized to believe they are responsible for their situation.

This dynamic is graphically illustrated in the Bevard County Older Americans Survey (Hayes, et al., 1975) in which only ten percent of the respondents admitted that they had difficulty because of their income, yet 25 percent of all those surveyed lived on incomes below the poverty level. Knowing that others who have worked hard all their lives are experiencing the same difficulties often helps relieve the sense of failure as an individual while more appropriately placing the blame on an oppressive social system.

Assessment of Needs

According to the Lewises, counselors are in an ideal and somewhat unique position to assess the environmental factors that influence human growth and development.

> Counselors have a deep personal awareness of the problems faced by their communities. They can identify unhealthy situations through their effects on individuals and then make the effort to alert the community as a whole and to identify potential allies with particular interest in the problems at hand (Lewis & Lewis, p. 358).

Thus, for those counselors who work directly with the elderly, assessment of needs can begin at the level of the individual counseling encounter. Since persons in positions of power are often more influenced by formal than informal documentation, it behooves the counselor to keep records of those needs that are the most pressing and most recurrent. A needs survey of elderly served by the counselor's agency can be a highly effective means of obtaining information about problems related to physical health, nutrition, housing, income, transportation, and culture.

Counselors, by presenting tabular data from their own record-keeping, can also be instrumental in getting their local governmental unit to undertake such a needs survey. An excellent example of a county-wide needs survey and subsequent recommendations for change is provided by the Bevard County Older Americans Survey (Hayes, et al., 1975).

Basic Concerns

Coordinating

One of the primary functions of any community agency counselor is that of coordinating the resources of the community to result in optimum benefit for counselees. This coordinating function of counselors need not be restricted to the intra-psychic psychological needs of their counselees. As the Lewises suggest, counselors ". . . can become just as aware of the resources for *change* within their communities, and make referrals to people's action organizations as routinely as they make referrals to specialized helpers of "individuals" (Lewis & Lewis, 1977, p. 358).

Reference was made in an earlier section of this chapter to the growing number of old-age advocacy groups. In addition to national organizations concerned with broad issues that affect all elderly citizens, numerous organizations committed to senior advocacy are cropping up in many large metropolitan areas that are concerned with issues at the local level. Counselors of the elderly need to become familiar with both the local and national organizations advocating on behalf of the elderly in order to make appropriate referrals.

Other action organizations, not devoted singularly to the needs of the elderly, can also be helpful in bringing about change for aged counselees. Legal assistance offices, women's centers, and ethnic community centers, are examples of action organizations that can be influential in resolving social/-political problems for the elderly. Prior to consciousness-raising, however, the elderly are not likely to use existing services because: (1) they have been socialized to resolve their own problems, and (2) they may be unaware of the services.

That the elderly are either reluctant to use existing services or uninformed of their availability can be inferred from the fact that although one out of every five poor persons is aged, the elderly make up only six percent of the clientele of legal assistance offices (Kleyman, 1974). Once the elderly have a renewed sense of self-esteem and are actively engaged in identifying factors that operate to oppress them, the counselor's role in effectuating services will consist primarily of making the elderly aware that the services exist.

Organizing

A group of politically active elderly persons can accomplish far more than they can as individuals. Counselors can help elderly persons organize around issues of relevance to their life experience by putting people with similar viewpoints in contact with each other and by arranging meetings where age-related issues and concerns can be discussed. Organizing the elderly should be a nonpartisan form of politicization with the singular goal of eliminating oppression experienced by the aged. With the exception of a few retirement communities for the very wealthy, no community of elderly is likely to be lacking for issues around which to organize.

Saul Alinsky (1971) has suggested that in order to organize a group of individuals into a political force, the organizer must first establish credibility with the people involved. Elderly people are understandably leery of younger persons who lack their experience, and sensitivity to the plight of the elderly gained during the consciousness-raising and needs-assessment activities can go a long way toward building the needed rapport. Hopefully, the listening skills that counselors learn in their first pre-practicum experiences will also prove useful in building credibility with an elderly clientele.

Most important, however, as an organizer the counselor should refrain from attempting to be a leader or spokesperson for the elderly. The counselor's role is to encourage elderly citizens to join forces so that they can present their concerns to the appropriate authority. No one can speak more eloquently and with greater conviction about the difficulties they face than the elderly themselves. Among any group of non-institutionalized elderly people there are likely to be several potential leaders. Sometimes the leader who emerges will be a retired professional person; other times a former blue collar worker. The leader obviously needs some facility with words, and understanding of organizational structure, and a fairly abundant supply of energy. The counselor should not attempt to hand-pick the leader (Alinsky, 1971).

An important organizational activity is the prioritizing of issues that the group intends to bring to the attention of those in power positions. Functioning as a resource person, the counselor can help develop a list of issues but should avoid involvement in the prioritizing process. The group should be encouraged, however, to select a winnable issue for its number one priority (Kleyman, 1974).

There are a number of problem areas experienced by the elderly, each of which may involve several issues that need to be confronted. For instance, following loss of income and health, loss of mobility is one of the most difficult problems the elderly face. One issue in this area has to do with the loss of a driver's license. Many states simply revoke the license of anyone who cannot pass a driver's test. Some states, however, allow elderly persons to keep their licenses but place restrictions on where and when they can drive. The provision of restricted driver's licenses in states where they are not presently available becomes an issue of major import to elderly citizens residing in these states. The provision for fare-free public transportation and structural accommodations for persons with physical limitations are two more issues. The availability of volunteer car pooling or public-supported taxi service is still another transportation issue.

Education is another problem area for the elderly that is often overlooked. As Baltes and Labouvie (1973) have pointed out, "Unprecedented amounts of money and effort have been invested in designing educational and social intervention programs for the young aimed at accelerating the rate of ontogeny; however, similar investments in modifying or monitoring the intellectual ontogeny of the aged are at best minikin" (p. 202). Thus, the availability of adult education, particularly that aimed at the needs of senior citizens, is an important issue. Other concerns like the relevance of course offerings for the elderly, times when offered, and location are important educational issues.

Common problem areas for the elderly other than transportation and education include income, medical care, nutrition, housing, security, and social and cultural activities. In any given community the elderly may be able to identify additional problems that they face which could be resolved *if* the community accepted responsibility for resolving the problem. For additional ideas about how to help groups organize against the forces of oppression, the reader should consult *Rules for radicals: A practical primer for realistic radicals* by Saul Alinsky.

Skill-Building

The Lewises contend that counselors should use their skill-building expertise to aid oppressed groups as well as to aid the organizations that employ them as counselors.

> Professionals can choose to shed their objectivity and place themselves and their expertise at the disposal of self-help and community action groups. Such groups can confront the rest of the world more effectively if they have had assistance in team-building in molding themselves into cohesive, caring entities. Many counselors utilize the theories and methods of organizational development to assist institutions. Those same approaches could be used just as effectively with the "have-not" groups attempting to have greater influence in the community at large (Lewis & Lewis, 1977, p. 358).

There are a number of skill-building procedures (e.g., group facilitation, problem solving, brainstorming, assertive training for individuals) that counselors should possess as a result of their professional training. A skill-building expertise they are not likely to have as a result of their professional education, however, is a knowledge of "group assertiveness" or "group confrontational" skills. Assertiveness and confrontation in this context is intended to imply anything from a group letter-writing campaign to boycotting and lobbying. Once aware of their shared experience of oppression and organized as a group around relevant issues, the elderly should be encouraged to exercise their Constitutionally guaranteed rights by confronting the appropriate authorities with their unmet needs.

Several examples of past success by the elderly through confrontation tactics can be provided. As a result of a threatened boycott of the 1971 White House Conference on Aging, old-age interest groups were able to extract several concessions from the Nixon administration (Atchley, 1977; Pratt, 1976). Kleyman (1974) cites several other examples. In one, a slight, elderly woman named Isabel van Frank pressed Black Panther Bobby Seale, as a candidate for mayor of Oakland, to do something about muggings of senior citizens in their city. As a result of her feisty confrontation, Seale helped organize a nonprofit escort service for the elderly that began operating three months later.

In another example, California Governor Reagan was cornered by 20 oldsters outside San Francisco's Ferry Building and questioned on a bill that would pass along Social Security increases to 315,000 aged poor, a bill Reagan had vetoed for two years. Presumably embarrassed by his own off-handed response to the elderly pickets in front of television news cameras, Reagan signed the legislation into law a few days later.

While these are exceptionally dramatic examples of confrontational tactics by elderly citizens, the more usual form of pressure comes through lobbying efforts by mail or in person. The point is, elderly persons can have an impact on the institutions that oppress them by banding together as a political force. When the elderly do speak out for their rights in public, they often have an important factor operating in their favor. Unlike most youthful protestors, authority figures are often reluctant to use any type of force to suppress their freedom of expression. For an outline of how the elderly can work on legislation and six steps to follow in organizing media relations, the reader is referred to *Senior power: Growing old rebelliously* by Paul Kleyman.

Advocacy

The Lewises (1977) maintain that:

> Ideally counselors try to bring about a situation in which all individuals can develop the strength and the expertise to take care of their own needs and to defend themselves against destructive environmental influences. In the interim, however, there is often a need to work in behalf of individuals or groups still lacking the power needed to defend themselves. Counselors can play an active role in protecting the rights of individual counselees, particularly when the helping agency or institution itself fails to treat the individual with dignity (p. 358).

It is an unfortunate fact of life that some elderly persons become less and less capable of defending their rights as they grow older. These individuals are frequently confined to nursing homes and they are unlikely to receive any counseling services other than those provided by the facility itself or by a public social service agency. It is important that social workers, development specialists, and other specialists employed in nursing homes for the elderly, who, by design or default, serve as counselors for the residents, perceive one of their functions as that of advocacy.

There are other instances in which counselors may find they must advocate on behalf of elderly counselees. Usually these are situations where individuals lack some necessary skills for dealing with the bureaucratic structure. As an example, an elderly minority couple may lack the prerequisite verbal skills needed to convince the Social Security Administration that they qualify for SSI benefits.

SUMMARY

The porportion of elderly citizens in the population of the United States has shown a steady increase from 4.0% in 1900 to 9.9% in 1970 and is projected to reach 11.2% in the year 2000 (Atchley, 1977). Although very few counselors work directly with the elderly population at present, it seems quite likely that as the elderly population grows and as more revenue sources are directed toward satisfying their needs, the aged will be the recipients of increased counseling services through adult education, senior centers, nursing homes, retirement housing projects, V.A. hospitals, and other community service agencies.

Counselors who work with the elderly need to recognize that the aged, as an oppressed minority group, are likely to present numerous adjustment problems that originate in the environment, not within themselves. The counselor who employs a behavior-change counseling approach when the source of the problem resides outside the counselee may be functionally supporting the forces of oppression that created the problem. The counselor who recognizes that some elderly counselee problems actually reside in the environment and who functions as a social-activist to change the environment will be serving to free the elderly from opression.

The six functions of a counselor/social activist for the aged are: counsciousness-raising, assessment of needs, coordinating, organizing, skill building, and advocacy. An important side effect of involving the elderly in consciousness-raising, organizing, and confrontational activities is that it raises the self-esteem of the elderly participant (Kleyman, 1974; Kuhn, 1974), a goal of both traditional and social-activist counseling. Like people of all ages, the elderly gain a strong sense of self-appreciation when they feel they have some say in the events that influence their lives.

Counselors have always served as agents of behavior change. Minority critics have suggested that this narrow view of the counselor's role may actually help perpetuate the source of many minority counselee problems. Both the behavior-change approach to counseling that is designed to resolve emotional crises within the individual and the social-activist approach to counseling designed to reduce external forces of oppression are needed in counseling the elderly.

REFERENCES

Adams, H.J. The progressive heritage of guidance: A view from the left. *Personnel and Guidance Journal*, 1973, *51*, 531-538.

Alinsky, S.D. *Rules for radicals: A practical primer for realistic radicals*. New York: Random House, 1971.

Atchley, R.C. *The social forces in later life*. Belmont, California: Wadsworth Publishing Co., 1977.

Baker, S.B., & Cramer, S.H. Counselor or change agent: Support from the profession. *Personnel and Guidance Journal*, 1972, *50*, 661-665.

Baltes, P.B., & Labouvie, G.V. Adult development of intellectual performance: Description, explanation, In C. Eisdorfer & M. Powell Lawton (Eds.), *The psychology of adult development and aging*. Washington, D.C.: American Psychological Association, 1973.

Banks, W., & Martens, K. Counseling: The reactionary profession. *Personnel and Guidance Journal*, 1973, *51*, 457-462.

Barron, M.L. Minority group characteristics of the aged in American society. *Journal of Gerontology*, 1953, *8*, 447-482.

Butler, R.N. Age-ism: Another form of biogotry. *Gerontologist*, 1969, *9*, 243-246.

Ciavarella, M.A., & Doolittle, L.W. The ombudsman: Relevant role model for the counselor. *School Counselor*, 1970, 17, 331-336.

Comfort, A. We know the aging process can be slowed down. *Center Report*, (Center for the study of Democratic Institutions), June, 1974, 18-23.

Cook, D.R. The change agent counselor: A conceptual context. *School Counselor*, 1972, *20*, 9-15.

Cottrell, F., & Atchley, R.C. *Women in retirement: A preliminary report*. Oxford, Ohio: Scripps Foundation, 1969.

Curtin, S.R. *Nobody ever died of old age*. Boston: Little, Brown, and Co., 1972.

Dennis, W. Creative productivity between the ages of 20 and 80 years. *Journal of Gerontology*, 1966, *21*, 1-8.

Drew, J.H. The effectiveness of an ombudsman. *Personnel and Guidance Journal,* l973, *51,* 317-320.

Dustin, R. Training for institutional change. *Personnel and Guidance Journal,* 1973, *52,* 442-427.

Dworkin, E.P., & Dworkin, A.L. The activist counselor. *Personnel and Guidance Journal,* 1971, *49,* 748-753.

Fields, C. Service delivery and consumer participation (Summary Report). In E.P. Stanford (Ed.), *Minority aging; Institute proceedings.* San Diego: Institute on Minority Aging, 1973.

Freese, A.S. Good news about senility. *Modern Maturity,* 1978, *21,* (1), 9-10.

Hayes, P.J.; Wahl, P.F.; Bedard, P.E.; Boyd, L.C.; & Hagen, P. *Brevard County older Americans survey—summary analysis and recommendations.* Merritt Island, Florida: Division of Health and Social Services and Brevard Council, Inc., 1975.

Henry, J. *Culture against man.* New York: Random House, Inc., 1963.

Kleyman, P. *Senior Power: Growing old rebelliously.* San Francisco: Glide Publications, 1974.

Kreps, J., & Clark, R. *Sex, age, and work: The changing composition of the labor force.* Baltimore: Johns Hopkins Univerisity Press, 1975.

Kuhn, M. Grass roots gray power. *Prime Time,* June, 1974, 4-6.

Kuhn, M. Liberation from ageism. *Interaction,* June, 1975, 5-6, 11.

Lewis, M.D., & Lewis, J.A. The counselor's impact on community environments. *Personnel and Guidance Journal,* 1977, *55,* 356-358.

Looney, D.S. Senility is also a state of the mind. *National Observer,* March 31, 1973, 1.

McConnel, C.E. Age discrimination and the Employment Service— Another look. *Industrial Gerontology,* 1977, *4,* 235-246.

Menacker, J. Toward a theory of activist guidance. *Personnel and Guidance Journal,* 1976, *54,* 318-321.

Montaigne. Of the affections of fathers to their children. *Essays,* 1580-1588.

Palmore, E., & Manton, K. Ageism compared to racism and sexism. *Journal of Gerontology,* 1973, *28,* 363-369.

Percy, C.H. *Growing old in the country of the young.* New York: McGraw-Hill, 1974.

Perry, P.W. The night of ageism. In Harold Cox (Ed.), *Focus: Aging*. Gilford, Connecticut: Publishing Group, 1978.

Pine, G.J. Troubled times for school counseling. *Focus on Guidance*, 1976, *8*(5), 1-116.

Pratt, H.J. *The grey lobby*. Chicago: The University of Chicago Press, 1976.

Rose, A.M. The subculture of the aging: A framework for research in social gerontology. In A.M. Rose & W.A. Peterson (Eds.), *Older people and their social world*. Philadelphia: F.F. Davis, Co., 1965.

Schultz, J.H. The economics of mandatory retirement. *Industrial Gerontology*, 1974, *1*, 1-10.

Schwab, D.P., & Heneman, H.G. Effects of age and experience on productivity. *Industrial Gerontology*, 1977, *4*, 113-117.

Streib, G.F., & Schneider, C.J. *Retirement in American society*. Ithaca, New York: Cornell University Press, 1971.

U.S. Bureau of Census Current Population Reports, Series P-60, No. 116, *Money income and poverty status of families and persons in the United States: 1977* (Advanced Report), U.S. Government Printing Office, Washington, D.C., 1978.

Warnath, G.G. The school counselor as an institutional change agent. *School Counselor*, 1973, *20*, 202-208.

Wheeler, H. Goodbye to mandatory retirement. *Modern Maturity*, 1978, *21*, 9-11.

Wirth, L. The problem of minority groups. In R. Linton (Ed.), *The science of man in the world crisis*. New York: Columbia University Press, 1945.

Medical Aspects of Aging

Glenys O. Williams

ABSTRACT

The majority of people over 65 feel well, even though their age group fills 40% of the hospital beds. Expectation of life is increasing, with the old-old requiring considerable health care. Changes in structure of the body due to aging alter the appearance. Diminished function affects the special senses, while failure of the brain, poor balance, and elimination difficulties are responsible for most common medical problems of old age. Many old people accept symptoms of disease as natural consequenses of aging, and delay seeking medical advice. Others react to aging with anxiety and hypochondriasis. Health screening of all over 70s is recommended as a preventive measure.

People at high risk of physical and mental disease are those recently discharged from hospitals; living alone; recently bereaved; with locomotor difficulties; and mentally impaired. Special attention needs to be paid to those in high risk categories. Distinctive characteristics of illness in the old are multiple disease, atypical symptoms, unusual and chronic course, and drug problems. Mental symptoms are frequently caused by physical conditions. Common precipitating factors for nursing home admission are senile dementia, incontinence, deafness, and inadequate home support.

This chapter contains very specific information on the medical aspects of aging. If counselors are to be effective in meeting the needs of the elderly, some knowledge of the medical implications of aging is important. Counselors reading this chapter should have more insight into the physical realities of aging. This information, coupled with typical counselor education, will be beneficial in working with the elderly.

INTRODUCTION

The majority of old people of all races and both sexes living in the United States report themselves to be in good to excellent health (U.S.D. HEW, HRA, 1977). In spite of this, 40% of the hospital beds in this country are filled by patients over 65. They have more medical problems, and they need hospitalization more often than the young. But the number and complexity of their diseases is far less important than their ability to remain independent and to cope with everyday life.

Longevity of the population continues to rise, with most women living eight years longer than men. The tendency for women to outnumber men is increasing. A male child born in 1976 is expected to live 68.9 years and a female 76.7 years. However, all people reaching the age of 65 have an average continued life expectancy of 16 years. The section of the population increasing most rapidly is the old-old, persons in the mid-70's, 80's and 90's, the majority of whom need a considerable amount of social support and health care. Most of the young-old, those in their 60s and 70s, are healthy and active.

Chronological age may have very little correlation with appearance. Genetic factors and the presence or absence of disease will help determine which 80 year old looks 65, and vice versa. Frequently it is extremely difficult to differentiate between the effects of aging and the effects of disease. During a long life, there is considerable wear and tear of tissues, prolonged exposure to environmental hazards, and the opportunity to accumulate several chronic diseases. The effect of these conditions may not become obvious until late in old age.

Growth implies a change both in structure and function. Much of the turmoil of adolescence is due to the young person getting used to a new "aging" body. During this period, remarkably rapid increases in height and weight, the appearance of secondary sexual characteristics, increased strength, and an awareness of sexual function occur.

The change from middle age to old age is less dramatic, but it too is accompanied by changes both in structure and function. The realization of physical aging causes psychological stress at the end of life, just as at the beginning.

CHANGES IN STRUCTURE DUE TO AGE

Bones.

Changes in body shape and appearance develop slowly over many years. Height may decrease as reduction of calcium in bones (osteoporosis) causes softening and compression of the vertebrae. This process also contributes to a characteristic feature of old age, curvature of the spine in the thoracic region (kyphosis). Shrinkage of the mandible causes altered facial appearance and difficulty in fitting dentures.

Skin.

As the skin becomes dry, thinner, less elastic, and wrinkled, it is responsible for much of the typical appearance of old age. Melanin pigment is deposited in irregular blotches instead of evenly as in the suntan of youth. Hair graying and thinning occurs, the loss being especially marked in men. Absorption of fat around the eyes causes the characteristic sunken-eye appearance.

Muscle.

Although weight may remain the same, some muscle tissue is replaced by fat and some by fibrous tissue, causing considerable change in the contour of arms, legs, and abdomen in particular. Decreased muscle strength is responsible for much of the difficulty old people have in such activities as walking upstairs, using a can-opener, lifting a saucepan, or rising from a low chair. For this reason, older people prefer chairs with high seats and arms.

CHANGE IN FUNCTION

Normal aging has been described as decreased physiological function (Reichel & Barnett, 1978, p. 222). The most profound effects of this decrease are on the special senses, the brain, balance, and elmination.

1. Special Senses

A. Vision. The eye begins to lose its power to change shape and focus on near objects (presbyopia) by the mid-forties. Later, cataracts develop in the lens in 95% of people over the age of 65 (Duke Elder, 1969, p. 4). This is the process in which the lens becomes progressively more opaque and eventually leads to blindness. However, it is easily remedied by surgery, either corrective spectacles, or intraocular artificial lenses.

Degeneration of the light-sensitive portion of the retina occurs fairly commonly and cannot be corrected. In central macular degeneration the central part of vision is lost and peripheral vision retained, so that the only features of a face that an old person may see are the hair, ears, and chin. For this reason, some elderly patients can only recognize people by peering into their faces.

An advantage of aging has been demonstrated by Erwin, (Note 4); vigilance, or visual perception over a 30-minute period, is consistently better in older people then younger. Palmore (1979) suggests that this may explain why older persons have traditionally been the watchmen, gatekeepers, and flocktenders in many societies.

In spite of the frequency of presbyopia, cataracts, glaucoma, and macular degeneration, well over 80% of the population retain reasonable sight even into the nineties. But a 60 year old needs 300% more illumination than a 20 year old to see as clearly (Weale, 1961, pp. 95-100), and an 80 year old may need 500% more. The design of an office used for counseling the elderly should take this need into account. Counselors should sit where they can be clearly seen, without glare. Desks or counters where the elderly have to read or write should be well-lit.

Sensory losses, such as decreased vision, are major contributing factors in balancing difficulty, loss of mobility, depression, and disorientation. For instance, a blind older person may be bewildered and anxious on arrival in a hospital. It is necessary for the speaker to introduce oneself clearly, encourage, and reassure the patient before beginning an interview (Cape, 1978, p. 90). Physical environments for the elderly should take sensory losses into account and be colorful, stimulating, and well-lighted (Pastalan, 1974). Contrasting colors for easy recognition of doors, walls, and floors have also been suggested (Coons, 1978, p. 122).

B. Hearing. Deafness is more common in men, possibly due to occupational noise exposure, while defective eyesight is commoner in women. Interestingly, visual problems tend to be reported early, but hearing defects denied (Weston, 1964, p. 273).

There is a statistically significant relationship between deafness and depression. Difficulties of communication with a deaf old persons often lead to their exclusion from everyday family conversations by frustrated, irritable relatives. In addition, family physicians have found communication with older patients to be a major problem (Williams & Clements, Note 3). The resulting social isolation can progress to paranoia, depression, and loss of orientation (Butler & Perlin, 1963, p. 300). Deafness is also a significant factor in precipitating admissions to nursing homes.

Presbycusis is the condition due to aging which causes slow progressive loss of hearing. Nerve cells deteriorate in the inner ear, initially causing loss of perception of high frequency tones, which include the consonants f, s, and th. As the condition becomes worse, normal speech cannot be heard. Deterioration in the central nervous system causes older people also to be unable (a) to distinguish sounds they want to hear from background noise, and (b) to understand sounds that they can hear. Slowness in processing hearing information in the brain causes difficulty in communication and makes many old people reluctant to take part in a conversation.

Hearing aids, which are worn by 5% of all old people, are probably needed by more and are helpful to those who can adjust to the indiscriminate amplification of sound produced. Sometimes, a miraculous cure can be achieved by the removal of wax impacted in the ear canal.

It is important when talking to old people to speak normally but slowly. Look them full in the face so that facial expression and lip reading can supplement the defective information they receive from their ears. Background noise should also be eliminated wherever possible.

C. Taste and Smell. There is evidence that the senses of taste and smell decrease with age, particularly in men. Lack of enjoyment of food due to inability to taste can lead to defective nutrition. The sensation of thirst is also considerably reduced, so that dehydration is often found in old people who do not recognize their need for fluids.

2. The Brain

Aging "may be a reflection of the breakdown of control mechanisms" which are situated in the brain (Shock, 1974, pp. 1-10).

The brain's optimal potential is reached between the ages of 16 and 20; after this there is a gradual decline, which increases after age 75. The total number of brain cells is reduced (Ball, 1977), reaction times are slowed, and information processing is impaired (Corso, 1975, pp. 119-144).

It is likely that brain failure in old age is the fundamental cause of (a) loss of agility, clumsiness and frequent falls, (b) misunderstanding and confusion, (c) loss of control of bowels and bladder, and (d) loss of ability to cope with sudden stress-physical, mental, or emotional. These four groups of problems are the most common medical problems found in old people (Cape, 1978, p. 79).

3. Balance

With age comes difficulty in maintaining balance and controlling posture. Posture is achieved by brain control of messages from the eyes, ears, neck position, skin, and anti-gravity muscles in the legs. Failure or weakness in any one of these areas can jeopardize the ability to stand and walk upright. Older women are more likely to sway when standing (Exton-Smith, Note 2), and also fall more frequently than men of the same age (Sheldon, 1960). Falls often cause fractured hips leading to hospitalization, then institutionalization, and finally permanent loss of independence. Handrails on both sides of steps or stairs in the home, counseling office, or institutions for the aged are a necessary safeguard. Similarily, loose mats on polished floors must be removed.

4. Elimination

Decreased physiological function is particularly evident in the kidney, which becomes less efficient. (See Drug Problems following). There is a marked tendency in old age to become preoccupied with bodily functions, particularly bowel function. Constipation is extremely common and is contributed to by weak muscles, unsuitable diet, and excessive use of laxatives.

ATTITUDES TO AGING AND DISEASE

The present generation of over 65s was brought up to be independent and stoic. Many of them consult a physician only at times of crisis or catastrophe. Before the advent of Medicare, they were unwilling to spare hard-earned dollars for the dubious benefit of a medical check-up. It must also be confessed that not all physicians have been sympathetic to routine checks on elderly patients.

Frequently patients will accept vague symptoms, and even disability, as an unavoidable consequence of getting old, and will not ask for help until a disease process is far advanced. For this reason, health screening of all persons when they reach 70 years has been recommended as a preventative measure (Andrews, 1971). As the following case histories demonstrate, a routine health check identified the causes of two patients' vague symptoms, with happy results for both.

> Mrs. S. was 74 and thought that was why she did not have her customary pep. It was an effort to walk upstairs; she had to stop halfway up because she was short of breath. She tired easily and found it too much effort to keep her house clean as she liked. Her bowels were a little constipated, but she dismissed all these symptoms as due to getting old. At the Well Elderly Clinic, it was found that she was anemic. The anemia was due to a bleeding tumor in her colon. Once the tumor was removed, she gained all her old energy back.

> Mrs. J. came to the Clinic because she was tired. She was 71 and attributed her fatigue to rushing from one meeting to another. During the winter she had found that cold was intolerable. Mrs. J's face was puffy, her voice was low, her pulse slow, and a blood test showed that her thyroid function was far below normal. Her hypothyroidism was treated with synthetic thyroid hormone and her symptoms of "aging" disappeared.

The "iceberg" phenomenon of disease in older people was demonstrated in a survey of three family practices (Williamson, Stokoe, Gray, Fisher, Smith, McGee, & Stephenson, 1964). The number of diseases not known to physicians was nearly twice the number of diseases known to them, showing the extent of unreported disabilities in their older patients. It has been suggested that a major educational effort is needed to persuade the elderly to report unpleasant or embarrassing symptoms. Counseling the elderly, who may be concealing symptoms, to seek medical advice would be an effective way to improve their quality of life.

As a result of major publicity campaigns, the benefits of blood pressure checks in the detection of hypertension, and more recently, cholesterol levels to identify people at risk for heart disease and stroke, have made many older people willing to avail themselves of such procedures. It is likely that future generations of older people will be more inclined to use preventive health measures and will be less willing to accept disabilities in old age.

There is another group of elderly people who react to aging very differently. Their response is characterized by anxiety, drug or alcohol dependence, and hypochondriasis. Since old age is accompanied by so much personal and social loss and approaching death, there is a real basis for such anxiety. Many of these people turn again and again to the physician for relief of physical symptoms. They may complain of pain in the chest, a racing heart, frequency of urination, abdominal discomfort, itching, or headache. They may increasingly assume the sick role and demand more attention and assistance.

Physicians must convince themselves by necessary diagnostic tests that there is no physical illness before reassuring patients, remembering that physical disease may develop insidiously in known hypochondriacs.

Because there is evidence of increased physical illness in patients before the onset of depression (Widmer & Cadoret, 1978), counselors and physicians must also be alert for symptoms of depression (See Depression). Team work between counselor, physician, and all available community resources is necessary in anxious patients to help them cope with the many stresses of their old age.

High Risk Elderly

Some elderly patients have a higher risk of developing physical and mental illness than others. Factors associated with high risk are (a) recent discharge from hospital, (b) living alone, (c) recently bereaved, (d) locomotor difficulties, and (e) mental impairment. In a group of people over 65 who had been recently discharged from a hospital, were living alone, or who had been recently bereaved, pathological depression was found in a high percentage (14%) and anxiety states in 4-6% (Lowther, MacLeod & Williamson, 1970).

Locomotor difficulties may be due to paralysis following a stroke or to more common conditions, such as obesity or poor foot care. Whatever the cause of limited mobility, the results are often predictable and affect many areas of life. Reduced activity and loneliness may follow and precipitate depression. Walking difficulty often causes serious falls, while inability to cook or go shopping may lead to nutritional deficiencies.

A major change in environment, such as moving to a nursing home, has been reported to be followed by sharply increased death rates of patients over 70, particularly during the first three months (Aldrich & Mendkoff, 1963). Mental health and physical survival are said to be adversely affected by such changes as institutionalization and involuntary relocation in the elderly (Lieberman, 1969; Webb, 1959). Those patients who do most poorly are (a) those in poor physical health, (b) those who are very old, and (c) men (Kasl, 1972). It seems that all these mental and physical stresses are more than an aging person can handle; their fragile state of homeostatic equilibrium is disturbed and sickness or death can result.

Preparation for the transition from home to long-term care institution has been shown to be helpful in reducing morbidity and mortality (Jasnau, 1967). However, in a recent study, Borup, Gallego, and Hefferan, (1979) disagree that relocation causes increased mortality. On a more positive note, they endorse programs designed to reduce the stress of the experience.

There is a pressing need for a service in which elderly people in high risk categories are actively sought out. Counseling and medical care could then be made available to those who are unable to cope with their difficulties, and to the remainder as a preventative measure.

SPECIAL CHARACTERISTICS OF ILLNESS IN THE AGED

1. Multiple pathology

By the time people reach 65, they have had the opportunity to accumulate several chronic diseases. Each patient in one geriatric ward had an average of five pathologic conditions (Skelton, 1977). In spite of this the vast majority of older people consider themselves well, even though in the view of their physicians, they frequently overestimate their state of health.

The success of the human race may be attributed to the fact that it has learned to adapt rapidly to circumstances. In this way many older people readily learn to compensate for such conditions as failing eyesight, arthritic joints, and shortness of breath due to arteriosclerotic heart disease. They feel healthy because their health is good enough to do what they want to do. But surgical replacement of a painful arthritic hip joint may make more exercise possible than that patient's failing heart can tolerate. Similarly, drugs for one condition may aggravate another. For instance, diuretics taken for hypertension can cause a severe flare-up of gout.

2. Atypical presentation

Atypical presentation is one of the most challenging aspects of disease in old people. Diagnosis can be extremely difficult because the body responds differently to the stress of illness in older age then in youth.

A. Temperature control. Control of body temperature is less precise and the body frequently does not respond to infection with an elevated temperature. A child with a urinary tract infection may have high fever and a febrile seizure; an adult will have slight fever and perhaps chills; but an elderly patient with the same infection may have no fever, just a little mental confusion.

Accidental hypothermia. This is the potentially lethal condition that kills older people who live alone every winter. The aged brain is unable to regulate body temperature, so shivering does not occur. The older person may be unaware of cold, and unable to move about to generate body heat. In addition, sedatives or disease may cause increased susceptibility to cold. Since one of the first signs of hypothermia is confusion, the victim cannot understand that warmth is needed urgently. The core body temperature may fall to 35 °C (95 °F) and coma and death follow. Prevention through anticipation is the best method of treatment, which underlines the necessity for special attention to high risk elderly.

B. Mental symptoms may be due to physical disease. It has been estimated that 30% of cases of acute dementia or confusion are due to a physical cause. Any older person who becomes suddenly confused should be examined to exclude the presence of a remediable condition (See Senile Dementia). "Senility" is a term which has been inaccurately applied to dementia and should be discarded. It implies that the patient's condition is hopeless and entirely due to old age. It also implies that the patient is only fit for chronic care in a nursing home or mental hospital and will inexorably deteriorate.

The following conditions frequently cause reversible confusion (or acute dementia) in elderly patients: (a) cardiac failure, myocardial infarction, (b) infections such as pneumonia or cystitis, (c) adverse reactions to drugs such as alcohol, digitalis, or sedatives, (d) depression ("pseudodementia"), (e) dehydration, (f) electrolyte disturbance, (g) brain damage due to trauma or stroke, (h) accidental hypothermia, and (i) anemia.

The stress of these physical conditions puts too much strain on the aging brain, which fails temporarily. The first symptoms of confusion are loss of memory for recent events and then disorientation in time and space. Associated with these are the inability to recognize even close relatives and perseveration (phrases or actions may be repeated over and over). In the early stages social graces may be well-preserved, disguising the confusion.

The "sundowner" syndrome is the condition in which an old person is confused during the evening or night. Often it is due to inadequate blood supply to the brain from a failing heart. These patients wander and shout during the night, but during the day are apparently normal.

C. Decreased pain sensation. There is evidence that the aged have diminished appreciation of pain originating in deep organs such as the heart. A myocardial infarction in a 40-year old usually causes excruciating chest pain, but in an 80-year old, the same amount of heart damage may be manifested only by fatigue, shortness of breath, or perhaps confusion. Elderly diabetics are particularly prone to have painless heart attacks. Similarly, duodenal ulcers may cause no symptoms before they perforate and the mortality rate is high as a result.

In addition, patients may be aware of pain, but unable to locate it accurately (Charlesworth & Baker, 1973, p. 649), delaying diagnosis until they are in an advanced state of shock. Acute appendicitis, for instance, is a serious disease which can rapidly progress to peritonitis; the mortality rate for over-seventies is 30%.

3. Unusual Course of Disease

Medical students, trained in teaching hospitals where the majority of patients are under 65, learn to expect rapid recovery from acute disease. Patients over 65 suffer acute illnesses about half as frequently as young adults, but they do not recover as rapidly. As a result, younger physicians have a tendency to find the treatment of older patients dissatisfying because it is difficult to see results (Williams & Clements, Note 3). The recovery of an old person from an acute episode such as a myocardial infarction, may be very slow and encouragement is needed continually. Successful rehabilitation of elderly cardiac patients requires a genuinely optimistic and positive attitude by members of the rehabilitation team (Harris, 1978, p. 45).

All professionals caring for such patients need to be aware of the different time frame of illness and recovery in elderly patients. In this way frustration and dissatisfaction will be avoided. Goals to be kept in mind are improving mobility, self-care, and independent living above all. Most will return to their pre-morbid state, but some will never recover their strength completely after an acute illness. In such people deterioration in aging seems to follow a step-wise progression, with sudden falls in ability followed by relatively stable periods.

Certain aged patients make totally unexpected recoveries showing that they still have remarkable reserves of physical strength and mental determination with which to confound their advisers.

The distinctive feature of the common diseases of old age, such as osteoarthritis, diabetes, osteoporosis, and hypertension, is that they are chronic diseases. Some of the diseases take years to develop, wax and wane, and finally leave the patient crippled but free of pain. Different forms of arthritis follow this pattern. Others, such as diabetes, force a change in life-style with dieting, urine-testing, and perhaps injections of insulin. The diabetic patient cannot forget the disease for one day after it is diagnosed. The patient with hypertension and without its complications, is generally completely symptom-free, but has to follow a medication regimen exactly and go for frequent checkups of blood pressure and weight. These diseases move in and become part of life. They can never be left behind or recovered from completely.

Another major disadvantage of chronic disease is that few physicians have been trained to be enthusiastic about taking care of them. In addition, adequate funds, for instance, for physical therapy to loosen up stiff joints or mobilize an older person after a stroke are very difficult to obtain. Many people find that drugs they have to take are prohibitively expensive. It is not surprising that so many elderly people become obsessed by their bodily functions, or that they develop depression in addition to their multiple physical, family, and social problems.

On the other hand, the aged are the only group with a national health insurance program, Medicare. This fact, along with a decreased incidence of accidents, are two of the advantages of aging listed by Palmore (1979).

4. Drug Problems

As a direct result of their multiple problems, it is not surprising that the old have large drug bills. In 1974, people over 65 in the United States spent $2.3 billion on drugs—more then 20% of the national total (Vestal, 1978). Many people also take several self-prescribed over-the-counter drugs, particularly analgesics, vitamins and laxatives. In this context, it must be remembered that alcohol is also a drug.

The incidence of adverse reactions and side effects to drugs increases with the number administered and with age (Hurwitz, 1969; Hurwitz & Wade, 1969). Aging may affect the fate of drugs within the body. For instance, the half-life of diazepam (Valium) in the body is 20 hours at age 20, and 90 hours at age 80 (Klotz, Avant, Hoyumpa, Schenker & Wilkinson, 1975). Reasons for this are decreased blood supply, changed body composition, and slower removal of the drug because of diminished kidney and liver effectiveness. Consequently, drugs may accumulate in the body and produce toxic effects. Smaller or less frequent doses are required than in the young. Unusual symptoms such as vomiting, fatigue, or confusion may frequently be signs of drug toxicity.

Multiple drugs are frequently necessary for old people, particularly those with cardiovascular disease. But there is a real danger that drugs may sometimes be prescribed for each symptom described by the patient. Physical symptoms may be produced as a "ticket" to see the physician, when the treatment that the patient really wants is a sympathetic ear. In this way, effective counseling can safeguard a patient from some of the hazards of modern medicine.

Communication with elderly patients has been seen to be one of the many problems identified by family physicians (Williams & Clements, Note 3), and this is frequently associated with difficulty in getting a patient to understand a treatment plan. Non-compliance by the elderly in taking medications has been variously ascribed to (a) child-proof containers which cannot be opened, (b) loss of memory, (c) failure of judgment, (d) lack of understanding by reason of language or culture, (e) eyesight too poor to read labels, (f) personal idiosyncrasy, and (g) financial difficulties. Relatives and visiting nurses can be invaluable in supervising a drug regime, which should be kept as simple as possible.

CRITERIA FOR NURSING HOME ADMISSION

Moving an elderly person to a long-term care institution should be based on a recommendation by the family physician. It should be carefully planned in advance. In practice, all too often moving to a nursing home results from a crisis, such as a fractured femur. Ideally, there should be a trial of home-based care first, with help from the family, friends, visiting nurses, and home health aides. The final decision should then be made at a conference involving the patient, family members, community service providers, and the physician. The factors listed below are those suggested as admission criteria for mental hospitals (Lowenthal, 1964), but are very suitable criteria for nursing home placement (Butler & Lewis, 1977, p. 207):

1. Disturbance in thinking and feeling, such as delusions or depressions.

Dementia is problably the main reason precipitating nursing home admission and 50-75% of the nursing home population has intellectual impairment (Besdine, Note 1).

2. Physical Illness.

Common conditions leading to admission are arteriosclerotic heart disease, stroke, osteoarthritis, frequent falls, incontinence, and deafness.

3. Potentially harmful behavior such as confusion or unmanageability.

4. Harmful behavior such as refusing necessary medical care or actual violence to others.

Senile dementia or brain failure is probably responsible for confusion, (3), and harmful behavior, (4), in the majority of patients.

5. Environmental factors such as the unavailability or incapacity of a responsible other person to care for the patient.

SOME COMMON MEDICAL PROBLEMS

Senile Dementia

Until recent years senile dementia was often atributed to hardening of the arteries to the brain. We now know that there are at least 50 different conditions that can cause dementia. Five to ten percent of people over 65, and 22% over 80, suffer from some form of dementia. It may be the fifth greatest killer in the United States.

Alzheimer's Disease. Difficulty in remembering names is a frequent complaint in old age, and frequently accepted as normal. But loss of memory may be the first sign of irreversible brain disease, which will progress through loss of judgment and confusion to dementia and death. This condition is not normal aging. It is senile dementia of the Alzheimer type (SDAT) and it accounts for about 55% of all cases of dementia in the elderly (Haase, 1977, pp. 27-68). It is more common in women than men and genetic factors may play some role. Stress in earlier life has been suggested as a risk factor (Kral, 1962), while slow virus infection and biochemical abnormalities may contribute to its development. There is no treatment.

The second most common cause of irremediable senile dementia is cerebrovascular disease and follows multiple strokes or hypertension. A recent encouraging report on the declining incidence of stroke, particularly in the elderly, may herald a new era in which one cause of senile dementia may be eliminated (Garraway, Whisnant, Furlan, Phillips, Kurland & O'Fallon, 1979).

Depression

Depression is relatively common in old age and is by far the most common manifestation of mental illness. It may be a reaction to aging itself, combined with a reaction to physical or environmental stress. Since 60-70% of mental and emotional illness is treated in the medical system, not the mental health system, a great many depressed old people are seen by family physicians. Frequently the patient thinks the problem is physical and presents symptoms such as constipation, loss of appetite, insomnia, or weight loss.

Mental symptoms of depression include feelings of hopelessness; lack of drive; loss of concentration, memory, and interest in sex; and diurnal variation in mood. Depression in the elderly can also lead to confusion, or pseudo-dementia, and it has been suggested that there are many depressed patients in institutions who have been erroneously labelled "senile."

The danger of undiagnosed depression is that it can lead to suicide, particularly in men in their eighties. Over 65s are responsible for one-quarter of all successful suicide attempts in this country, and there are few unsuccessful attempts in the elderly. Counselors should be alert to signs that a depressed patient is suicidal. The following is a list of major diagnostic clues for suicide in old age (Butler & Lewis, 1977, p. 207): depression (with no anger outlet); withdrawal; bereavement (especially within the first year after loss); isolation: widowed, single; expectation of death from some cause; less organization and complexity of behavior; induced helplessness; institutionalization; physical illness; alcoholism; desire and rational decision to protect survivors from financial disaster; philosophical decision: no more pleasure or purpose; meaninglessness of life; decreased self-regard; organic mental deterioration; and changes in sleep patterns.

The tragedy of suicide and the suffering caused by unrecognized depression, is that depression is an eminently treatable disease. Counseling, use of antidepressant drugs, and electroconvulsive therapy are all effective modes of treatment.

Insomnia

Insomnia is common in old age. It has been estimated that the need for sleep diminishes with age, and that an 80 year old does not need more than five hours sleep in 24 hours. Given the tendency of many 80 year olds to nap in the afternoon, the likelihood of a long night's sleep is diminished. However, insomnia is also a common sympton of some mental diseases. The anxious patient will tend to toss and turn after going to bed, unable to go to sleep, (primarily insomnia). The depressed patient may either wake in the middle of the night and be unable to go back to sleep for several hours, or wake early in the morning (terminal insomnia). Identifying the type of insomnia is extremely valuable in determining diagnosis. The symptoms of a normal grief reaction, such as occurs after bereavement, are the same as depression. However, if the symptoms continue for more than six months, the depression is pathological and requires medical treatment.

Genito-Urinary Problems

Many old people accept as normal the fact that they have to get up at night to go to the bathroom, go frequently during the day, and sometimes have accidents. Urgency of urination in the elderly is also unfortunately accompanied by small bladder capacity and the physical inability to move quickly. Urinary incontinence, the passage of urine at an inconvenient time and place, may be intermittent or a continuous dribble.

The most common causes of incontinence in old age are (a) loss of control by the higher centers in the brain, (b) muscle weakness, and (c) increased sensitivity of the bladder due to an infection.

Loss of control by the brain may be precipitated by mental or physical stress, such as admission to the hospital for an acute illness. Usually such incontinence disappears on recovery and return home to familiar surroundings. When brain damage is severe, such as in the late stages of Alzheimer's disease, no such recovery can be expected.

Inability to control urine is embarrassing, particularly to women; unpleasant odors are caused; and the patient may be afraid to engage in social activities. Frequently the problem is concealed, but should be suspected in a patient who persistently refuses to go out in the absence of an obvious reason.

Hormone creams, bladder retraining, biofeedback, and surgery all offer some hope of improvement.

Difficulty of urination in old men is frequent and is most commonly due to benign hypertrophy of the prostate. Surgical treatment is generally successful.

Cancer

The incidence of cancer rises with age. This is thought to be due in part to the cumulative effect of contact with carcinogenic materials over a long period. It is also possible that cancers developing in younger age groups are destroyed by the immune system. In old age, this body defense mechanism is impaired and the cancer continues to grow.

The most common cancer of the elderly, skin cancer, in areas exposed to sunlight, is very easily cured. The next most frequently occurring cancers appear in the prostate, breast, stomach, and bowel. Since they may be associated with symptoms common in age, such as constipation, it is important to make the elderly aware of the potential danger of such symptoms.

Generally, an older patient with cancer has a better prognosis than a young patient with the same type of cancer, possibly because of the reduced quantity of hormones circulating in the older person. Therefore, older patients can often be treated less aggressively than the young, and may die of a previously existing disease before the cancer spreads. Exceptions to the rule of a good prognosis in old age cancer are thyroid cancer and malignant melanoma, both of which run an accelerated course.

Today most cancer specialists offer older people the opportunity of treatments available for all age groups. Improved surgery, chemotherapy, and radiation therapy have made possible comfortable prolongation of life for many. Even so, only about one-third are cured (Serpick, 1978). For the remaining two-thirds, new combinations of drugs are available for pain relief and unpleasant symptoms. Physicians have come to realize that prolonging life at all costs is often not the best for the patient, and respect the wishes of patients who prefer quality of life to quantity. Here again, the patient is often best served by a team of professionals.

Cardio-vascular disease

Diseases of the cardio-vascular system account for most visits by old people to their physicians and most causes of death over 65. Blood pressure increases with age and it is interesting that the races are affected differently. In blacks, hypertension is more widespread and more severe. Forty percent of all persons in this country between 75 and 79 have hypertension, and this puts a large segment of the population at risk for stroke and heart failure (Harris, 1978, p. 45).

Symptoms in the elderly may be misleading, but often symptoms of cardiovascular disease include chest pain, shortness of breath, and swelling of the ankles. Fatigue, loss of appetite, and confusion may all be due to cardiac failure secondary to hypertension. Headache and dizziness, though commonly attributed to raised blood pressure, usually have other causes.

Many forms of treatment are available and weight loss and salt restriction play an important part. A number of older people find it impossible to follow such instructions, but the fear of becoming paralyzed by a stroke makes others very careful to remember their blood pressure pills and receive regular check-ups. When an aged heart continues to fail in spite of adequate therapy, much support and help are needed.

SUMMARY

Some knowledge of the effects of normal aging on the human body and common medical problems in the old enables professionals to approach elderly clients and patients with increased understanding and empathy. In spite of all the deterioration and disease that occurs in age, the majority of old people continue to perform well and live independently because there is such an immense reserve of function in each body system. Many remain upright and alert, meeting and overcoming the stresses of everyday life successfully, though perhaps in a more leisurely manner than they did when they were younger.

REFERENCES

Aldrich, C.K., & Mendkoff, E. Relocation of the aged and disabled. *Journal of the American Geriatrics Society*, 1963, *11*,, 185-194.

Andrews, G.R.; Cowan, N.R.; & Anderson, W.F. The practice of geriatric medicine in the community. In MClachlan, G. (Ed.), *Problems and progress in medical care: Essays on currect research* (5th series). London: Oxford University Press for Nuffield Provincial Hospitals Trust, 1971.

Ball, M.J. Neuronal loss, neurofibrillary tangles, and granulovacuolar degeneration in the hippocampus with aging and dementia. *Acta Neuropathologica*, (Berl), 1977, *37*, 111-118.

Borup, J.H.; Gallego, D.T.; & Heffernan, P.G. Relocation and its effect on mortality. *Gerontologist*, 1979, *19*, 135-140.

Butler, R.N., & Lewis, M.I. *Aging and mental health*, (2nd edition). St. Louis: The C.V. Mosby Company, 1977.

Butler, R.N., & Perlin, C. Physiological-psychologicalpsychiartic interrelationships. In *Human aging*. Washington, D. C.: U.S. Government Printing Office, 1963.

Cape, R. *Aging: Its complex management*. Hagerstown: Harper and Row, 1978.

Charlesworth, D., & Baker, R.H. Surgery in old age. In J.C. Brocklehurst (Ed.), *Textbook of geriatric medicine and gerontology*. Edinburgh: Churchill Livingstone, 1973.

Coons, D.H. Milieu therapy. The social-psychological aspects of treatment. In W. Reichel (Ed.), *Clinical aspects of aging*. Baltimore: The Williams and Wilkins Company, 1978.

Corso, J.F. Sensory processes in man during maturity and senescence. In J.M. Ordy & K.R. Brizzee (Eds.), *Neurobiology of aging*. New York: Plenum Press, 1975.

Duke Elder, S. *A system of ophthalmology*. St. Louis: C.V. Mosby Company, 1969, *11*, 4.

Garrway, W.M.; Whisnant, J.P.; Furlan, A.J.; Phillips, L.H.; Kurland, L.T.; & O'Fallon, W.M. The declining incidence of stroke. *New England Journal of Medicine*, 1979, *300*, 449-452.

Haase, G.R. Diseases presenting as dementia. In C.E. Wells (Ed.), *Dementia* 2nd edition). Philadelphia: F.A. Davis Company, 1977.

Harris, R. Special problems of geriatric patients with heart In W. Reichel (Ed.), *Clinical aspects of aging*. Baltimore: Williams and Wilkins, 1978.

Hurwitz, N. Predisposing factors in adverse reactions to drugs. *British Medical Journal*, 1969, *1*, 536-539.

Hurwitz, N., & Wade, O.L. Intensive hospital monitoring of adverse reactions to drugs. *British Medical Journal*, 1969, *1*, 531-535.

Jasnau, K.F. Individualized versus mass transfer of nonpsychotic geriatric patients from mental hospitals to nursing homes, with special reference to the death rate. *Journal of the American Geriatrics Society*, 1967, *15*,, 280-284.

Kasl, S.V. Physical and mental health effects of involuntary relocation and institutionalization on the elderly—a review. *American Journal of Public Health*, 1972, *62*, 377-384.

Klotz, V. ; Avant, G.R.; Hoyumpa, A.; Schenker, S.; & Wilkinson, G.R. The effects of age and liver disease on the disposition and elimination of diazepam in adult men. *Journal of Clinical Investigation*, 1975, *55*, 347-359.

Kral, V.A. Stress and mental disorders in the senium. *Medical Services Journal*, Canada: 1962, *18*, 363-370.

Lieberman, M.A. Institutionalizaiton of the aged: Effects on behavior. *Journal of Gerontology*, 1969, *24*, 330-340.

Lowenthal, M.F. *Lives in distress: The paths of the elderly to the psychiatric ward*. New York: Basic Books, Inc., 1964.

Lowther, C.P.; MacLeod, R.D.M.; & Williamson, J. Evaluation of early diagnostic services for the elderly. *British Medical Journal*, 1970, *3*, 275-277.

Palmore, E. Advantages of aging. *Gerontologist*, 1979, *19*, 220-223.

Pastalan, L.A. The stimulation of age-related sensory losses: A new approach to the study of environmental barriers, In *New outlook for the blind*. New York: American Foundation for the Blind, 1974.

Reichel, W., & Barnett, B.L. Care of the geriatric patient. In R.E. Rakel & H.F. Conn (Eds.), *Family Practice* (2nd edition). Philadelphia: W. B. Saunders Company, 1978.

Serpick, A.A. Cancer in the elderly. *Hospital Practice*, 1978, *13*, 101-112.

Sheldon, J.H. On the natural history of falls in old age. *British Medical Journal*, 1960, *2*, 1685-1690.

Shock, N.W. Physiological theories of aging. In M. Rockstein, (Ed.), *Theoretical aspects of aging*. New York: Academic Press, 1974.

Skelton, D. The future health care for the elderly. *Journal of the American Geriatrics Society*, 1977, *25*, 39-46.

United States Department of Health, Education and Welfare, Health Resources Administration. Health United States, 1976-1977. *DHEW Publication No. (HRA)*, 77-1232, 1977.

Vestal. R.E. Drugs and the elderly. National Institute on Aging. Science Writer Seminar Series, United States Department of Health. Education and Welfare. *DHEW Publication No. (NIH)*, 78-1449. 1978.

Weale, R.H. Retinal illumination and age. *Transactions of the Illuminating Engineering Society*, 1961, 26, 95-100.

Webb. M.A. Longitudinal socio-psychologic study of a randomly selected group of institutionalized veterans. *Journal of the American Geriatrics Society*, 1959, 7, 730-740.

Weston, T.E.T. Presbycusis, a clinical study. *Journal of Laryngology and Otolgy*, 1964, 78, 273.

Widmer, R.B., & Cadoret, R.J. Depression in primary care: Changes in pattern of patient visits and complaints during a developing depression. *Journal of Family Practice*, 1978, 7, No. 2:293-302.

Williamson, J.; Stokoe, I.H.; Gray, S.; Fischer, M.; Smith, A.; McGee, A.; & Stephenson, S. Old people at home: Their unreported needs. *Lancet*, 1964, 1, 1117-1123.

REFERENCE NOTES

1. Besdine, R. *Treatable dementia in the elderly*. U.S. Department of Health, Education and Welfare. National Institute on Aging, Task Force Report, 1978. In preparation, 1979.

2. Exton-Smith. Lecture to Conference on Geriatric Medicine, University of Western Ontario, London, Canada, May 1976. Quoted by Cape, 1978, pp. 116-117.

3. Williams, G.O., & Clements, W.M. Family physicians and geriatrics: Practice experience, age and attitudes. *Canadian Family Physician*, in press.

4. Erwin, C. *Vigilance performance in elderly subjects*. Duke University Medical Center, Durham, North Carolina. In preparation. Quoted by Palmore, E., 1979.

Counseling the Elderly for Sexual Identity

Lauralee Rockwell

ABSTRACT

This chapter presents the idea that the ability to perform sexually is central to a person's identification as a man or a woman throughout the life span. Aging persons experience the pressures of cultural myths and values about the appropriate sexual behavior for older persons. Psychological and phsiological facts of sexuality in older men and women are presented. While there is a diminishing of sexual capability as people age, sexual behavior is seen as appropriate and pleasurable throughout the later growing years for healthy men and women. Counselors are urged to examine their own biases and prejudices toward the sexual behavior of older persons and to become aware of the possibilities for their aging clients to respond sexually throughout a life time. Specific procedures which have been found useful in working with sexual dysfunctions in older persons are presented and discussed.

INTRODUCTION

For the vast majority of people, sexual identity is determined easily at birth. Children are identified as male or female and proceed through life being taught and accepting sex roles and behaviors thought to be appropriate for their identified or assigned gender. A person's sexuality becomes a central core of identity. In all societies sex is used as a category to divide the tasks needed to be done in that society. Males may be assigned the warrior-hunter-provider type tasks and females the nurturant-child-rearing tasks. It is often assumed in our Western civilization that feminine characteristics are the opposite of masculine characteristics. Men are perceived as competitive, strong, assertive/aggressive, active, and independent. Women are perceived as emotional, cooperative, dependent, and sensitive. The performance of sex role tasks leads to an expectation that various personality traits will be exhibited by the person performing the task.

The stereotypic separation of the sexes begins early. Boys are bought toys usually associated with masculinity; guns, soldiers, tools, and sports equipment. Girls are bought toys usually associated with femininity; dolls, stoves, paints, and nursing equipment. As children grow, the household chores are divided according to sex; the boys taking out the garbage and other "heavy" work; the girls helping mother with the dishes, dusting, and taking care of the other children. Stereotypical ideas about the appropriateness of a particular task for one or the other of the sexes continue throughout life. Biology for these people becomes destiny.

Some persons live in situations where sex roles and behaviors are confused. Such people may have difficulty in establishing themselves in an appropriate gender, feeling early in life that they are really members of the other sex. Evidence in the recent Masters and Johnson publication (1979) supports the idea that persons with a homosexual orientation exhibit the same sexual patterns as heterosexuals including needing assistance with the same kinds of dysfunctions. In all societies, with the exception of transsexuals, the vast majority or people accept and seem content with their biological designations. Regardless of its form, the sexual identity of a person is basic to all other aspects of human existence.

There is a need for counselors who work with the aging to understand the centrality of sexuality in the life process. If sexuality can be maintained, life can be maintained and enjoyed. It is the purpose of this chapter to review some myths about sexuality and aging persons, to present some of the research findings about the sexual behavior of older persons, and to discuss their implications for counselors.

SOCIOCULTURAL PERSPECTIVES TOWARD SEXUALITY IN OLDER PERSONS

The early socialization process of today's elderly is often sexually constricting (Kalish, 1975). There is social pressure to break the stereotypical sexual patterns in work and social customs. Changes have occurred and will continue to re-shape our expectations of gender identified tasks. However, for the elderly, it is particularly difficult to change the habits of thinking and behaving of six or more decades. This is particularly true in regard to sexual behavior and the social roles that arise from it.

Misconceptions are many. There is a belief that sexual feelings and needs are no longer a part of the development of older people. If people continue to express sexual desire as they reach what people consider old age, that desire is considered inappropriate by many people. Thus, older persons are conditioned to believe that which was so important in being a man or in being a woman is no longer needed or to be looked upon as an appropriate part of a self image.

It is believed that older people who express an interest in sex or who report sexual behaviors are liars. Sexual activity seems to be relegated to the young and the beautiful. Consider how difficult it is for people to imagine their parents engaging in a variety of sex acts. How much more difficult to conceive of grandparents performing the same acts! The aging who have sexual desires often believe themselves that the expression of sexual feelings at their age is obscene and that sexual activity beyond sixty is nonexistent. They have been subject to the myths and ideas about sexual behaviors of older people throughout their lifetime, and many have accepted those myths and values. The old values and myths become self-fulfilling prophesies.

Changing social sexual mores may bring confusion in older people. An older woman may express her need to touch and feel the warmth of another human being by being free with hugs and kisses with others. An older man who exhibits the same behavior for the same reasons may be perceived as a "dirty old man." If he is single and able to attract a very young wife, he is perceived as masculine and virile. An older woman who takes a younger husband is not looked upon with the same approval.

Sexual worries which older people have are rooted in social myths (Wasow & Leob, 1977, p. 55). Physical changes may cause both men and women to worry about their sexual attractiveness and ability to perform. There is a myth that there is an absolute supply of semen. The emission of semen throughout a man's life will use it up and hasten old age. Without semen a man becomes less a man and less useful to society. He would certainly be less likely to seek sexual contact.

A woman who has reached menopause may believe that that stage of her development means the end of her sexuality. She may reject her partner's efforts and cause each of them to lose a pleasurable activity.

The values which older people have learned in their youth about the appropriateness of sex for older persons restrict not only the kind of sexual behaviors they might enjoy but even the idea of engaging in sex at all. Older people who do show physical affection by kissing, hugging and/or holding hands are perceived by younger people (and depicted in films, magazines and TV) as either cute or somehow obscene. This adds to the idea that older people become childish or perverted in sexual expression as they get older.

It is interesting that a 1975 Lou Harris poll indicated that many older people who had accepted the myths and stereotypes about older people, did not consider themselves a part of those myths and stereotypes. In another study (Wasow & Loeb, 1977, pp. 60-63) older persons in a nursing home had similar tendencies. The elderly reflected the mores of society in that they approved of sexual activity for elderly people in general but not for themselves in the home. The nursing staff had the same views.

It is easy for aging people to focus on the negative aspects of aging. There is a deterioration of all functions which is inevitable. The slowing down process takes place over a number of years and the usual increase of aches, pains and slower recoveries may be more apparent than the many opportunities which are available to them because of their age. While sexual activity may decline with age (Kinsey, Pomeroy, & Martin, 1948; Masters & Johnson, 1966, 1970), there is still considerable controversy over why this reduction occurs. The changes are biogenic to some extent, but psychological and social factors also contribute.

Counselors need to be aware of the myths which might affect the continued sexual functioning of their older counselees and assist them to cope with their very human and natural sexual desires and needs.

PERSPECTIVES ON AGING AND SEXUALITY

What are some of the changes in sexual functioning which can be expected by men and women as they age? There are great individual differences in sexual behavior as there are in all areas of human existence. One must consider always the general health of a person, motivation for sex, usual fatigue level, past patterns of sexual behavior and the availability of partners. An individual's self esteem and sexuality are inseparable factors in continuing sexual behaviors in old age.

Women

Menopause is an overt phase in the sexual development of women, one specific event in the process, the cessation of menstruation. The major biological change during this time is the aging of the ovaries along with a decline in the output of eggs and the sex hormones estrogen and progesterone.

Some of the physical symptoms of menopause are "hot flashes," headaches, dizziness, pains in the joints and palpitations. At least as many as 50 percent (perhaps 80 to 90 percent) of all women suffer some of these uncomfortable menopausal symptoms, only 10 percent are severely affected, and a sizable proportion— at least 10 percent and perhaps as many as 50 percent—display none of these symptoms (Hyde, 1979, p. 83). While some women see menopause as a signal that their sexual days are finished, others perceive it as a sign to be freer in their sexual behavior. This increased sexual behavior may be perceived as a threat by a male whose sexual prowess is on the wane.

The most commonly cited dysfunction of the elderly female is the lack of vaginal lubrication as a result of estrogen deficiency. Not only is there a decline in vaginal lubrication, but also the vaginal walls become thinner and less elastic and the woman might experience pain during intercourse. The contractions of an orgasm may become uncomfortable and the orgasm shorter and not as strong (Wasow & Loeb, 1977, p. 57).

The use of articifial lubricants, such as K-Y jelly or estrogen replacement therapy, may be used to help relieve the physical symptoms of menopause, and sometimes the psychological symptoms such as irritability and depression. Physicians prescribe estrogen in its natural form (e.g. Pre-Marin) or in a synthetic form.

Although the biology-culture controversy still rages, the practical implications are that estrogen replacement therapy may be very helpful to many menopausal women, particularly for relief of physical discomfort (Hyde, 1979, p. 86).

There is an 80 percent decrease in libido; 70-75 percent difficulty in sexual arousal; and 50 percent reduced orgasmic responsiveness in the sexual functioning of the uremic female. One-fifth of uremic women experience dyspareunia (pain during coitus) (Abram, et al, 1975). Some of the etiologic factors may be possible estrogen deficiency, neurologic factors, concurrent illness, and drug use.

Following a mycardial infraction, there appears to be a low incidence of sexual dysfunction for the post-coronary woman.

Men

Physical changes occurring in men are more noticeable because the male genitalia are more noticeable. As the male grows older, it may take longer to achieve an erection and more direct stimulation may be necessary. The erection may not be as hard and the angle of erection may become greater. It may take longer for an ejaculation to occur and the orgasm may be less intense. There may be a longer time between erections.

The most commonly cited dysfunction of the male is the inability to achieve orgasm. Ninety percent (90%) of the cases of impotence in the older population are psychogenic, while the other ten percent (10%) are organic (Kent, 1975). Finkle and Finkle (1977), two urologists, have studies various methods for treating male impotence and have concluded that most sexual problems of older men are psychogenic rather than organic. Psychogenic impotence is generally periodic and selective. If a man can have an erection while under the influence of certain drugs, with a new partner, or is capable of masturbation, or may have an erection while sleeping, his lack of potency is probably not organic.

The most common organic cause of impotence is diabetes mellitis. About fifty percent (50%) of male diabetics become impotent before age 60 and the incidence of impotence increases with the growing years. While potency decreases gradually, sexual desire seldom declines with potency.

Other causes of organic impotence and dysfunction are drugs (alcohol, marijuana, certain tranquilizers, e.g. chlorpromazine and resperpene), over-eating and obesity, interactions of stress, hormonal activity, general health, and aging (Weg, 1976). Cancer and other debilitating diseases often cause long-term impotence—beyond control of the individual. Urinary prostrate infections may cause temporary impotence until the infection is cleared. Only total removal of the prostrate (prostatectomy) causes impotence (Kent, 1975).

Men do not experience "menopause" as we think of it for women. However, men do experience a very gradual decline in the manufacture of both testosterone and sperm by the testes, although viable sperm may still be produced at age 90 (Hyde, 1979, p. 86).

The enlargement of the prostate gland is one of the most common physical problems for men. It is believed to be related to changes in hormone levels. Prostate enlargement occurs in 50 percent of men who reach age 80, and may cause urination problems.

There is a 90 percent depressed libido and 80 percent erective difficulties in the sexual functioning of the uremic male (Abram, et al, 1975). Disturbances of sexual function are, in general, proportionate to the degree of uremia. Testicular atrophy, impaired spermatogenesis, depressed testosterone, diabetes, infection, and hypertension may be some of the etiological factors.

Following a mycardial infarction, there is a high incidence of sexual dysfunction and avoidance for the post-coronary male.

The organic causes for such dysfunctions are infrequent, however. The psychological factors will be discussed in the next section.

Some problems of sexual identity in aging persons are of a biological-medical nature. It seems best to leave these to the doctor-patient relationship. Whether surgery, the administration of estrogen, testosterone, or other hormonal treatments will enhance a person's view of self, can be determined only by medical personnel. However, counselors can assist the aging by acting as liaison persons between patient and doctor. Medical doctors, too, are influenced by the same social values that often influence older persons to reduce or eliminate their sexual behavior as inappropriate for their age level.

PSYCHOLOGICAL PERSPECTIVES ON AGING AND SEXUALITY

Awareness of a declining sexuality begins around the age of fifty with the sharpest declines reported in groups ages 45-50 and 51-55 (Pfieffer, 1972). The Pfieffer study was a crosssectional, self-report study of middle and upper socio-economic people. Sex was important in the lives of the majority polled with more men expressing continued interest in women. In every age category more women than men reported cessation of sexual activity. Both men and women who had stopped their activity indicated that it had been the male's responsibility for stopping. In a group of husbands and wives who were interviewed separately, there was a high level of congruence between what husbands and wives said about the frequency of their sexual activity, the time of cessation, and whose responsibility it was for the cessation.

Does the fact that men report more sexual activity than women in every age group suggest that the double standard of society is carried into old age? Men who are sexually active may be perceived as powerful, strong, and healthy. Sexually active men are MEN! Women who are sexually active may be perceived as promiscuous, lewd or vulgar. Active sexuality detracts from being a woman. A man's identity in society is closely tied to actual or perceived sexual prowess. A woman's identity may be more closely tied to the nurturing caring roles in which she is cast.

Individual sexual differences abound. The pattern of sexual behavior established early and continued seems dominant. While the decline exists there are some persons who continue to be active and interested into the eighth and ninth decades. In one study (Pfieffer, 1968), the 78 and over group expressed more interest in sex than the 72-77 year old age group. Pfieffer postulated that these were a group of biologically advantaged persons. That is, just as there are persons genetically endowed in athletics, so are there persons endowed in their sexual prowess. One might also speculate that these people had not succumbed to social notions of what was proper behavior for their age. A continuance of sexual activity and interest may result in the maintenance of self-esteem and a healthy sexual identity.

There are many reasons why people give up sexual activity. As people grow older in a youth-oriented culture, they may see themselves as inappropriate sex objects. Illnesses for long periods of time may preclude sexual activity, and it may not be resumed upon recovery. Operations (such as mastectomy) may cause a wife to feel unattractive to her husband and to avoid revealing herself to him in a sexual manner. Lack of estrogen may cause a marked reduction in libido. The woman may put on weight and develop facial acne, making the woman feel less sexual. The loss of a spouse through death, divorce, or separation may take away the availability of a sex partner. Social mores inhibiting a woman from seeking out a sex partner may be so ingrained that she would give up sexual activity altogether. Men tend to marry women who are younger than themselves and to die at earlier ages. Women are likely to cease sexual activity on the death of a spouse.

The psychological perspectives on aging and sexuality can be categorized into immediate causes and prior learning (Kaplan, 1974). Prior learnings are the things people learned earlier—for example in childhood—which now inhibit their sexual response. Immediate causes are various things that happen in the act of lovemaking itself that inhibit the sexual response. The following four factors have been identified as immediate causes of dysfunction: (1) anxieties such as fear (2) the contructing of barriers to the experience of erotic pleasure; (3) failure of the partners to communicate; and (4) failure to engage in effective, stimulating sexual behavior (Hyde, 1979).

Anxiety caused by a fear of failure or fear of being unable to perform can create a vicious circle of self-fulfilling prophecy. A man who fails to achieve a quick erection may eventually find himself becoming impotent.

To engage in intercourse, the man must be aroused and have an erection, therefore the demands for performance are great. The demand for performance in women is the demand that they have orgasms. Women are beginning to understand what men have felt for years—the fear of performance.

Spectatoring, a term coined by Masters and Johnson, is one of the most common barriers to the experience of erotic feeling. People act like spectators or judges of their own sexual performance. "How am I doing?" "I wonder if I'll make it this time." "Good Job!" "Could stand some improvement." The older couple experiencing some fears and anxiety about the decline of their sexual responses may find themselves beginning to be compulsive about evaluating their sexual performance, therefore inhibiting sexual response.

Failure to communicate is one of the major causes of psychological distance for aging couples. As the physical body ages, interests, desires, and sexual needs may change. Sexual partners must make known to their partners, either verbally or nonverbally, what feels good and what turns them on. Sexuality may mean intimacy, bodily contact, affection, or just a romantic situation.

Depression is a frequent companion to old age. It is characterized by intense feelings of sadness resulting from a loss of personal power, a friend, a family member, or a spouse. Marital conflict, such as hating one's sexual partner, and intrapsychic conflict also contribute to the psychological perspectives aging persons have about their sexuality.

IMPLICATIONS FOR THE COUNSELOR

Because some older persons look on counseling as a sign of weakness, they believe their willingness to take part in the counseling process reveals to others a mental illness or a need to be told how to live their own lives. Thus, much caution and care must be taken by the counselor in dealing with the very threatening topic of sexuality.

Counseling for the aging about their sexuality should not be limited to crises. There may not be time for a patch and salvage job. Counselors of the aging need to develop and to disseminate educational programs which provide information about our changing bodies before the changes arrive. There is a tendency to believe that as people grow older they are more knowledgeable about changes going on within than they were about changes that occurred during adolescence.

The study of older people is still in its beginning stages and information about sexual changes is needed. Informational programs should be formulated to use in direct teaching of those who wish (and need) to know. The knowledge of what is happening to one's sexuality should not be left to the close friend or to risque jokes about older people. Just as counselors needed to know how secondary sex characteristics developed in adolescence, they need to know about the decline of sex characteristics.

Counselors can work with administrative and staff personnel in institutional settings. Counselors can help them to understand the need of older persons for closeness to other human beings, for being valued, and for being sensual. These qualities can be maintained even when intercourse is no longer available. Perhaps all that is needed is permission.

There is a need for educating the public through the media. More depictions of older people as alert, aware, open-minded, desirous, or continuing to enjoy each other sexually would certainly be helpful in combatting the image of a dried up, squeaky-voiced character in a rocking chair with only memories of the man or woman who used to be.

In working with older individuals, counselors need to follow the same principles as in dealing with other age groups. First, to become comfortable with one's own sexuality, values, and ideas about sex and older people, counselors need to clear up the myths they have cherished. Counselors need to know about the physiology and psychology of all stages of adult sexual development.

All bodily systems are in a state of decline at a time when a person may be asked to cope with changes in the environment, changes in and the loss of loved ones, and changes in friends. For some the rapidity with which the changes come can be overwhelming. Counselors can supply supportive counseling so that people might adjust to their changing conditions in more positive ways. Sometimes all that is needed is relatively simple imformation, reassurance, and an opportunity to discuss matters of sexuality in an understanding and supportive atmosphere. Questions left unanswered can sometimes lead to feelings of inadequacy, anxiety, depression, and guilt.

Counselors need to have an understanding of varied sexual problems and needs of the aged, including masturbation and homosexuality. Older people may still hold to the myths about masturbation and sexual fantasies in dreams and feel guilty. Counselors may ease their guilt, and in the cases of those institutionalized, help the staff understand the needs of persons to make themselves feel good.

Older gays also demonstrate patterns of long-term partnerships (Kelly, 1977). They suffer societal discrimination as gays as well as the usual problems of age stigmatization encountered by older straight Americans. The number of gay men involved in partnership liaisons increases with age but then decreases to almost none due to death or "divorce." Bereavement is an important factor in the experience of aging gay persons. The counselor can form a specially oriented support group to help this population with their special needs and concerns.

Other topics about sexuality which aging persons can process in group counseling are anxiety, availability or lack or partners, normal physiological changes, and sexual myths associated with aging.

There is also a need for marriage or couple counseling of aged persons. Some areas of concern are: more time with spouse or too much time without purpose, change of partner's interest and needs, and changing of roles—losing some and the further development of others. Frequently aged persons are involved in second marriages and need help in handling the memory or idealization of previous partners.

SUMMARY

When counselors are knowledgeable, caring, and active in helping people maintain their sexual identities, more older people will have more enjoyable and happier years. Much more needs to be learned about the way we grow old and how we can better enjoy the life that has been given to us.

Aging people are at a high risk for sexual dysfunction; but, if their health is good and sexual attitudes are positive, a rewarding sex life is possible for the older people who make some adjustments for their changing needs.

REFERENCES

Abram, H.S.; Hester, L.R.; Sheridan, W.F.; & Epstein, G.M. Sexual function in patients with chronic renal failure. *Journal of Nervous and Mental Disease,* 1975, 160: 220-226.

Brine, J.M. Psycho-social aspects of aging: An overview. In M. Ganikos & K. Grady (Eds.), *Counseling the aged: A training syllabus for educators.* Washington, D.C.: APGA, 1979.

Finkle, A., & Finkle, P. How counseling may solve sexual problems in aging men. *Geriatrics,* 1977, 32, 84-89.

Hyde, J.S. *Understanding human sexuality.* New York: McGraw-Hill, 1979.

Kalish, R.A. *Late adulthood: Perspectivies on human development.* Monterey, California: Wadsworth, 1975.

Kaplan, H.S. *The new sex therapy*. New York: Brunner/Mazel, 1974.

Kelly, J. The aging male homosexual: Myth and reality. *Gerontologist*, 1977, 17, 328-332.

Kent, S. Impotence as a consequence of organic disease. *Geriatrics*, 1975, *30*(1), 155-157.

Kinsey, A.; Pomeroy, W.; & Martin, C. *Sexual behavior in the human male*. Philadelphia: W.B. Saunders, 1948.

Macione, A. Physiological changes and common health problems of aging. In M. Ganikos & K. Grady (Eds.), *Counseling the aged: A training syllabus for educators*. Washington, D.C.: APGA, 1979.

Martin, C.E. Sexual activity in the aging male. In J. Money & H. Musaph (Eds.), *Handbook of sexology*. Elsevier/North Holland: Biomedical Press, 1977.

Masters, W.H., & Johnson, V. *Homosexuality in perspective*. Boston: Little, Brown, 1979.

Masters, W.H., & Johnson, V. *Human sexual inadequacy*. Boston: Little, Brown, 1970.

Masters, W.H., & Johnson, V. *Human sexual response*. Boston: Little, Brown, 1966.

Pfieffer, E.; Verwoerdt, A.; & David, G.C. Sexual behavior in middle life. *American Journal of Psychiatry*, 1972, *128*(10), 82-87.

Pfieffer, S.; Verwoerdt, A.; & Want, H. Sexual behavior in aged men and women. *Archives of General Psychiatry*, 1968, *19*, 753-758.

Rubin, I. *Sexual life after sixty*. New York: Basic Books, 1976.

Van Keep, P.A., & Gregory, A. Sexual relations in the aging female. In J. Money & H. Musaph (Eds.), *Handbook of sexology*. Elsevier/North-Holland Biomedical Press, 1977.

Vermeullen, A.; Rubens, R.; & Verdonck, L. Testosterone secretion and metabolism in male senescence. *Journal of Clinical Endochronology and Medicine*, 1972, *34*(4), 730-735.

Wasow, M., & Loeb, M.B. The aged. In H.L. Gochros & J.S. Gochros (Eds.), *The sexually oppressed*. New York: Association Press, 1977.

Weg, R.B. Normal aging changes in the reproductive system. In I. Burnside (Ed.), *Nursing and the aged*. New York: McGraw-Hill, 1976, 99-112.

Retirement as a Transition Point in Human Development

Phillip A. Perrone
and
Katherine Perry Supiano

ABSTRACT

The authors have attempted to synthesize major research works of social scientists in identifying issues and prescribing procedures which counselors should consider when counseling clients involved in the retirement transition. Moreover, they suggest limiting the scope of counselor intervention to those individuals who are more likely to benefit from counseling. Hopefully, these ideas for counselor intervention will eventually by tried and evaluated so counselors can base their behavior more on experiences of counselors rather than the ideas of counselor education.

The transition into retirement has received increasingly greater attention in recent years as increasing numbers of older individuals join the retired ranks. Retirement has been viewed by many investigators as a crisis event, primarily due to the emphasis placed on the work role in our culture. Nearly all retirees through the year 2000 will have been raised in an era when one man's worth and identity were measured to a large extent by his job, and the woman's worth measured largely by the work status of her husband and the "appearance" of her home and family. While it will be shown that retirement is not perceived as a crisis by all retirees, more older persons are seeking counseling as a means of resolving life changes associated with the retirement process.

The purpose of this chapter is to aid counselors in identifying problems related to retirement so as to facilitate the constructive personal growth of clients during this life transition. The focus of the chapter will be confined to the better adjusted majority of retirees and pre-retirees seeking assistance with retirement related concerns.

INTRODUCTION

Retirement may be defined as the transition from active participation in the paid labor force to a non-wage earning role in society. This change is typically viewed by society as a specific event; that is, "the point at which an individual separates oneself or is separated from a job and has no intent to seek another job" (Atchley, 1977, p. 158). This perspective is too delimiting for the counselor who prefers to consider clients in their developmental entirety. We concur with Atchley's conceptualization of retirement as "a process that begins when the individual realizes that someday one will leave one's job and ends when one becomes so feeble or impoverished that one can no longer play the retirement role" (Atchley, 1976, p. 3).

The retirement transition period exerts a profound impact on the life style of clients and has been viewed by many investigators (Mack, 1958; Maddox, 1970; Shanas, 1972) as a critical period in the life cycle. Holmes and Rahe (1967) rated social transitions in terms of stressful intensity and ranked retirement as tenth in magnitude of required adjustment. Depicting retirement as a crisis event does not imply that it is a socially undesirable occurrence; rather, it requires "a significant change in the ongoing life pattern of the individual" (Holmes and Rahe, 1967, p. 217), and the necessary utilization of both adaptive and coping strategies.

It may reasonably follow that some individuals adjust to retirement more successfully than others. Research has been conducted to determine factors affecting adjustment to retirement with several "causes" emerging from the literature. Poor health is the primary cause of early, voluntary retirement and is a major factor in retirement dissatisfaction (Payne 1953; Streib & Schneider, 1971). Tuckman (1956) noted that retirement due to health reasons was resented as much as compulsory retirement.

Another factor accounting for retirement dissatisfaction is loss of income. Several researchers have cited decreased income as a factor in low retirement morale (Payne 1953; Pollman, 1971; Streib & Schneider, 1971). However, this appears to apply only to those individuals with already low levels at the time of retirement (Simpson & McKinney, 1966).

In his analysis of variables affecting adjustment to retirement, Atchley (1976) states "among those who encounter difficulty in adjusting to retirement, financial problems head the list (40%), followed by health problems (28%), missing one's job (22%), and death of a spouse (10%). Thus, among the 30% of retired people having significant adjustment problems, only about 7% have problems related to missing their jobs, while about 23% have adjustment problems which stem from conditions under which the retirement role must be played" (p. 110). Atchley's basic point is that retirees have only two extrinsic adjustments; loss of job and loss of income. It is factors relating to the individual's capacity to respond successfully to change that accounts for the greatest variability in adjustment.

Lowenthal (1972) has developed a lifecycle model of retirement in which retirement is depicted as a special case of normal adaptation tasks occurring near the end of the life span. Lowenthal emphasizes the ongoing nature of adaptation, noting that responses to stressful events are a function of adaptive behavior established throughout the life course. It follows then that previous adaptation style is a relevant factor in assessment of the retiree/client.

IMPLICATIONS FOR COUNSELING

Given the many factors which influence retirement adjustment, it is important for counselors to accurately assess clients' situations prior to intervention. Such assessment would include information concerning personality and coping mechanisms, social milieu, health, and income. In light of the developmental nature of the retirement process, reassessment and evaluation of this original information should be a continual component of the counseling endeavor.

In intial contacts with clients, counselors should provide some basic data regarding the retirement phenomena. It is important to be aware of the nature of a client's retirement decision (was it voluntary or unvoluntary?) and the effect retirement will have on personal income. Also important is the availability of social and familial support during this transition. The amount of extended support may indicate the amount of counselor support the client requires.

Assessment of the client's history of adaptation to stressful events provides the counselor with insight into the client's current coping ability. Much of this information may be gleaned through observation of the client and reviewing previous coping behavior. Neugarten, Havighurst, and Tobin (1968) have developed a categorization of major personality types found among the elderly. Their findings were based on a longitudinal study of several hundred persons, aged 50 to 80 over a six year period. In general, these investigators found that older persons who are regularly engaged in various social roles have greater life satisfaction. However, they found individuals with high life satisfaction and low social activity, and vice versa (p. 173).

Four personality types emerged from their analysis: the integrated personality, the armored defended personality, the passive-dependent personality, and the unintegrated personality. The integrated personality is represented by well functioning individuals with complex inner lives, intact cognitive abilities, and competent egos. They are all rather flexible, maintaining a comfortable degree of internal control of events and demonstrating high life satisfaction irrespective of the amount of role activity.

The armored defended personality includes individuals who are "striving, achievement oriented with high defenses against anxiety and the need to maintain tight control over life" (p. 176). Those who can "hold on," ignoring "retirement" issues are relatively satisfied. Others fight a maintenance battle, continually retreating and drawing an ever restrictive social perimeter, yet retaining a moderated degree of satisfaction as long as they can successfully "retrench."

The passive-dependent personality encompasses "persons with strong dependency needs who are moderately satisfied as long as they obtain responsiveness from significant others" (p. 176). There is also an "apathetic" pattern within this category, where passivity is the striking feature accompanied by low activity and low satisfaction.

The fourth personality type, unintegrated, includes individuals with gross defects in psychological functioning and deteriorated socialization and thought processes. Such individuals demonstrate profound dysfunction and require intervention strategies not applicable to this discussion. While these personality "types" should not be viewed as an all encompassing categorization of aged personality, they do enable the counselor to hypothesize the client's adaptive style.

The first three personality types can provide potential clientele for counselors. Each type may require differential approaches depending on the individuals preferred and needed level of social activity (e.g., group procedures may be more beneficial than individual interventions). Moreover, the various personality types not only suggest varying degrees of counselor responsibility within the relationship , but the counselor obviously will need to initiate the counseling relationship for the less assertive personality types. Generally, integrated individuals will be more likely to perceive the need for assistance, more likely to seek out help, will assume more responsibility in the relationship, and will have stronger egos, needing less support.

Armored-defended persons are less likely to perceive a need for assistance and often require non-threatening initiative on the part of the counselor. These persons may be best suited for an individual approach, followed by a support group when ready. Specifically, they may need help in establishing adequate defenses prior to risking exposure and change. A continued support system may be needed.

The passive-dependent personality presents a unique situation to the counselor as victimized significant others may need more assistance than the passive dependent individual. A family/-system approach, where new behavioral patterns are developed to lessen the dependency, is one possible approach.

Counseling goals and strategies must be adapted to these various personality types. The process becomes more complex when one recognizes that a significant percentage of persons at the onset of retirement will be married. Thus the counselor may be dealing with two personality types as well as the interaction and interdependence of the two. This calls for considerable couple and family counseling.

A second area to assess is client attitude and values. Surely, how one regards retirement affects how one will subsequently adjust to that transition. Individuals with negative attitudes toward retirement may find their fears were "justified" by way of a self-fulfilling prophecy, or that their fears were unwarranted by a satisfying retirement. In contrast, persons with unrealistically positive attitudes may also be setting themselves up for disappointment if retirement does not fulfill their expectations.

Lowenthal (1972) has noted that stress occurs as a result of preceived incongruities with and between one's purpose and one's behavior. Perceived incongruity is idiosyncratic and influenced by the quality and quantity of feedback received and the manner in which the feedback is received and processed. Some people are overly sensitive, others insensitive, and still others may be devoid of external as well as internal feedback mechanisms. For these persons, behavior nearly functions in a vacuum. The vacuum exists for individuals who shut out feedback.

Counselors can provide feedback, provide support so existing feedback is more readily received, and help persons process feedback more accurately or more appropriately. It is important to note that at retirement, referent groups and time frames change. These changes require major adjustments if they were not anticipated, or if retirement was an abrupt event rather than a gradual process.

Prior to retirement most persons were confronted with the realization that time, energy, and prior accomplishments were working against achieving all one's life goals. Moreover, human nature is such that achievement of goals rapidly fades from one's memory as new goals emerge and the individual becomes preoccupied with higher levels of attainment. Persons from before World War II were socialized to achieve, to set goals and pursue them relentlessly.

Another significant transition occurs when the individual is faced with the realization that not all goals are achievable. Consequently, there is the need to shift from goal oriented, other-directed behavior to inner-directed, inter- and intra- personal goals. Dependence on external extrinsic gratification can be a thing of the past if the person can successfully make the transition. Remarkably few people know how to enjoy the process of living as much as achieving a product.

Another view of inner directed and outer directedness is seen in the work of Rokeach (1968, p. 197) who identified both terminal (life goal) values and instrumental (life process) values in his

Counseling for the Growing Years

research. It might provide counselors and older clients a useful framework if these two sets of values were presented. With little elaboration these two sets of values are listed below:

Terminal Values	Instrumental Values
A comfortable life (a prosperous life)	Ambitious (hard-working, aspiring)
An exciting life (a stimulating, active life)	Broadminded (open-minded)
A sense of accomplishment (lasting contribution)	Capable (competent, effective)
A world at peace (free of war and conflict)	Cheerful (lighthearted, joyful)
A world of beauty (beauty of nature and the arts)	Clean (neat, tidy)
Equality (brotherhood, opportunity for all)	Courageous (standing up for your belief)
Family security (taking care of loved ones)	Forgiving (willing to pardon others)
Freedom (independence, free choice)	Helpful (working for the welfare of others)
Happiness (contentedness)	Honest (sincere, truthful)
Inner Harmony (freedom from inner conflict)	Imaginative (daring, creative)
Mature love (sexual and spiritual intimacy)	Independent (self-reliant, self-sufficient)
National security (protection from attack)	Intellectual (intelligent, reflective)
Pleasure (an enjoyable, leisurely life)	Logical (consistent, rational)
Salvation (saved, eternal life)	Loving (affectionate, tender)
Self-respect (self-esteem)	Obedient (dutiful, respectful)
Social recognition (respect, admiration)	Polite (courteous, well-mannered)
True Friendship (close companionship)	Responsible (dependable, reliable)
Wisdom (a mature understanding of life)	Self-controlled (restrained, self-disciplined)

Life is not an either or process, but counselors may find it necessary to help individuals recognize and accept more instrumental values as guides to living during the retirement process.

REFERENCES

Atchley, R.C. *The social forces in later life*. Belmont, California: Wadsworth Publishing Co., 1977.

Atchley, R.C. *The sociology of retirement*. Cambridge, Massachusetts: Schenkman, 1976.

Holmes, T.H., & Rahe, R.H. The social adjustment rating scale. *Journal of Psychosomatic Research*, 1967, 2, 213-218.

Lowenthal, M.F. Some potentialities of a life cycle approach to the study of retirement in F. Carp (Ed.), *Retirement*, New York: Behavioral Publications, 1972, 307-336.

Mack, M.J. An evaluation of a retirement planning program. *Journal of Gerontology*, 1958, 13, 198-202.

Maddox, G. Adaptation to retirement. *Gerontologist*, 1970, 10, 14-18.

Neugarten, B.L.; Havighurst, R.J.; & Tobin, S.S. Personality and patterns of aging. In B.L. Neugarten (Ed.), *Middle age and aging*. Chicago: University of Chicago Press, 1968, 173-177.

Payne, S.L. The Cleveland survey of retired men. *Personnel Psychology*, 1953, 6, 81-110. 81-110.

Pollman, A.W. Early retirement: A comparison of poor health to other retirement factors. *Journal of Gerontology*, 1971, 26, 41-45.

Rokeach, M. *Beliefs, attitudes and values*. San Francisco: Jossey-Bass, 1968.

Simpson, I.H., & McKinney, J. (Eds.). *Social aspects of aging*. Durham, North Carolina: Duke University Press, 1966.

Shanas, E. Adjustment to retirement: Substitution or accommodation? In F. Carp (Ed.), *Retirement*. New York: Behavioral Publications, 1972, 219-243.

Streib, G., & Schneider, C.J. *Retirement in American society*. Ithaca, New York: Cornell University Press, 1971.

Tuckman, J. Retirement attitudes of compulsary and non-compulsary retired workers. *Geriatrics*, 1956, 569-572.

Counseling the Aged, Dying, and Bereaved

Donald Steele

ABSTRACT

Death and bereavement are aspects of life that are difficult to understand and accept. The purpose of this chapter is to discuss these issues emphasizing how both have been viewed in the counseling literature. Counselor attitudes on these issues are critical to establishing a therepeutic relationship.

Usually, in issues of death and bereavement, counselors must work not only with the elderly person but with the rest of the family. Perhaps the most important question counselors need to ask themselves in working with dying or bereaved elderly is, "Do I want to intervene?" This chapter gives counselors a rationale for answering this question in the positive.

Finally, the use of a developmental approach in educating the elderly about death and bereavement is addressed. Counseling intervention strategies are also offered from a developmental perspective.

INTRODUCTION

Death. dying. grieving, and aging are four words fraught with negative connotations. These connotations have made it easy to avoid contact and intervention with people who are experiencing these concerns. The words refer to sorrow, depression, endings, and darkness which lead to avoidance of the topics in polite discussion and, more importantly, avoidance of those who are actually dying and grieving.

Three questions to be posed about these topics are:

1. Why intervene with the aged, dying, or bereaved?
2. How can we intervene with the dying or bereaved elderly?
3. Do I want to intervene?

The answers to these questions are central to counselor interaction and assistance of the elderly. Question number three is perhaps the most important and most difficult to answer. Without the willingness of the counselor to intervene, no action can be carried forth.

Information about dying, death, aging, and bereavement abounds in social science, medical, and counseling literature. The history of the literature on the subject demonstrates that we have excellent information. Jackson (1956) gave us *Understanding grief*, Feifel (1959) wrote *The meaning of death*, and Fulton (1965) published *Death and identity*. All of these works provided understanding and insight into death and grief with some guidelines to intervention. In spite of this, practitioners by and large ignored the topic.

In 1969 Ross produced *On death and dying* in which she challenged us to look at the reasons for our avoidance of death, the dying, and the grieving. Ross offers several answers, the fundamental one being that death is frightening to each of us. Until we are willing to face and accept our own feelings about death, we will not be willing or able facilitators for those facing death. She asks and answers the question: "If we cannot face death with equanimity, how can we be of assistance to our patients? We will make rounds and talk about the weather. . ." (Ross, 1967, p. 31).

Counseling for the Growing Years

Counselors, intending to be of assistance to the bereaved or dying elderly person, need not worry about locating information. Instead, counselors need to attend to personal matters which stand in the way of effectively using available information.

For helpers and researchers, it should be noted that death is not a solitary topic to be dealt with academically. Death must be dealt with as it intrudes on the living and the dying. Although the intrusion is the taking of an individual life, at least two can be affected by this intrusion. It can be anticipated that two similar, but strikingly variant reactions, can be anticipated. One person may be affected because of the death of oneself. A second person may have to react to the death of a significant other. Normal response to both of these forms of death intrusion will generate feelings of loss, but these feelings will differ enough to make it important, in this chapter, to distinguish and discuss feelings about dying and feelings about grieving in separate sections.

DEATH AND THE ELDERLY

Death is common in the experience of the elderly. The simple fact that the average age of older Americans is 71.6 years cannot be ignored. As each person approaches this number and notes decreasing physical ability, that person is reminded of the fact that death is a factor in one's own life. Moreover, few persons move through life without experiencing the death of significant others, friends, acquaintances, and loved ones. No matter how well one tries to remain shielded from death, it cannot be ignored.

Contact with death among the elderly may bring about resignation or understanding in some people. Cumming and Harey (1961) have suggested that this might be a form of disengagement whereby the elderly cut themselves off from others, thereby preparing themselves for death. If this hypothesis is true, it should not be confused with desiring personal death. Readiness or resignation may take the form of relief when the pains and trouble of life have become too heavy to bear. Readiness also may take the form of a simple acknowledgement that death is near or to be expected without embracing or wanting its occurrence. Some elderly, on the other hand, will reject any thought of their own death or acceptance of the death of a loved one.

A portion of the elderly population will embrace death. Twenty five percent of suicides are among the elderly (Kastenbaum, 1971). These individuals choose to end life for reasons of physical pain, feelings of uselessness, or loneliness. Death is more common in the lives of the elderly. Yet there is little evidence that the elderly react to it in ways substantially different from the rest of the population. Since, however, they are affected by it more often than others, counselor attention is warranted.

COUNSELOR PREDISPOSITION FOR ASSISTING

Effective counseling about death with the elderly requires that counselors be knowledgeable about their own feelings about death. It further means that counselors should know the attitudes and belief systems they have developed. Finally, counselors need a deep respect for the elderly. Counselors need to be aware of personal reactions to death and bereavement. Ross (1969) has clearly emphasized this point. Counselors unaware of their feelings will find that they are unable to be effective in many cases because they do not understand that their feelings cause avoidance of clients or cause them to dwell overly on client's problems.

In the matter of death, counselors may have anxiety resulting from their unresolved personal losses or concerns about death. Knowledge of these anxieties will help counselors work more effectively with clients. Counselors must be aware of their blind spots, private needs, irrelevant attitudes, biases or moral prejudices which may cause them to react to their own personal needs and not to the client. Tauber (1954) and Bandura et al. (1960) have noted that anxious therapists avoid situations which arouse anxieties and, in general, appear less confident. Others have noted reactions including a tendency to be overly conciliatory, paranoid, more powerful, or constantly reassuring (Reich, 1951).

Counselor introspection is important if counselors wish to increase potential effectiveness. Besides personal feelings about death, counselors need to concern themselves with feelings about loss of loved ones and loss of clients with whom they have established contact. The elderly are more likely to die than others in the population. Therefore, the incidence of terminated counseling relationships due to death is greatest with this population. When the counseling relationship is terminated because of the client's death, counselors must be prepared to face their feelings of grief and bereavement. Sensitivity to this event will help counselors prepare for these feelings before they occur. Denial of such feelings, however, can result in damage to other personal and professional relationships.

Besides feelings, counselors have belief systems about death based on faith or philosophy. Counselors should know their belief system and biases so as to define the limits of interaction with the client. It would be wrong for any counselor wittingly or unwittingly to impose another belief system, or limit the clients' ability to express the belief system of their choice. Ross (1973) made the point that no single religious faith or philosphical belief system by itself affects how one approaches death. What has an effect is how a person has lived out that religious belief or philosophy.

A final factor that counselors must consider is their attitude toward the aging. In the starkest statement of this point let us ask, "Does the counselor believe that the aged are worth helping?" In other words, do we truly value our clients as being worthwhile human beings even though they may have nothing measurable to offer to society or to us. If the counselor's answer to this is no, one would do well to reexamine one's role. Counselors who do not value their clients have little to offer them.

THE DEATH OF THE AGED

Is an old person's death more acceptable than a young person's? A study by Sudnow (1967) indicates that this may be so. Values are placed on life in accord with perceived contribution to society. When two people, one elderly and one younger, arrive at an emergency room at the same time, the younger is more likely to receive treatment faster, if priorities have to be set. Likewise, a younger person will garner more herioc efforts than the older (Sudnow, 1967). Similarly, we hear people remark when an old person dies that "one should expect such" or "they had a good life." The inference is that the aged are least productive, have less to offer, and that they have had their chance. In essence, the elderly appear to have less societal significance when compared to younger persons.

This is usually the thinking of those who are not old and who are not dying. Staff, counselors, and friends may hold such beliefs and make decisions based on this type of thinking. This thinking is not usually the thinking of the aged about death. When confronted with dying, the elderly patient will react as others who are dying. Counselors working with the elderly must, as in working with any client, listen to hear what the client needs and then proceed to help. Old or young, the client is a human with personal feelings.

One's Own Death

Reaction to one's own death is the reaction to the loss of one's own life. The meaning which life has for a person will greatly affect the reaction to that loss. A life that has been rich, and continues to be so, is more difficult to give up than a life of pain and loneliness. Many elderly have had opportunities to see their bodies decline and to prepare for dying. These latter may be more prepared to accept death, but this does not necessarily mean they are desirous of it.

Reaction to one's own death has been outlined by Ross (1969). In her work she noted and discussed five stages. Unfortunately, these stages have been accepted by many as following one another in stepwise fashion. The writer has disclaimed such a notion (Ross, 1973). All people do not react to all events in the same way nor do feelings and behavior follow one another in stepwise fashion. The misconception persists and is ex-emplified in practice. This is clearly shown in the following physician's statement, "I can now recognize that a patient is an-gry. How do I move that patient along through *bargaining* and *depression* to accept it?" Such a statement indicates a lack of understanding that human emotions do not follow one another in close order. Emotions ebb and flow, replace, overlap, and conflict with one another.

Another approach to conceptualizing reactions to death, one that will be used here, is derived from the work of C. Murray Parkes (1972). Parkes describes a series of feelings and behaviors that occur in people. The feelings and behaviors take place over time and vary according to the value of life, meaning, and psychological make-up of the individual experiencing them.

Realization that one's life is going to end is frequently difficult to accept. The reaction is to deny initially.with acceptance coming gradually. Some elderly experience shock less dramatically than younger persons facing similar news. The elderly have watched their bodies decline and have some expectations about the finiteness of life.

Disbelief when it is a reality may last a short time or persist through to the moment of death. It may disappear only to return at a later time. Where it persists it may be a defense against a terrible reality which is not wanted and cannot be faced (Ross, 1969). Slowly the reality begins to show itself and the dying learn that their illness is real, and that new ways of relating to others must be found.

Knowledge that one is dying may produce feelings of anger, guilt, jealousy, sorrow, depression, and loneliness. Anger is an expression by a person that death is unwanted. It may be aimed at God, the physician, or family members. Anger may be expressed at the unknown in the form of questions like: "Why is this happening to me?" or "Why is the pain so great?" or Why can't I just end it?" Anger may be expressed nonverbally in refusals to eat or in acting out or self-destructive behavior, such as suicide (Kastenbaum, 1971). Some anger may be quite legitimate: "Why was the diagnosis wrong?" "Why don't I get good care?" Other anger is simply a way of gaining control over an uncontrollable situation.

Guilt is another common feeling for the dying person. Some guilt reflects true regret over ommissions or commissions of the past. Dying people who feel they could have lived a more satisfactory life may have legitimate concerns to discuss. Some guilt is a search for a satisfactory answer to the unknown. Persons who can answer the question: "Why did this happen to me?" by locating blame in themselves, have an answer to the question—albeit an unsatisfactory one. A final manifestation of guilt is inverted anger. For some it is unacceptable to blame God or a doctor for what has occurred. Yet a reason needs to be found. The easy way out is to blame oneself for real or imagined acts that lead to the final illness (Clayton, 1968).

Sorrow, depression, and "the blues" are common feelings. These feelings not only result from feelings about "dying," but may come from being helpless, experiencing long term pain, or being unable to finish some special task. The realization of dying is bleak for many and will bring forth sorrow or depression. Support and comfort are mandated at such times. When chronic pain is a factor, medications may need to be adjusted.

Many dying patients will work their way through these feelings and come to a resignation or acceptance (Ross, 1969) of their situation. Others will die before this occurs. Another small group will find a way to end life before it takes its natural course.

Grief for Another

Grief felt at the loss of a loved one occurs over time and is considered by most writers to be a process of feelings and behaviors which occur for the four fold purpose of:

1. testing the reality that the deceased is gone,
2. breaking bonds with the deceased,
3. establishing new relationships with the environment, and,
4. establishing new relationships with other persons (Parkes, 1972).

Silverman (1972) outlined the course of grief in three phases, impact, recoil, and recovery. The ultimate goal of the bereaved is to recover sufficient equilibrium in order to be able to live a reasonably happy and productive life without the deceased.

Many of the feelings and behaviors previously described for the dying also occur for the survivor. The difficult task for the elderly survivor is to work through the feelings and work toward supplanting the roles which the deceased played. Recovery requires that the bereaved be able to live life without the deceased. This means that either the bereaved learn to perform some of the roles which the deceased performed or that one finds others with whom to establish relationships that can fulfill roles that the deceased previously played.

Unfortunately, many elderly are unable to make new friends or to learn new tasks because of illness or immobility. Many others are in ill or failing health, have lost many of their friends, and have difficulty looking toward a fulfilling future. Considerations

Counseling for the Growing Years

such as these will compound the grief which the survivor feels and may make it more difficult to reestablish a meaningful life without the deceased.

A strong feeling of helplessness accompanies bereavement. The bereaved are helpless in regaining the lost person, are helpless in feeling better, and helpless in learning new ways of relating to their environment. For many of the elderly, bereaved loneliness, depression, and helplessness contribute to poor health and even to death (Parkes, 1972). Loss of an important person at a time in life when there is little likelihood of substituting a meaningful replacement is for many a most severe blow.

To determine a person's reaction to the death of a loved one, one must consider how the death affects all areas of living. Loss can be uni- or multi- dimensional. Loss of a lover, cook, bookkeeper, companion, and/or breadwinner can have differing effects on a survivor. Knowledge at which role or roles were most important can provide a clue to the survivor's reaction.

DEVELOPMENTAL INTERVENTION

If the popular concept that death and aging represent decline and termination is true, it is difficult to fathom how one would take a developmental approach to dying and aging. As Neugarten (1977) points out, "developmental usually implies movement toward a higher or more differentiated end point. Therefore, it is an awkward term in describing aging." It is even more awkward in describing death! The counselor wishing to work with the aging (and with the dying or bereaved aging) from a developmental perspective has to come to terms with attitudes about life and living. A developmental approach can be used. The counselor needs to go far beyond the act of encouraging clients to be happy because they will grow from this experience or that "all will be well because God will provide." One way of helping is to utilize a developmental perspective to view death as the completion of life's work. From this vantage point death reflects meaning of life. Death is a marker point from which life can be assessed; it provides multiple opportunities to help clients grow in the face of the inevitable.

Counselors taking a developmental approach can become involved though education and intervention.

Education

A developmental approach to education permits a counselor's work to begin before people are dying, aged, or bereaved. Preparation and understanding about death can begin at any age, but should begin in the pre-school period. Counselors can help parents to understand that their children seek honest answers at their level of comprehension. When death occurs or when questions about death arise, they should be answered directly and honestly (Grollman, 1967).

When children reach school age, counselors can become more active and educate by means of bibliotherapy. There are numerous fictional and nonfictional works which can provide a basis for discussion of death. Experiences can be designed to facilitate discussion. Also, there will be times when death arises in the school, perhaps the death of a pet, the death of another student, or the death of a child's parent or grandparent. This should be viewed as an opportunity for counselors to become involved in talking and answering questions that children raise. This work can be continued beyond the school years.

More structured education to assist persons on understanding death, bereavement, and aging can be given through courses, seminars, or workshops. Understanding what is normal and expected can be an excellent way to prepare for aging and dying (Brantner, 1972). Attention may be drawn to matters of value through questions like: "Life is limited and death is real, what implications for living arise from this? If people are valued because of their inherent value, can suggestions be made about how the aging and dying are to be treated?"

Preparation and education for death needs to focus on economics, emotions, ceremonies, religion, and social considerations. Counselors can help pupils and adults to consider their values and attitudes about wills, funerals, and insurance. Such matters are not merely economic issues (Mitford, 1963). Rather these matters have emotional significance. Decisions about such matters should account for feelings of those who will survive. Funerals in particular need to be given more than economic consideration. Funerals have value for survivors and survivors ought to have some say in how they will be carried out. Fulton (1976) has suggested that those who minimize ceremony at the time of death have greater depression and anxiety and consume a higher quantity of drugs and alcohol. Funerals do offer psychological benefit to survivors.

A final task for education is the offering of information that will assist people to better aid the dying or bereaved. Much aid that can be offered to the aging, dying, and bereaved does not need to be professional in its origin. Understanding can be gained through support groups and through personal contacts. Excellent models for planning self-help groups have been developed and reported throughout the United States and Great Britain (Silverman, 1974; Steele, 1975).

Intervention

Counselors can be effective intervenors with the aging, dying, and bereaved. Skills already in the repertoire of well-trained counselors help them to build relationships and provide information. A counselor intervening with this population may have the following goals:

1. To provide support in dealing with stress. This is best done through listening and helping the person clarify feelings.

2. To provide an opportunity to place the event of one's own death or the loss of an important other in perspective. Growth, development, and integration are all possible at this point. Usdin and Hofling (1978) point out that the aged have much to talk about. The history of a long life can be dealt with in a life review that focuses on bringing together the past and making decisions for whatever is left of the future. Not everyone will be pleased with how they have lived their lives (Usdin & Hofling, 1978). The opportunity to discuss conflicts and resolve them is important. This can be facilitated at the end of life so that a person may find congruence between action and belief.

3. There may be practical things that need to be done and the counselor can help a person complete these tasks.

4. There may be important relationships which need review. The dying may wish to clarify previously unfinished matters with others who are important to them.

Not all dying scenes are pleasant and not all bereaved aging are lucid. Counselors doing their best will find that there are a number of fears that need to be addressed. The fear of dying is often fear of loneliness, fear of the unknown, and fear of loss of control. Similarly, the loneliness of the bereaved may be expressed in fear, conflicts, or strong efforts to maintain independence. Empathy and respect are two counseling characteristics that will be very helpful in assisting the elderly.

Another important intervention exists in working with the family of the dying. A surviving older spouse needs special attention. Efforts need to be made to assure that the surviving older spouse gets good physical care, especially if the dying person's life is prolonged. Many difficulties that occur for survivors are the result of poor physical care during the time of a spouse's long term illness. Within this period of time, the spouse and other family members may need assistance with their feelings and emotions. Support and the freedom to express themselves openly is most helpful. Some events which need special attention include helping people say goodbyes, expressing past regrets, and planning for the future. As much as possible, the DYING should be included in all these discussions.

A final counselor activity with the dying and aging is follow up. Involvement with the family after death is important. Grief is a process of making psychologically real an event which is not desired and for which coping plans do not exist. The counselor's task is to help survivors express and work through feelings so that they can reach a point of recovery or a point of acceptance so a new beginning can take place or integration can be accomplished.

The death of a loved person ends the role the deceased filled for the survivor. Besides the loneliness and pain of no longer having the person available, there are new roles to be learned, new tasks to be performed, and new ways of relating to old friends and acquaintances. Since the survivor is aged, it may be more difficult to learn new ways of coping. Counselors can assist the grieving to work through their feelings and to learn new tasks of surviving. The aged survivor may also need to establish new friends and relationships at a time in life when opportunities are minimal. The surviving aged person may also need special assistance with learning how to properly take care of oneself.

SUMMARY

Counseling the aged about death and grief can be a rewarding experience. It requires that the counselor have good counseling skills, knowledge of self, knowledge of the feeling states that accompany death and grief, knowledge of aging and their needs, and finally the knowledge of community resources. Application of developmental theory at this phase of life may entail providing support for the aging as they attempt to find meaning in a life which is drawing to a close. The elderly have lived long lives. They are people with feelings. They have value. When death becomes a concern for them, they need assistance. Effective counselors will find their lives enriched because of their encounters with those who have already experienced the life that they have yet to live.

REFERENCES

Bandura, A.; Lipsher, D.; & Miller, P.E. Psychotherapist's approach-avoidance reaction to patient's expressions of hostility. *Journal of Counseling Psychology*, 1960, *24*, 1-8.

Brantner, J. Personal communications. University of Minnesota. 1972.

Clayton, P.; Desmarais, L.; & Wanokur. C. A study of normal bereavement. *American Journal of Psychiatry*, 1968. *125*(2). 168-178.

Cumming, E., & Harey, W. *Growing old: The process of disengagement*. New York: Basic Books. 1961.

Feifel, H. *The meaning of death*. New York: McGraw Hill. 1959.

Fulton, R. *Death and identity*. New York: John Wiley & Sons. 1965.

Grollman, E. *Explaining death to children*. Boston: Beacon Press. 1967.

Jackson, E. *Understanding grief*. Nashville: Abingdon, 1956.

Kastenbaum, R. Premature death and self-injurious behavior in old age. *Geriatrics*, 1971, *26*, 70-81.

Mitford, J. *The American way of death*. New York: Fawcett, 1963.

Neugarten, N. Personality and aging. In J. Birren & K.W. Schuie (Eds.), *Handbook of the psychology of aging*. New York: Van Nostrano. 1967.

Parkes, C.M. *Bereavement: Studies of grief in adult life.* New York: International Universities Press, 1972.

Reich, A. On countertransference. *International Journal of Psychoanalysis,* 1951, *32,* 25-31.

Ross, E.K. *On death and dying.* New York: Macmillian, 1969.

Ross, E.K. Lecture, Wausau, Wisconsin: 1973.

Silverman, P.R. *Helping each other in widowhood.* New York: Health Sciences Publishing Company, 1974.

Steele, D.W. *The funeral director's guide to programming for the widowed.* Milwaukee: National Funeral Directors Association, 1975.

Sudnow, D. *Passing on: The social organization of dying.* Englewood Cliffs, New Jersey: Prentice-Hall, 1967.

Tauber, E.S. Exploring the therapeutic use of counter transference data. *Psychiatry,* 1954, 331.

Usdin, G., & Hofling, C.J. (Eds.). *Aging: The process and the people.* New York: Brunner-Mazel Publishers, 1978.

Counseling the Elderly and Their Families

Steve Peltier

ABSTRACT

The purpose of this chapter is to sensitize counselors to the effects of aging on the family and to examine the role of family counseling in working with the elderly. The first part of the chapter looks at the concept of family development. The second section addresses goals and processes of family counseling. The third section deals with specific issues of institutionalization, retirement, and death and the role family counseling can play in assisting families through ensuing transition periods.

INTRODUCTION

There are two primary roles that counselors can take when working with families with elderly members. First, counselors can assist the elderly and their adult children in understanding governmental regulations, and in identifying programs which will be most beneficial for dealing with stress that accompanies shifting family roles. Many problems expressed by elderly counselees can be traced to tense home situations. By working with family members, counselors can assist families in making changes that will relieve stress and alleviate symtomatic behavior. The focus of this chapter will primarily be on this second role.

Contrary to myth, elderly family members are not abandoned (Spark & Brody, 1970). While most elderly do not share the same residence with their adult children, there is more physical and emotional attachment between generations than commonly believed. There is also a significant body of research which demonstrates that families are effective support systems for the elderly and are responsive to critical needs of elderly persons (e.g. Shanas, 1968).

There are a number of reasons for working with families of the elderly. First, families provide support systems for the elderly person. Second, the family is a group that is easily identifiable and relatively easy to mobilize to assist the elderly member. Also, the family usually makes the final decision regarding the future of its elderly (Cath, 1972). In addition to changes in elderly members that might necessitate a family counselor, it has been found that the aging process has an impact on other family members (Rathbone-McCuan, 1976). It has been found that older family members play a significant role in the dynamics of the family (Boszormenyi-Nagy & Sparks, 1973; Spark & Brody, 1970).

Aging and the Family

While models for "healthy" families have been developed for the early phases of the family life cycle, there are few, if any, models for "healthy" aging families. To understand what constitutes a healthy developmental pattern for this population, it is necessary to understand family interactions at the aging phase of the family life cycle.

From 1900 to the present, the percent of elderly in our population has increased from 4% to 10% (Brody, 1974). As a result of this increase, there has been a corresponding increase in the number of multigenerational families. As of 1968, 70% of people 65 or older have grandchildren and 40% of the people 65 or older have great-grandchildren. While only 25% of the elderly live with an adult child, 84% live within one hour of one of their children, usually a daughter. Eighty percent of the elderly see an adult child at least once a week and two-thirds see an adult child every day or two. Seeing their children usually means seeing their grandchildren at the same time. This seems to indicate that the elderly have a substantial impact on roles and patterns within the family with respect to their children and grandchildren.

The elderly have been called the big "Losers" (Brody, 1974). They lose spouses, siblings, peers, and children. They also have other sets of losses such as familiar environments, physical and mental capacities, roles both inside and outside of the family, earning power, and ultimately life itself.

Each of these changes in older family members cause changes to occur in roles and functions of other family members. These changes occur in emotional and expressive portions of the relationship and in more instrumental components of the family.

This chapter has been divided into three parts. The first part is an examination of the concept of family development and presents a framework for understanding the process of change in the family. The second section includes a review of the assumptions, goals, and processes involved with family counseling. The last section discusses specific situations in which family counseling is an appropriate mode of intervention.

FAMILY DEVELOPMENT

Family development is an active acquisition and a selective discarding of roles by family members as they seek to meet the changing functions required of them as they adapt to life stress as a family system (Hill & Mattesich, 1977). Family development focuses on the emergence of norms, roles, and other family characteristics that are necessary for the family to remain as a unit. Changes in responsibility and differentiation of family members as the family moves through various periods of its life cycle is an additional focus. The process begins when a man and a woman marry. They have responsibility for each other and themselves. With the addition of children, they take on additional responsibilities. As children move through adolescence and gain confidence, the nature of support shifts and parents take less responsibility for their children. As parents age, the role of responsibility shifts to the adult child who must take more responsibility for the care of parents.

The process of family development is closely tied to the individual development of family members. A significant number of researchers have looked at influences on family development in early stages of the life cycle and found that family members provide role models that assist in the social development of the child (Rogers, 1964; Troll, 1971). Additional research has been accumulating at a much slower rate that shows that continued contact with elderly family members increases the likelihood that elder members will provide models for their adult children that are used in formulation of social roles necessary for later stages of adulthood (Troll, 1971).

The distinction between family development and individual development is interactional in nature. The aging of an individual family member may correspond to the aging of the family, but this does not necessarily have to be true. Family development occurs only if there is change in relationship or interactional characteristics of family members.

Filial Maturity

As the aging process continues, adult children also change their roles in respect to older family members. This pattern of development in adult childhood has been labeled "filial maturity" (Blenker, 1965). This period of role change is characterized by the development of the adult child's capacity to be depended on by aging parents. This is not role reversal, in which the adult child takes a parental role, but rather a supportive role with respect to aging parents.

While this is a developmental phase for the adult child, it is also seen as a developmental phase for the whole family (Brody, 1974). Elderly members must have the capacity to be dependent and permit the adult child to take the filial role. Other family members, spouse, siblings, and extended family need to provide support for both members. Ideally the filial crisis should occur and be resolved as a normal developmental phase rather than as an acute crisis. Usually, for families seen in counseling, this is not the case. Gaps of unresolved problems which result have a direct bearing on how the family copes with changing relationship roles.

Change in the Family System

Change in the family system comes from three primary sources (Rogers, 1964). The first change revolves around physical maturation of individuals. As people age, society and family age and sex norms relevant to their roles change. In addition, abilities also change. These changes limit or expand types of activities and roles individuals can assume. Second, change results from expectations of family and society. If family or society change stereotypes or expectations of elder members' roles, there will be a corresponding change in family interaction patterns. The third area which fosters change originates in the desires, aspirations, and values of the individual. An individual's "life view" can cause members of the family system to change.

FAMILY COUNSELING

The influence of families on elderly members has been examined from a number of perspectives including marriage counseling (Peterson, 1973; 1974), social work (Bloom & Monro, 1972; Brody, 1966; 1974), and family therapy for both individual families (Boszormenyi-Nagy & Spark, 1973; Herr & Weakland, 1978; Spark & Brody, 1972) and groups of members from institutionalized families (Manaster, 1967).

Most of the discussion of family counseling and its uses relates to two issues: institutionalization (Brody & Spark, 1966; Cath, 1972; Miller & Harris, 1967) and death or loss (Berezin, 1970). Recently authors have started to look into other issues such as retirement (Peterson, 1973; 1974) and sexuality (Peterson, 1973).

Family counseling is defined as any therapeutic intervention which has as its major focus the alteration of the family system. Counseling may include only one member (Bowen, 1978), the whole nuclear family (Minuchin, 1974), the extended family (Boszormenyi-Nagy & Spark, 1973), multiple family groups (Laqueur, 1972), or a variety of other combinations.

Family counseling shifts therapeutic focus away from the individual within the family to the family as a whole. The assumption is that cause of the problem is stress in the family system and that resolution of problems will be beneficial for all family members and for the family as a unit.

Systems Theory

Family counseling looks at how the family unit is functioning and uses that unit and its members to initiate change. Many of the assumptions used in family counseling are derived from systems theory. Systems theory, as the name suggests, looks at a system (dyad, family, group, or organization) and describes how change takes place within the system (Bertalanffy, 1968).

Systems theory postulates that:

1. Individuals are responsive to others within the larger system.
2. Wholeness exists such that change in one person will cause change in other parts of the system (family). Conversely, an individual can not change unless the family system changes.
3. Families will resist change in an individual family member in an attempt to maintain equilibrium or homeostasis.
4. Families are more than the sum of the individual family members.
5. Family units have qualities which result from interaction of family members.
6. Family systems require constant feedback and tend to resist change.
7. Family systems operate on a set of explicit and implicit rules which regulate behavior.
8. Causality is circular in that a response to a stimulus becomes a secondary stimulus for another response (Bertalanffy, 1968).

Goals for Counseling

The focus of counseling with families and their elderly members is to help resolve situational problems, not to treat psychopathology. This goal necessitates use of brief counseling-problem solving approaches which are cheaper and more efficient. Families come into counseling with specific problems. Outcome goals are developed from issues that families present.

There are two primary goals in family counseling. The first is to assist the family to reorganize its roles and responsibilities so that the family's dysfunctional structure will not continue to support the symptom of the elderly counselee. By assisting family members to modify or change their roles, the counselor enables the family to move through the developmental crisis to the next stage in the family's development.

The second goal is to make explicit rules that family members use in their interaction with each other. In dysfunctional families most rules are implicit and allow family members to interpret them to their own advantage. By making rules explicit, family members know what expectations are placed on them. This allows for expectations to be challenged and changed as the family, or it's members, desire change.

Process of Family Counseling

There are three major points in the therapeutic counseling process. In practice they cannot be separated, but for purposes of discussion they will be discussed individually. The first is characterized by the counselor "joining the family." The counselor and the family come together to form a system. In this phase of counseling, the counselor attempts to become involved with the family in a way that makes it possible to assess the underlying structure of the family.

Second, in assessing the structure of the family, the counselor should concentrate on a number of dimensions. Preferred family interaction patterns should be observed and alternative patterns used by the family should be identified. The flexibility of the system should be examined, as should it's capacity for elaboration and restructuring. Third, counselors should observe individual's sensitivity to other family members' actions. Sources of stress and support in the family's environment should be identified. The family's developmental stage should be examined and its performance compared to tasks appropriate for that stage. Finally, the counselor needs to explore ways in which the elderly counselee's symptoms or problems are used to maintain the family's preferred interactional patterns.

The third stage of the counseling process is intervention. Interventions are used to provide the family with new ways of looking at themselves. This is essentially a re-defining and re-label-ing of many of the family's experiences. The emphasis should be on positives in the family's situation.

Counseling interventions are designed to transform conflicts that are being discussed into ones occurring in the session. Counselors achieve this by using commands or suggestions to various members in the family. Counselors also shift their allegiance from one coalition to another as the situation dictates to challenge and/or support power groups in the family.

The first task for counselors is to increase tension by testing the limits of the system. This helps counselors to identify patterns the family uses to deal with stress. Counselors should help the family understand how their usual patterns of interactions may be obstacles to achieving the change they desire.

When counselors have identified dysfunctional interaction patterns, they need to challenge the family system. They have four choices in selecting interventions: (1) they can obey the pattern, yet attempt to change the quality of the interaction (e.g. when two highly competitive adult children are asked to try a more cooperative approach to solve a problem); (2) they can disobey the pattern without explicitly pressing for different interactions (e.g. when they deliberately direct their attention toward the elderly member rather than siding with the members who sought counseling); (3) they can disobey the pattern while expliciting requesting the use of new patterns (e.g. when they direct a peripheral adult child to take a more direct role in the counseling process); and (4) they can elminate the traditional patterns (e.g. when they decide who is to be present during the counseling sessions.

SPECIFIC PROBLEM SITUATIONS

There are a number of situations that commonly involve elderly persons and their families. Some situations primarily involve the elderly family member and spouse while others encompass additional family members. In both cases, family counseling can be effective in opening communication lines and relieving stress that is felt by the family and its members.

Institutionalization

In many cases, the family makes the final decision as to whether an older member will be placed in an institution. Usually family decisions reflect one of four circumstances. First, placement may be a culmination of stress in family-older member relationships. Stress may be between adult children and their spouses.

A second difficulty arises when there are crises of somatic and/or psychiatric illnesses in elderly family members or when physical illnesses are such that professional care/or constant monitoring is required. Dementia and other psychiatric illnesses may also necessitate that the family seek institutionalization.

A third circumstance that can pressure families to consider institutionalization revolves around living conditions of elderly members at the time of increasing disability. The family may perceive that an elderly family member is not able to care for oneself and that the living situation has deteriated to a point where it is unsafe and/or unhealthy. Insitutionalization may provide the family with a viable solution.

A fourth situation occurs when the family is unable to meet economic demands of chronic health care for the physically ill elderly. The relatively meager assistance from Medicare for health care and the complete absolution of family financial responsibility for physically ill older family members constitutes a significant factor in the placement of the ill family member.

Also, institutionalization of an elderly family member may be seen as a sign of abandonment by other family members. Adult children of institutionalized parents may live with guilt about their inability to meet parental needs. Society offers few direct supports for individuals caught in this dilemma.

Family counseling can be used in the above situations to assist all family members in reaching the filial maturity stage and to assist the elderly to accept their development. In addition, family counseling can help families develop support systems for aging members and provide psychological support for the family as it works through the developmental crises resulting from institutionalization.

It is important at this point to reiterate that the "problem" of the elderly person may be symptomatic of more pervasive problems in the family, and, therefore, the family rather than the elderly member should be viewed as the "counselee."

Participation of the family from inception of counseling provides an opportunity for problems to be resolved constructively. Counseling can relieve stress of the immediate crisis and serve as a preventive measure at later crisis points. Effective communication between family members and the counselor can assist institutions working with the elderly to structure programs to meet the needs of elderly members.

Retirement

Retirement can be a major crisis in the lives of both men and women. Shifting roles that accompany transition from worker to non-worker are prime reasons for stress that effect the elderly and their families (Neugarten & Guttman, 1968). Problems of adjustment to retirement frequently precipitate emotional upset in the elderly that leads to hospitalization (Wolff, 1967).

There are a number of reasons for increased stress at this particular transition point. There is a loss of self-esteem in the retired person. With increased leisure time and with diminished responsibilities, retired persons can begin to feel useless and superflous. Retired persons frequently perceive that their role in the family changes from that of a provider to that of being a "burden." Additionally, retirees experience a loss of co-workers, friends, and other social contacts.

An additional source of stress occurs when individuals or couples are forced to alter activity paterns that were developed over many years. Being together for 24 hours of the day instead of the ten hours they were accustomed to can prove to be trying. Individuals may rely on roles learned on the job which are often inappropriate for "new" dyadic relationships.

Pre-retirement programs are being developed to help people become aware of stress involved with retirement. Most successful programs investigate support systems that "the soon to be" retired person has developed. These experimental programs have discovered that it is very difficult to foster adjustment if both husband and wife are not involved in the therapeutic process (Peterson, 1973). In fact, in many cases, total family involvement is advisable.

There are two primary means of intervening with families at this crisis point. The first is to involve the spouse and as many other family members as possible in pre-retirement counseling. This provides a forum for family members to discuss role changes, their consequent anxieties, and implications of retirement for all family members.

A second approach uses group procedures which allow couples to share their concerns and possible solutions for retirement issues that concern them. This approach provides the couple a support group to assist them in making the transition from work to retirement.

Death and Dying

The topic of death and dying probably has been the most examined issue facing the elderly. Much of this investigation has looked at the individual and not at systems surrounding the person. The primary function of family counseling is to open lines of communications between family members and to assist them in talking about death, its meanings, and its implications.

The elderly member who is dying cannot be helped in a meaningful way if the family is not involved. As the dying member is less able to continue to assume previous roles (i.e. provider, supporter, confidante), other family members must begin to assume these roles and provide stability for the family. Roles of family members change from onset of illness and continue to fluctuate until long after the dealth of an elderly member. The counselor can assist family members to identify roles that are needed to assist the family in filling them.

Most elderly persons who are dying need to discuss death with their families, be with their families at death, and feel the warmth of their primary relationships (Peterson, 1974). During these family sessions, concerns, fears, resentments, and guilt can be aired. Therapeutically, at the same time another process is occuring, the dying family member is slowly detaching from world and family. It is important for the counselor to continue to work with the family to help them understand this detachment process. This process is often misunderstood as a rejection of the family by the dying member. The counselor's task is to help the family understand this phenomena as being within the natural order of events.

SUMMARY

The focus of this chapter has been on the effect of aging on the family and ways counseling can assist in resolution of issues that affect the family. The concept of family development has been discussed as it applies to the family with an elderly member.

Specific issues of institutionalization, retirement, and death were discussed as well as ways that family counseling could help the family through transition periods.

At the present time, little effort is directed at encouraging families with elderly members to seek out counseling to resolve problems and/or relieve the stress of certain situations. As more becomes known about the effects of family counseling with the elderly, counselors may see the need to develop family counseling skills to better serve the needs of the elderly and their families.

REFERENCES

Berezin, M.A. The psychiatrists and the geriatric patient: Partial grief in family members and others who care for the elderly patient. *Journal of Geriatric Psychiatry*, 1970, *4* (1), 53-64.

Bertalanffy, L. General system theory—A critical review. In W. Buckley (Ed.), *Modern systems research for the behavioral scientist*. Chicago: Aldine Publishing Co., 1968.

Blenkner, M. Social work and family relationships in later life with some thoughts on filial maturity, in social structure and the family. In E. Shanas & G.F. Streib (Eds.), *Generational relations*. Englewood Cliffs, New Jersey: Prentice Hall, 1965.

Bloom, M., & Monro, A. Social work and the aging family. *Family Coordinator*, 1972, 21, 103-115.

Boszormenyi-Nagy, I., & Spark, G.M. *Invisible loyalties: Reciprocity in intergenerational family therapy*. New York: Harper & Row, 1973.

Bowen, M. *Family therapy in clinical practice*. New York: John Aronson, 1978.

Brody, E. The aging family. *Gerontologist*, 1966, *6* (4), 201-206.

Brody, E. Aging and family personality: A developmental view. *Family Process*, 1974, *13* (1), 23-28.

Brody, E. & Spark, G.M. Institutionalization of the elderly: A family crisis. *Family Process*, 1966, *5* (1), 76-90.

Cath, S.H. The geriatric patient and his family: The institutionalization of a parent: A nadir of life. *Journal of Geriatric Psychiatry*, 1972, *5* (1), 25-46.

Herr, J.H., & Weakland, J.H. The family as a group. In I.M. Burnside (Ed.), *Working with the elderly: Group processes and techniques*. North Scituate, Massachusetts: Buxbury Press, 1978.

Hill, R. & Mattescich, P. *Reconstruction of family development theories: A progress report*. A paper presented at the National Council on Family Relations Annual Meeting, San Diego, California: October, 1977.

Laqueur, H.P. Mechanism of change in multiple family therapy. In C.J. Sager & H.S. Kaplan (Eds.), *Process in group and family therapy*. New York: Brunner/Nazel, 1972.

Manaster, A. The family group therapy at Park View Home for the aged. *Journal of the American Geriatrics Society*, 1967, *15* (3), 302-306.

Miller, M.B., & Harris, A.P. The chronically ill aged: Paradoxical patient-family behavior. *Journal of the American Geriatrics Society*, 1967, *15* (5), 480-495.

Minuchen, S. *Families and family therapy*. Cambridge, Massachusetts: Harvard University Press, 1974.

Neugarten, B., & Guttman, D. Age-sex roles and personality in middle age. A thematic appreciation study. In B. Neugarten (Ed.), *Middle age and aging*. Chicago, Illinois: University of Chicago Press, 1968.

Peterson, J. Marital and family therapy involving the aged. *Gerontologist*, 1973, *13* (1), 27-31.

Peterson, J. Therapeutic intervention in marital and family problems of aging persons. In A. Schwartz & I Mensh (Eds.), *Professional obligations and approaches to the aged*. Springfield, Illinois: Charles C. Thomas, 1974.

Rathbone-McCuan, E. Geriatric day care: A family *Gerontologist*, 1976, *16* (6), 517-521.

Toward a theory of family development. *Journal of Marriage and the Family*, 1964, 26, 262-270.

Shanas, E., et al.. *Old people in three industrial societies*. New York: Atherton Press, 1968.

Spark, G.M., & Brody, E. The aged are family members. *Family Process*, 1970, *9* (2), 195-210.

Spark, G.M., & Brody, E. The aged are family members. In C.J. Sager & H.S. Kaplan (Eds.), *Process in Group and family therapy*. New York: Brunner/Mazel, 1972.

Troll, L. The family in later life: A decade review. In C. Broderick (Ed.), *A decade of family research and action*. Minneapolis, Minnesota: National Council on Family Relations, 1971.

Wolff, K. Family conflicts and aging: Psychodynamics of the aging process. *Northwest Medicine*, 1967, *66*, 50-55.

Financial Counseling: General Economic Background and Information for Helping Elderly Clients

Robert M. Soldofsky

ABSTRACT

Understanding the changing age structure in the twentieth century and beyond is essential to an appreciation of the general economic and specific personal financial conse-quences of these changes. The proportion of the population 65 and older increased from 4.3% in 1910 to 12.2% in 2000. The social security system started operating in 1937. Social welfare expenditures were extremely small until that time, but grew rapidly to absorb about 32.0% of the Gross National Product by 1976. The rising social security payroll taxes are increasing the political tensions between the older and younger persons in American society. The personal financial problems of elderly persons are being aggravated by contin-uing rapid inflation and by longer lives.

Firm financial planning for retirement may start 5-10 years before the actual retirement date. Gathering cash-flow infor-mation for the retirement years is essential as well as prepar-ing in advance for possible part-time employment. A visit to the local Social Security Administration well in advance of retirement is prudent. Four financial problems that are likely to be most serious, and other specific important problems, are discussed. These problems include old age and survivors benefits, supplemental security income, medigap insurance, property taxes, income taxes, medicaid, funerals, and finan-cial-legal topics such as wills.

INTRODUCTION

This chapter is divided into two sections. The first section provides a background of the most relevant economic, financial, and demographic developments that counselors are likely to find vital for their understanding of societal conditions within their work setting. The second section deals with specific financial issues that are important in both the preretirement and retirement phases of life.

The clients that financial or holistic counselors of the elderly are most likely to see are those with well below median cash flow and financial resources. A large proportion of these persons may be utilizing public assistance. Circumstances beyond their control often deal very harshly with these individuals. Rising inflation and increasing life spans are in the process of moving the oldest people in our society towards the poverty level. Those persons who are above the median in cash flow and wealth most often obtain counseling from lawyers, bankers, securities dealers, insurance agents, realtors, and specialized estate planners.

GENERAL ECONOMIC BACKGROUND

The changing demographic structure of the nation is basic to one's understanding of current and impending problems facing elderly people. The combination of our aging population and declining birth rate have set up a rising dependency ratio—the ratio of retired to working populations—that is increasing the extent of income transfer from employed to retired persons. Growth in the proportion of retirees and those approaching that condition has obvious political implications. Reasons for early, timely, and delayed retirement will be reviewed and goals for replacement cash flow will be discussed. A final topic to be discussed in this chapter is the impact of the rising cost of living on elderly persons.

Population Dynamics

The four-generation family is becoming more frequent now than the three-generation family was at the turn of the century. A new personal problem that is arising is how persons near or at their own retirement are going to be able to provide for the personal and financial comfort for parents who are 75 or more?

Table 1

CHANGING POPULATION AGE 45 AND OLDER
(in millions)

	1900	1930	1950	1974	2000
Age 45-54	6.4	13.1	17.4	23.8	35.7
Age 55-64	4.0	8.5	13.4	19.5	22.9
Age 65 and over	3.1	6.7	12.3	21.8	30.6

Table 1 reports proportions of the older population from 1900 through 2000. Population estimates are used for the latter date. Table 2 is more dramatic in that it shows the rising number and portion of people who will be 65 or older by the year 2000. Table 3 is still more dramatic—even disquieting—in showing that the percentage growth of persons in the 75-84 and 85-plus groups will be exploding during the remainder of this century. This growth is disquieting because it is these groups that will demand transferal of significant resources to them for their care.

Table 2

POPULATION: 65 AND OLDER, AND TOTAL U.S.

Year	Total Population (millions)	65 and Older	65 and Older as % of Total
1910	92,407	3,986	4.3
1930	123,077	6,705	5.4
1950	151,684	12,362	8.2
1977e	216,745	23,431	10.8
2000p	260,378	31,822	12.2

e estimated
p projected

Table 3

POPULATION PROJECTIONS, TRENDS WITHIN THE 65-PLUS AGE GROUP, 1977-2050

(Percent Change)

Sex	1977-2000	2000-25	2025-50
Both sexes, 65 plus	+35.8	+60.0	+ 9.0
65 to 74	+19.6	+77.5	+ 6.7
75 to 84	+56.0	+41.1	+14.0
85 plus	+84.1	+32.4	+91.6
Male, 65 plus	+33.2	+64.0	+ 5.7
65 to 74	+21.3	+79.1	- 6.3
75 to 84	+54.7	+44.1	+13.5
85 plus	+64.4	+29.9	+92.9
Female, 65 plus	+37.6	+57.3	+11.2
65 to 74	+18.3	+76.2	- 7.1
75 to 84	+56.8	+39.4	+14.3
85 plus	+93.2	+33.4	+91.1

Our society is providing better working and living conditions for most people, improving medical care, and improving nutrition. As educational and income levels continue to rise, these improvements become available to an increasing proportion of people. The overall result is an increase in the average life span. The changing age structure is a force that has been leading toward wider coverage in social insurance programs. The extent of income (tax) transfers between the working and non-working segments of the population is a source of increasing economic and political tension. The retirement age is likely to be increased beyond 65 to about 68 or even to 71 in order to balance income transfer within our system.

The general shift toward population over 65 is startling. This shift is reflected in Tables 1 and 2. The ratio of persons 65 and over to people in the 18 to 64 class is useful for analytical purposes. In 1970 this ratio stood at 17.6%, which means that for every 100 persons in the 18-64 age group there are 17.6 who had to be supported. By 1977 this ratio had increased to 18.2; it is likely to rise steadily to 20.0 by the year 2000 and to spurt to 29.6 by 2025. This spurt reflects outcomes of the baby boom of the post World War II period and lower birth rates of the 1960s, 1970s, and probably the continuing low birth rates of the 1980s. For historical completeness, the dependency ratio was 11.6% in 1940, and 14.1% in 1950.

A factor that affects the dependency ratio is that labor force participation rates among those age 55 and older is declining. By age 62 about 30% of the working population has withdrawn from employment and at age 65 that figure rises above 50%. As recently as 1950 about 70% of the labor force was still working at age 65. Continuing declines in labor force participation will increase social security and other taxes that the working force will be expected to pay to maintain the present level of insurance and public benefits.

The tax burden

When the social security system started in 1937, its tax rate assessment on employee and employer was 1% up to a maximum wage of $3,000 per year. The principal of equal tax payments and amounts on both employee and employer remains in effect, but the levels of income for which it applies are continuing to accelerate. By 1955 the tax rate was set at 2% on maximum taxable wages of $4,200. In 1955 the average annual wage was about $3,500 in nonagricultural employment. By 1970 the tax rate was 4.8% on a maximum taxable wage of $7,800. The average wage in that year was about $6,000. The estimated annual average wage for the latest available year, 1978, is $10,600. The social security tax rate and tax base are scheduled to rise as shown in Table 4. Present estimates prepared by the Social Security Administration suggest that the maximum wage on which social security taxes will be paid will rise to about $93,600 in the year 2000.

Table 4

HOW SOCIAL SECURITY TAX WILL INCREASE

(The table summarizes the financing arrangements for Social Security enacted in 1977. Amounts are rounded to nearest dollar.)

| Year | Mazimum Earnings Taxed | Tax Rates | | Maximum Employee Tax |
		Employer-Empoyee	Self-Employed	
1978	17,700	6.05%	8.10%	1,071
1979	22,900	6.13	8.10	1,404
1980	25,900	6.13	8.10	1,588
1981	29,700	6.65	9.30	1,975
1982	31,800*	6.70	9.35	2,131*
1983	33,900	6.70	9.35	2,271
1984	38,000	6.70	9.35	2,412
1985	38,100	7.05	9.90	2,686
1986	40,200	7.15	10.00	2,874
1987	42,600	7.15	10.00	3,046

*The maximum earnings base for taxation is fixed by law through 1981. Thereafter, it is to be adjusted automatically according to the national rise in average earnings. Figures above for the maximum earnings taxed and the maximum employee tax, accordingly, are projections, for the years beginning 1982.

Source: U.S. Congress, House Ways and Means Committee

Intense and heated discussions have taken place in Congress about the climbing tax burden needed to finance social security programs that have been legislated. In recent years until the 1977 Amendments, Social Security Trust Funds, which are accumulated differences between receipts and disbursements, were dwindling. Increases were needed to keep benefits at legislated levels and Fund balances from going into the red. The debate continues about whether legislated increases in social security taxes should be allowed to go into effect. An alternative is to draw upon general tax revenues of the United States for a part of the social security program. Of course, that alternative would result in higher personal and corporate income taxes.

Persons earning about $26,000 in 1980 will pay 6.13% or $1,404 in social security taxes and a *marginal* rate of 40% in Federal Income Taxes, or about $6,000. They may also be paying state income taxes of another $1,000 and sales taxes of about $200. In addition, they will be responsible for hidden excise taxes on gasoline, cigarettes, and many on other things. If they own their own home, they will pay property taxes directly, and if renting will pay property taxes indirectly.

All of these taxes will total about $9,000 or about one-third of their earnings. In addition, individuals may be buying life and health insurance, paying for a car and a house, and paying into private pensions to which they and their employers contribute. Rising social security tax payments, which are based on the rising tax rate and maximum taxable wage levels, are having an impact on everyone! Tensions between younger tax payers and persons to whom these earnings are transferred through the federal and state governments are likely to grow.

In national terms social welfare expenditures have grown from $23.5 billion in 1950 to $331.4 billion in 1976, or a growth rate of 10.7% per year. These expenditures have increased from 8.9% to 20.6% of the Gross National Product (GNP) which stood at $1,611 billion for 1976. Total taxes have risen from about 22.0% of GNP in 1950 to 32.0% of GNP in 1977.

One must point out that about 73% of these 1976 social welfare expenditures can be directly and clearly related to the social security programs. These large and identifiable outlays in 1976 were as follows: Old-age, survivors, disability, and health insurance for $146.6 billion; Medicare for $90.4 billion, and Supplemental Security Income for $3.0 billion. Parts of these cash payments did not go to elderly persons, but there is no way to disentangle payments to the elderly from the multitude of programs that exist. For example, part of the outlay for food stamps and veterans programs did go to elderly persons. However, one can be quite sure that maternal care programs and elementary school programs did not cater directly to elderly persons.

A great national concern is that the continuing growth of programs for the elderly, our most rapidly growing population, may overwhelm and discourage many of our productive workers. One example of what may happen is suggested by the fact, according to a 1979 Social Security Adminstration study, that people aged 65-69 required about 3000 days of short-stay hospital care per 1,000 persons per year. For people in their late 70s, the corresponding rate was 4,700 days per year; for people over 85, about 8,300 days per year were required. Our aging population is very likely to require an astounding increase in personal and medical services.

Retirement age

Since the Social Security Act of 1935 arbitrarily set the retirement age at 65, that age has become a target around which large numbers of people formulate their goals. Aside from reasons of health, the most important reasons for early retirement have been, in decending order of importance: low work commitment, wealth and existence of two pensions, and job dissatisfaction. Other important reasons include social pressures, loss of a job (especially during a recession), and change in the permissable retirement age to 62 under social security. Reasons for delayed retirement include generally good health which provides the capacity to work for additional years beyond 65, rising inflation, and increased personal financial inducements. Under the 1977 Social Security Amendments, delaying retirement one year beyond 65 will increase benefits by 3% per year, up to age 72. Some people have had to return to work after retirement because of inflation, rising state and local taxes, or depletion of financial resources.

Replacement cash-flow levels

The term cash-flow rather than income is used because income has a technical definition for federal income tax and other purposes. Social security benefits represent cash flow, but they are not taxable. Those parts of benefit payments from private and state-sponsored pension funds that represent recovery of after-tax contributions by employees are not taxable, but employers' contributions and income earned on employees' and employers' contributions are taxable. Replacement cash flow of about 60%-66 2/3% after retirement at age 65 is generally adequate to provide a retirement standard of living equal to pre-retirement levels.

In 1979 social security benefits for a single person retiring at 65 who had always earned up to the maximum taxable level would have been $533.30 per month or $6,636 per year. That amount would provide a replacement cash flow of 37.5% for someone who had been at the $17,700 income level in 1978. For a married couple both of whom just turned 65 and only one of whom worked for 40 quarters, the benefit payment would be $9,954 or 50% more. One should note that social security payments have a built in social insurance benefit so that individuals who earned an average of one-half the rising taxable maximum during all of the years they worked would get a benefit approximately equal to 60% of the maximum benefit. Average earnings of one-fourth of the maximum will provide almost 40% of maximum benefits.

Starting in 1972 Congress provided that social security retirement payments increase by the cost of living, but these increases lag one year behind cost of living changes. Prior to 1972 Congress periodically legislated increases in social security payments. A woman who retired in 1965 with a maximum benefit payment of $135.90 per month would have received a payment of $336 in July 1978.

The public retirement systems do not provide for luxurious living in retirement. Estimates are made annually by the Bureau of Labor Statistics for low-budget, intermediate-budget, and high-budget retired couples. For the summer of 1977, these figures for metropolitan areas were as follows: $5,151, $7,198, and $11,203 respectively.

Poverty cash-flow-level estimates are also made annually. For 1977 the estimated poverty level cash flow for one person was $2,906 and for two people it was $3,666. This cash-flow level is so low that the Bureau of Labor Statistics points out that no one could live for long on the starvation diet and substandard living conditions for which it would provide.

Retirement cash flow for a cross-section of the elderly population drops rapidly as a function of age. For example, in 1967 average wages were about $5,300. Table 5 shows the income distribution for single persons in four age groups starting with the 65-69 age group. Note that in that year very few persons over 75 had an income equal to the average wage and that incomes decreased as a function of age. These patterns condense the lifecycle earning experiences and levels for 1967. For 1968 the poverty income level for one person was calculated to be $1,667 and for 1967 the low-budget level for a retired couple in a metropolitan area was $2,730. The longer one lives in a society with rising inflation, the more likely that person will sink to the poverty level. People generally have found, and will continue to find, it impossible to save enough to provide for a comfortble living standard if they live to an advanced age.

Table 5

NONMARRIED AGED: INCOME DISTRIBUTION BY AGE, 1967

Total Money Income	Age			
	65-69	70-74	75-79	80 and Over
Less than $1000	14	15	21	39
$1000-2499	36	46	50	45
$2500-4999	26	28	20	12
$5000-9999	19	10	7	3
$10,000-14,999	3	1	1	1
$15,000 and Over	2	1	1	____*
Total Percent	100	100	100	100

Source: Lenore E. Bixby, Demographic and Economic Characteristics of the Aged (Washington, D.C.: U.S. Government Printing Office, 1975).

*Less than 0.5.

Counseling for the Growing Years

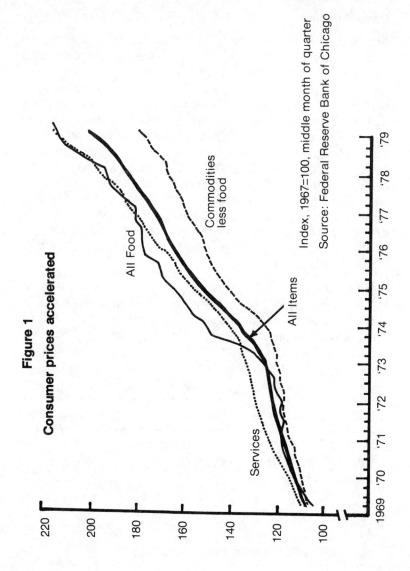

Figure 1
Consumer prices accelerated

Index, 1967=100, middle month of quarter

Source: Federal Reserve Bank of Chicago

Cost of living

The Consumer Price Index (CPI) is the most popular and most nearly appropriate measure of changes in the general price level for present purposes. It represents the measured price increases in a given market basket of consumer purchases. Quality changes generally are excluded and the "market basket" is changed occasionally. The base period of 1967 is still being used even though it is obvious that changes have occurred. Figure 1 shows the extent of these consumer price increases from 1969 to 1978. The rate of price increase accelerated to 7.7% in 1978 and is likely to average above 10% for 1979. The future course of price inflation is uncertain, but very few economists believe that it is likely to drop back to the approximate 3%-4% levels that were typical of the period from the end of the Korean Conflict in 1952 to the beginning of the Viet Nam adventure in 1968.

The inflation rate, as measured by the CPI, is unlikely to drop below an average of 6% per year for the rest of the century. Many believe that a 10% rate will be closer to reality. If inflation continues at the present rate, consequences, terms of continued rising prices, will be as follows:

No. of years	Annual Inflation Rate		
	3%	6%	10%
	(index of prices)*		
10	134	179	259
20	181	301	673
30	243	574	1,745

*Base index number of 100

Accelerating inflation is a continuing and real worry for older Americans. First, only a part of the retirement replacement income usually is tied to the CPI. Second, life expectancy at age 65 is now 16.8 years for males and 21.8 years for females. These figures are increasing. Millions of people are living into their 80s and 90s. Third, the CPI is based upon the market basket of an urban-middle-class family of four and does not fully represent the outlay of an elderly person or couple. The elderly couple's budget mentioned above is a better representation of their expenditure patterns. It shows a considerably larger proportion of outlays for medical care, an element that is increasing faster than the overall CPI. Food prices and housing also have risen faster than the overall CPI.

Fourth, quality changes that raise the standard of living are not represented. For example, the change from black and white to color television is not represented. Fifth, improved and more expensive living conditions, such as installation of central air conditioning or upgrading of thermal insulation, would not be included. New and/or more expensive medication, physical therapy, and surgical procedures are not represented. Therefore, when older persons say that their standard of living continues to fall during retirement, their perception is correct. Finally, taxes are excluded from the CPI. Hence increases in sales, income, property, and gift taxes raise living costs without being reflected in the CPI.

FINANCIAL COUNSELING: ISSUES AND INFORMATION

This section discusses substantitive issues, such as preretirement planning and estate planning, separately from sources of information. Generally, there are organizations; books, articles, and pamphlets; and resource people to whom one can turn for information.

Most individuals who seek counseling from a public source will have well below average income and wealth. Few retired persons will have a cash flow of more than $10,000 per year in 1979-80 prices. Those with higher incomes—and even many of those with considerably lower incomes—will seek out other professional or semi-professional help.

Rehearsing cash inflows before retirement

When retired people are asked when, in their opinion, retirement planning should begin, responses scatter from before 21 years of age to older than 60. Realistic planning for financial aspects of retirement can not be done very far in advance of the decade prior to retirement. Of course, for many years prior to retirement, employed persons are likely to contribute to pension plans, annuity policies, and investments of other kinds in preparation for retirement. By the time most people are within 5-10 years of their likely retirement age, most of their financial plans and their future paths are rather well defined. Individuals should be able to make clear estimates of their likely replacement cash flow by the time they are 57 if retirement is to be at 62, or at age 60 if retirement is to be at age 65. After a preliminary look at these results, individuals may decide to try to continue gainful employment until age 70 as facilitated by 1978 Ammendments to the Age Discrimination in Employment Act.

Assistance is available through organizations such as the American Association of Retired Persons (AARP) to determine one's anticipated cash flow, financial resources, and likely expenses. One can simulate or rehearse what these levels are most likely to be. The major sources of cash inflow for most retirees will be payments from private pensions, civil service pensions, and social security. Some people will have income from ownership of securities and property as well. One needs to gather estimates of cash inflow and outflow, and to evaluate the adequacy of cash flow at the earliest likely retirement date. For many that date will come when they are 62 years of age, when reduced social security benefits become available.

Estimates of payments from private or public employers may be provided routinely or may have to be requested. The Social Security Administration will help individuals prepare estimates of their old age and survivors benefits (OASI), and also provide forms on which to make their own estimates. Table 6, prepared by the Social Security Administration, provides rough 1979 estimates of what benefits are likely to be until 1990 under assumed tax rates, wage increase rates, and earnings levels. These tax and earned income maximums are now "firm" and will be under the present law through 1987. It is possible, however, that this law might be modified one or more times before that date.

Table 6

BENEFIT PROJECTIONS FOR STEADY WORKERS RETIRING AT AGE 65

(1979 TRUSTEES REPORT ASSUMPTIONS, ALTERNATIVE II)

Year of Retirement	Annual Earnings ($)			Annual Benefits ($)			Replacement Rate ($) 1/		
	Low	Average	Maximum	Low	Average	Maximum	Low	Average	Maximum
1978	5,300	10,612	17,700	2,945	4,567	5,727	60.3	46.7	34.7
1979	5,741	11,495	22,900	3,256	5,082	6,390	61.4	47.9	36.1
1980	6,203	12,419	25,900	3,615	5,657	7,177	63.0	49.2	31.3
1981	6,768	13,550	29,700	4,000	6,280	7,980	64.5	50.6	30.8
1982	7,270	14,555	32,100	3,921	6,037	7,658	57.9	44.5	25.84
1983	7,703	15,423	35,100	3,920	6,140	7,879	53.9	42.2	24.5
1984	8,118	16,254	37,800	4,115	6,436	8,331	53.4	41.7	23.7
1985	8,551	17,121	40,200	4,312	6,738	8,799	53.1	41.5	23.3
1986	9,011	18,042	42,300	4,595	7,180	9,458	53.7	41.9	23.5
1987	9,528	19,077	44,700	4,886	7,629	10,124	54.2	42.3	23.9
1988	10,098	20,218	47,100	5,168	8,086	10,775	54.2	42.3	24.1
1989	10,704	21,431	49,800	5,443	8,499	11,414	53.9	42.0	24.2
1990	11,344	22,713	52,800	5,736	8,954	12,086	53.6	41.8	24.3

Source: Social Security Administration

/1 Replacement income is defined as percentage of *prior* year earnings replaced by initial social security benefit in year of retirement.

Individuals may receive pension benefits starting at various dates for military service, civil service, or from private employers. All elements of vital information should be accumulated and reviewed in the planning stage.

Parts of retirement benefits may become available at different ages. In some cases these dates can vary. Military pensions for retired reservists who have completed a minimum of 20 years of service start at age 60. These military benefits are adjusted annually for cost of living changes.

An increasing number of organizations are providing preretirement seminars that cover all phases of planning. The extension of manditory retirement to age 70 undoubtedly will increase this trend. Information to help individuals plan may be obtained from a number of organizations, such as the AARP and a Federal Administration on Aging agency in most states or cities.

Job training and retraining for "retirement"

For social, psychological, physical, and economic reasons, people should consider some form of continuing—usually part-time— employment after "retirement" or after they start receiving benefits from one or more of their pension and/or annuity plans.

The Comprehensive Employment and Training Act Amendments (CETA) authorizes special training programs for persons over 55 years of age. Funds for this program have now been authorized until 1982 and Congress will undoubtedly continue to fund this program. Amendments made in 1978 to the Older Americans provide about $400 million dollars per year through fiscal 1981 for the direct employment of low income poor in a wide variety of community service jobs. Some 81,000 people may be employed on these jobs in 1981. These training programs and jobs are under the direction of the Secretary of Labor. Information should be available through public employment service offices, senior centers, and area agencies on aging.

The 1978 Age Discrimination in Employment Act Amendments abolish mandatory retirement for practically all federal workers, and prohibit mandatory retirement before age 70 for covered workers in private, state, and local employment. If a person is dismissed and alleges that the true basis is age discrimination, suit may be brought through the assistance of a field office of the Legal Services Corporation, a government sponsored organization, or through other public agencies.

Income additions

Reductions in social security benefits will be experienced if earned income (wages and salaries), exceed rising limits above which retirement benefits are reduced. In 1978 if a person between the ages of 65 and 72 earned $4,000 and was receiving benefits, $1 was deducted from that person's benefits for each two dollars earned. This earnings threshold rose to $4,500 in 1979, will rise to $5,000 in 1980, to $5,500 in 1981, and to $6,000 in 1982. In 1982 this earnings test will be eliminated for persons 70 and older. These limits are subject to change and should be continually checked.

Retirement timing

From the societal viewpoint, retirement at about 68-70 years is now preferable because of the changing dependency ratio. From a personal viewpoint, much retirement timing will depend upon health, financial resources, family responsibilities, the outlook for inflation, and the willingness and ability to continue some part-time work—perhaps until one is about 75-80 years old.

The process of rehearsing or preplanning the financial and personal consequences of retirement will help greatly in fixing the range of dates and the exact date for full or partial retirement. Currently only about 75% of all men are reported as being in the labor force at age 62, about 50% at age 65, and 25% at age 70.

Several things help to explain the personal goal of 65 as the retirement age for so many people. Social security payments are reduced substantially before age 65. If one retires as early as the 62nd birthday, benefits are about 80% of what they would be if that person were 65. Benefits increase about 6.75 per year on the basis of age alone from age 62 to age 65. They also increase if credited earnings in the added years of employment are higher than they were 10-20 years earlier. Between age 65 and 72, benefits increase 3% per year if a person continues to work. Federal and state income taxes provide for added tax exemptions and other special benefits for those 65 and older.

Immediate preretirement steps

Timely receipt of Old Age and Survivors Benefits (OASI) depends upon individuals filing their intentions properly with the Social Security Office. Proof of age is required. Persons should obtain a copy of their birth certificate in advance. If no birth certificate can be obtained, the earliest official record of age may be used. A birth certificate and marriage license of a spouse and/or widow will be required before that person can start to draw benefits. At the same time, the intention to retire is filed if the individual is entitled to any additional OASI benefits in the year of retirement. One need not be retired to obtain a Medicare Card and hospital and medical insurance benefits.

Prudent persons would file their Medicare cards three months before they are 65 because such cards are generally needed to obtain Medicare benefits. Private health insurance companies will pay hospital bills on their specific policies only above what Medicare *should* pay. Fortunately, the Medicare hospital insurance is retroactive to the 65th birthday. In the meantime, the individual would have had to finance one's own payments before reimbursements. Part B of Medicare, which covers physicians and other services, is not retroactive. The medical insurance cost for Part B, which is set at $ 8.70 per month starting July 1, 1979, will go up 10% per year if one does not enroll in it when one is 65. One frequent surprise for many people is that Medicare does not cover outpatient drugs.

One precaution that should be taken during the preretirement period is to file a request with the Social Security Administration for an earnings statement every three years. The reason for this request is that a detailed annual record of earnings for the most recent three years is provided. These earnings are easiest to examine for accuracy. All prior earnings are lumped together. Also, one can request the number of quarters with which one is credited for the purpose of receiving social security benefits later.

If one is employed and insured by an organization, one should check, prior to retirement, to discover what insurance will be continued through the retirement years. In some cases, life insurance may be available at a reduced rate and without examination through the employer's insurance company.

Financial problems in retirement

In this subsection the major topics considered are income maintenance, insurance, taxes, and legal-financial issues.

In a long conversation with Ms. Martha L. Quint, attorney at law and legal services coordinator of the Heritage Agency on Aging, six problem areas that occur most frequently in the counseling of the elderly were identified. The Heritage Agency of Aging, which is headquartered at Kirkwood Community College in Cedar Rapids, is funded by the Iowa Commission on Aging. Amendments in 1973 to the Older Americans Act of 1965 provided for the existence of a network of such agencies.

Four topics were identified that may have extremely severe consequences are: benefits under (OASDI), Old Age, Survivors, and Disability Insurance; Supplemental Security Income (SSI); "Medigrap" insurance; and property tax credits. The first two items are treated under income maintenace, the third under insurance, and the fourth under taxes. Another topic that comes up frequently is Medicaid—benefits for the very poor that are in addition to Medicare. A final area that falls in the legal-financial topic may be called adult protective services. This topic deals with legal concerns surrounding such things as how titles to property are written and names in which checking and similar accounts are held.

The major programs directed by the Social Security Administration are Old Age and Survivors Benefits (OASI), Disability Insurance, Medicare, and Supplemental Security Income. The dollar amount of outlays under these programs was given above. Current data may be found in the *Social Security Bulletin*. Relatively few disputes arise under the old age and survivors benefit programs. More than 18 million people are now receiving retirement benefits. Almost 61.% of this total have taken early retirement. Almost 3 million persons receive supplemental security incomes. There is an unknown amount of overlapping between these various programs.

Disability claims are subject to much more dispute and more appeals than the OASI programs. The degree and duration of the disability must be shown. Proof of disability is administered differently in different states. Generally, disability payments may not start before five months from the date of disability. That date itself may be a matter of dispute. One needs to find the exact, current, and local definitions of disability. Information can be obtained through local or regional Social Security Administration Offices. General information can be obtained from current official publications and from the 1978 book, *Social security-today and tomorrow* by Robert M. Ball.

Over three million veterans receive retirement and disability benefits under social insurance programs. More than two million survivors or veterans also receive benefits. Service connected disability payments are made for disability levels rated as being more than 10% and additional payments may be made for wives and children of such diabled veterans. Veterans with non-service connected disabilities who are 65 or over, and who pass under income and asset tests, may also be entitled to benefits.

The number of veterans is so large that counselors may well find themselves working with elderly veterans or veterans' survivors. In that event one should be in contact with a Veterans Administration Office. General information bulletins can be obtained from these offices.

Very low income elderly may be entitled to food stamps as a part of programs started in 1965. Regulations under these programs seem to be in constant flux. Current information about eligibility for this program is available in county social service or welfare offices.

The Medicare insurance program was established in 1965 by federal legislation. The Hospital Insurance part of the Medicare program, for which virtually all persons over 65 are eligible, is paying about 11 million bills annually for a total of about $15 billion. About 80% of the number of billings and 95% of all outlays are for inpatient hospital treatment. The other claims are paid for home health care and residence in a skilled nursing facility.

Home health services are part-time services that are necessary for medical reasons. These services may be deemed to be essential by a physician. The home health agency providing the service must be qualified to perform these services under the Hospital Insurance program. For details about home health services and skilled nursing facilities, one must consult guide books published by the Social Security Administration or call one of its field offices.

Counseling for the Growing Years

The Medical Insurance part of Medicare, often called "Part B," helps to pay reasonable fees for doctors' services, outpatient hospital care, home health care and other health services not covered by Medicare Hospital Insurance. This insurance must be applied for and purchased. The price is $8.70 a month starting July 1, 1979. Increases are likely in future years. Under this Supplemental Medical Insurance (SMI), the patient must pay the first $60 of a physician's charges and 20% of all remaining reasonable covered physician's charges. This latter feature is called "coinsurance." The use of coinsurance in this instance and elsewhere is an effort to prevent over use of insured services and to help keep down total costs. Home health services may be provided under SMI just as they are under hospital insurance, except that a three-day stay in the hospital is not necessary.

Supplemental Security Income is available for persons with very low income and minimal outside resources. For example, the cash flow for eligibility was set at $208 per month in Iowa in 1979. Eligibility levels are determined at the state level. Interested parties are advised to contact their local Social Security or Social Service office.

The Supplemental Security Income program provides for both cash payments and payments directly to qualified vendors who provide medical services to the eligible aged, blind, and disabled. In 1975 cash assistance was provided for 2,360,000 elderly persons and Medicaid payments exceeded $5 billion for the year. An average of $331 was paid per recipient. Most Medicare payments for the elderly were for skilled nursing facilities and intermediate care facilities. Smaller amounts were used for inpatient hospital care, prescribed drugs, and physicians services.

Once an elderly person has been declared eligible for Medicaid, the Medical Insurance will be assumed. In the event of hospitalization, the $60 deductible and 20% of coinsurance will also be paid.

Unless the provider of services is qualified under Medicaid, Medicaid will not pay the 20% coinsurance under Medicare or the cost of other essential medical services. Medicaid will pay the cost of such things as visits to a physicians office, dental services, and prescribed drugs for use outside of a hospital.

However, some services require advance approval of the social service agency handling the case. Many physicians do not participate in these programs because of time and costs involved in filling out required forms.

INSURANCE

Medical insurance

One of the most troublesome areas for elderly persons is that of obtaining—or seeking—health insurance for areas not covered by Medicare. Medicare pays approximately 38% of the total health costs of persons over 65. Thus the quest for additional health insurance is understandable.

"Medigap" insurance, a form of health insurance to provide coverage for items not covered by Medicare, recently has been the subject of scandalous practices and the focus of Congressional investigations. The coverage of some policies, such as the Blue Cross-Blue Shield medicare supplements or "wraparound" policies are designed to fill a specific gap noted, and generally come quite close to doing so at a reasonable cost. However, there are broad areas of outpatient medical needs such as dental care, eye care, hearing care, private duty nursing, and visiting nursing for which little or no health insurance is available.

Hospital Indemnity policies, policies which pay a specified daily amount, also exist. Some of these policies pay amounts in addition to Medicare or pay only when Medicare entitlements run out. Other policies are written to pay on eligible services *not* covered by both Medicare and Medicaid.

Many elderly persons are deceived into purchasing two or more policies with overlapping coverage. Also, limited benefit policies, such as cancer policies, are sold frequently to persons over 65. The limitations and exclusions of such policies make them have dubious usefulness.

If counselors are in doubt about "wraparound" insurance to supplement medicare, hospital indeminity policies , or limited benefit policies, they can check with reputable insurance agencies, state insurance commissioners, or academic specialists in insurance.

Automobile insurance

Ability to transport one's self is almost essential. The inability to drive a car, for example, for physical, financial or insurance reasons can be quite serious. When appropriate, counselors can help elderly clients find satisfactory automobile insurance.

Funeral insurance

Forms of paid up life insurance to cover funeral expenses are treasured by some people. Funeral expenses are notoriously high and, in many cases, may be pushed higher if advanced plans are not made. Insurance, or some other source of funds, to cover outlays by survivors frequently proves to be beneficial.

Many people are joining cooperative funeral societies which facilitate the planning of simple, dignified funerals. There are more than 150 such independent non-profit associations in the United States. Most of them are associated with the Continental Association of Funeral and Memorial Societies. Their address is included in the Bibliography.

TAXES

Federal income taxes, state income taxes, and local property taxes are continuing obligations of citizens 65 years of age and older who have taxable income and/or own real property. However, federal and state tax codes provide for special forms of tax relief and special assistance in preparation of tax forms for senior citizens.

In 1980 no federal income tax form has to be filed for a single person 65 or over with taxable 1979 income below $4,300, a married couple filing jointly with one spouse over 65 with taxable income below $6,400, and a married couple both of whom are over 65 with taxable income below $7,400. These threshold amounts have continuously moved up and are likely to continue to do so.

At age 65 a person is allowed an extra personal exemption of $1,000 for 1979 income. As long as a person turns 65 before the end of the tax year, the extra exemption can be claimed for the full year. A legally blind person over 65 is entitled to a third personal exemption.

Cash-flow items excluded from income computation include social security benefits, railroad retirement benefits, public assistance benefits, mortgage assistance payments under Section 235 of the National Housing Act, gifts and inheritances and veterans' benefits and proceeds from veterans' benefits.

All or part of other retirement and pension benefits are fully taxable. If an individual did not contribute funds to the retirement plan provided by the employer, all benefits are taxable income. If the person did contribute to the financing of pension benefits, and if an amount equal to contributions is to be received within three years or less from the beginning of payments, those payments are not taxable until all of the individual's cost or investment is recovered. All pension benefits received be paid. If the recipient's costs are not expected to be recovered within three years, the computation is more complex. Basically, a part of the pension or annuity benefits received each year will be taxable and a part will be tax exempt. The percentage of nontaxable benefits is fairly close to payments into the plan, divided by the product of annual benefits and actuarial life expectancy of the person at the time of the first payment. Help with this computation may be obtained by the client from the IRS.

One of the most important benefits in the *Internal revenue code* is the provision to exclude the gain on the sale of a principal residence on a *once-in-a-life-time* basis. The law was changed in the 1978 Revenue Act to allow this provision for persons 55 years of age or older to exclude up to $100,000 in gain if their residence was sold after July 27, 1978. There are some problems in phrasing in this revised provision of the *Code*. Therefore, extreme care must be exercised in application.

Persons, including those over 55, selling their residence, may transfer any gain into a new residence if that residence is purchased within 18 months of the sale of the prior residence. If the new residence costs less than the adjusted selling price of the old residence, there will be a tax on the gain. As in all cases, exact details of the *Code* need to be checked when a provision is used. If a person wishes to make or to revoke an election to use the once-in-a-life-time excludable gain, the person may do that by filing an intention within three years from the due date of the return or two years from the date the tax was paid.

The IRS is trying to develop a corps of Volunteer Income Tax Assistants (VITA), to aid those who need help. A specialized corps to help those 60 or over is to be trained. Counselors for the elderly may contact the IRS to take this course, when it is given in their area, or contact a senior citizen center or a State

Agency on Aging to locate persons who are members of VITA. The IRS lists in its various forms the WATTS numbers which may be called for assistance. These WATTS numbers may be found in telephone directories. Special large-type packets of instructions, *Tax benefits for older Americans*, are available and may be ordered by telephone.

State Income tax forms need to be filled in most states for those persons who have taxable income. Rules vary from state to state. Some states have special provisions for taxation of those 65 and over. These may differ from those of the IRS. Generally, state revenue departments also provide training for volunteers who wish to help disabled, blind, and elderly persons who need to file income taxes. If state income taxes have been withheld and the person has no tax obligation, a form should be filed to claim a refund.

Property tax relief

In many states property tax relief is granted to the elderly poor. Counselors should find out whether such relief exists in their state, the exact terms of the property tax relief, and the method of filing for such relief. Typically, such information will be available in the county tax assessor's or treasurer's office.

In Iowa, elderly, low-income persons who rent their living quarters rather than own them also will be given property tax refunds if they file for it. Elderly Iowans living in nursing homes may get property tax refunds if they can show that rental service is part of their nursing home bill.

LEGAL-FINANCIAL PROBLEMS

Two of the most important areas under legal-financial problems are "adult protective services" and wills and estates.

Adult protective services

A frequent and troublesome question is how to establish ownership of checking and savings accounts in order to give a trusted person access to them in the event of an emergency. If an elderly person places one's own name on such accounts along with that of a son or a daughter (for example, as a joint tenant with the right of survivorship), the child has an uncontestable right to write checks against the account. Cases are not infrequent in which a child or other trusted person has withdrawn funds and left the the senior citizen in a disastrous position.

The reason for placing a second name on the account is to protect the older person in the event of becoming incapacitited and unable to take care of one's affairs.

One way to protect the elderly is to utilize the durable power of attorney in which the designated party would have access to funds for specific purposes for a determinable period of time. Lawyers and some bankers will assist in preparing simple, but important, legal forms for this purpose.

Tenancy in common involves an undivided ownership for each of the parties. All legal actions must be agreed upon by all parties. The parties need not have equal interests in the property in question. In the case of joint tenancy with the right of survivorship, either party has complete access to the property. In this case, upon death of one of the joint tenants, the property passes to the remaining person(s).

Upon death, the tax implications of joint tenancy with right of survivorship and tenancy in common become quite different, especially as the size of the estate grows. In a tenancy in common, the portion of the value to which the deceased was entitled would be included as a part of the estate for tax and settlement cost purposes. Under joint tenancy with the right of survivorship the other party or parties would come into ownerhip of the property without any state estate tax becoming due. But, upon death of the subsequent owner, the estate taxes could be substantially more than twice as large because of the highly progressive nature of the estate tax structure. The IRS probably will attribute the entire amount of the property as though it were contributed soley by the surviving joint tenant. This action could increase the survivor's estate and the taxes on that estate at a later date. With advance planning and the aid of a qualified lawyer, however, the contribution of each spouse to the cost of the property can be established.

The laws of each state must be studied to learn the exact meaning and implications for the ways in which title to personal and real property is held. Although most state bar associations will supply pamphlets on such matters of adult protection services, estate planning, and other legal-financial areas, these summaries are too brief for practical purposes. An experienced, local, independently practicing attorney employed by a financial institution may be helpful in such matters.

Wills and estates

A will is a document that directs how an individual wants one's property distributed after death. If one dies without having a will, (intestate), property will be distributed according to state law. Such distribution is very likely to be different from what the deceased would have wished.

If a person makes a will, an executor is normally named. Typically a child is named as the executor, but must be willing to accept the responsibility. A bank can be designated as coexecutor to provide for continuity, but charges for bank services may be very high for a small estate—even one under $500,000.

Plans need to be made for the disposition of clothing, personal jewelry, household items, and for the bulk of the property which will constitute the estate of the deceased. As a formal attachment to the will, or as a separate statement of wishes and intentions, clear and complete directions for disposal of clothing should be made well in advance.

Dishes, silverware, family heirlooms, pictures, and the like should be inventoried well before death and the preferred disposition indicated. Some household items might be designated for sale with the proceeds to go to a charity or to the body of the estate. If such instructions are not left, problems could arise in the division of these items among those who might like to have them irrespective of their legal rights.

Under the United States Gift and Estate Tax Law of 1976, the exemption before there is a federal tax is $161,565 in 1980 and $175,625 in 1981. The minimum tax rate is 10% on the first $10,000, 41% on the amount between $1,000,000 and $1,250,000, and 70% on taxable estates above $5,000,000. In addition each state will have its own estate tax laws. In Iowa, the maximum rate is 8% on property above $150,000 after considering an $80,000 exemption for a deceased husband or wife.

Given these large inheritance tax rates, it is understandable that substantial effort be made to reduce these taxes. The counselor is unlikely to have many clients whose estates would be large enough for them to be subject to the inheritance tax. However, estate plans should be reviewed every few years and counselors should encourage persons to make or update their wills.

Basic Concerns

Some steps can be taken to reduce estate taxes. Gifts up to $3,000 per year may be made by each spouse to whomever that person wishes. These gifts need not be limited to members of the family. Large gifts made within three years of death may not be excluded from unified gift and taxable estate structures.

Consideration needs to be given to the strategy involved in making gifts. If property that is likely to appreciate rapidly is given away early, the estate tax rate may be much less, but the donor may regret the decision if funds are needed before death.

Much of estate planning involves the use of either a revocable or irrevocable trust. A revocable trust will not reduce estate taxes, but it may reduce the burden of managing one's own property. If a trust is revocable, the grantor can dissolve it at any time. An irrevocable trust cannot be altered, amended, or revoked by the person who sets it up. No power is retained over the trust or its property. The grantor is frequently designated to receive the income from such a trust for the rest of one's life and medical and other outlays may be paid from the body of the trust if advance provision is made for such acts. Such a trust must be set up a minimum of three years prior to death in order to save estate taxes and settlement costs.

Life insurance proceeds are included in the deceased person's estate in almost all cases. If the insured retains any rights over the policy during one's lifetime, proceeds become part of the estate. Such rights include the right to change the beneficiary or to cancel the policy. Life insurance may be used to help build an estate, to provide for burial expenses, to provide for living expenses while an estate is being settled, and to help preserve a family business.

After a death, the value of an estate must be carefully estimated. The expenses involved in preparing such estimates and other expenses incident to the operation and disposition of the property are deductible items for the purpose of computing estate taxes.

SUMMARY

No person can be expected to have the range of knowledge and detailed current information needed for all aspects of financial planning for the elderly and for those approaching that stage of life. After some years one may have a basic store of information at hand, in books and pamphlets, and in one's active memory. However, details in each and every one of the topics touched upon are likely to be changing in irregular and unexpected patterns. No single news source or loose leaf service is likely to cover the range of financial and legal topics that may be of interest to clients.

A basic list of books and pamphlets may be purchased. Some things are provided free of charge through the Social Security Administration and Internal Revenue Service. A list of materials and sources is appended to this chapter, but this list is in no way complete. An effort was made to reference authorative and substantial sources. Nevertheless, the reader is encouraged to be continually aware of new, relevant material.

A financial counselor for the elderly may try to have excellent personal contacts on the local, regional, state, and federal level in order to obtain timely and accurrate information. Personal acquaintances at the nearest Social Security Administration and Social Services offices also would be essential. Contacts could be made with an agency on aging as well as with private groups such as the Gray Panthers or the American Association of Retired Persons. Individual lawyers and bankers may have an interest in counseling for the elderly. In all cases, work of the counselor should be geared toward providing the elderly with pertinent information so they can use relevant materials for their continual growth and development.

Since the information on financial and legal counseling with the elderly is not readily available,the following selected bibliography has been included to assist counselors.

REFERENCES

Financial Information on the Elderly

Arak, M.V. Indexation of wages and retirement income in the United States. *Quarterly Review of the New York Federal Reserve Bank*, Autumn, 1978, pp. 16-23.

Boskin, M. Social security and retirement decisions. *Economic Inquiry*, January, 1977, pp. 1-25.

Fox, A. The earnings replacement rates of retired couples. *Social Security Bulletin*, January, 1979, pp. 17-44.

Johnson & Higgins. *American attitudes toward pensions and retirement*. New York: 1979. (Based on a poll conducted by Louis Harris and Associates, Inc. Johnson & Higgins is a New York City firm of actuaries.)

Moon, A., & Smolensky, E. (Eds.). *Improving measures of economic well being*. New York: Academic Press, 1977.

Munnell, A.H. The impact of inflation on private pensions. *New England Economic Review*, March/April, 1979, pp. 18-31.

Sass, S.G. *An actuary's primer for social gerontologists*. Paper presented at the International Congress for Gerontology, Jerusalem, Israel, June, 1975.

Schulz, J.J. *The economics of aging*. Belmont, California: Wadsworth Publishing Co., 1976.

Sheppard, H.L., & Rix, S.E. *The graying of working America*. New York: The Free Press, 1977.

Thompson, G.B. Impact of inflation on private pension of retirees, 1970-4. *Social Security Bulletin*, November, 1978, pp. 16-29.

Thompson, L.H. Toward the rational adjustment of social security benefit levels. *Policy Analysis*, Fall, 1977, pp. 485-508.

Wilson, T. *Pensions, inflation, and growth: A comparative study of the elderly in the welfare state*. London, Great Britain; Heinemann Educational Books, 1974.

Financial and Legal Counseling Information

Aging. U.S. Department of Health, Education and Welfare, Administration on Aging. (See Organizations for address. Issued 6 times per year. Subscription $9.25. Order from Superintendent of Documents, Government Printing Office. Has helpful articles on research results and new developments.)

Ashley, P.P. *You and your will: The planning and management of your estate*. New York: McGraw Hill Book Co., 1977.

Ball, R.M. *Social security: Today and tomorrow*. New York: Columbia University Press, 1978.

Blodgett, R. *The New York Times book of money*. New York: Quadrangle Books, 1976.

Changing Times—The Kiplinger Magazine. (Numerous articles on money management and occasional articles of great specific interest to the elderly and their counselors. For example, "Health Insurance Policies," December, 1978, pp. 5-11 is an excellent guide to the pitfalls in buying "medigap" and other health insurance policies.)

Contemporary crafts marketplace. Ann Arbor, Michigan: RR Bowker, 1977. (Address: RR Bowker, Order Dept., P.O. Box 1807, Ann Arbor, Michigan 48106.)

Corrick, F. *Preparing for your retirement years*. New York: Pilot Books, 1972.

Federal benefits for veterans and dependents. Washington, D.C.: Government Printing Office. Address: Superintendent of Documents, Government Printing Office, Washington, D.C. 20402. Order No. 051-000-00087-1.

Gross, P.H. *Successful personal money management: A practical guide for your financial planning*. New York: McGraw Hill Book Co., 1977.

Harl, N.F. *Where there's a will—Estate planning*. Ames, Iowa: Cooperative Agricultural Extansion Service, Iowa State University, 1976.

Myers, R.J. *Social security*. Homewood, Illinois: Richard D. Irwin, Inc., 1975.

National directory of housing for older people. Washington, D.C. 20036. (National Council on Aging)

National directory of retirement residences. New York: Frederick Fell, Inc., 1973 (386 Park Avenue South, New York: 10016).

Otte, E. *Rehearse before you retire* (3rd edition). Appleton, Wisconsin: Retirement Research, 1977.

Porter, S. *Sylvia Porter's money book* (rev. edition). New York: Doubleday & Company, Inc., 1976.

Roos, I. Why the underground economy? *Fortune*, October 9, 1978, pp. 92-98.

Rosefsky, R. *Rosefsky's guide to financial security for the mature family*. Chicago: Follett Publishing Co., 1977.

Social Security Bulletin (monthly). U.S. Department of Health, Education and Welfare, Social Security Administration. (Subscription $14.00. Order from Superintendent of Documents, Government Printing Office.)

Swartz, M.J. *Don't die broke—A guide to secure retirement*. New York: E.F. Hutton, 1978.

Uchtmann, D.L., & Bock, C.A. *Planning Agricultural estates after the tax reform act of 1976*. Urbana, Illlnois: Cooperative Extension Service, College of Agricultural, University of Illinois, 1978.

U.S. Department of Health, Education and Welfare—Social Security Administration. *Your medicare handbook*. Washington, D.C., U.S. Government Printing Office, 1979.

Wilberdlng, M.F. (Ed.). *What everyone needs to know about law*. Washington, D.C.: U.S. News and World Report, 1975.

Section III

Special Issues

Counseling for the Growing Years

OVERVIEW

This section focuses on specific issues that affect particular groups of elderly. The elderly are by no means a homogeneous group. Among other variables, differences in culture, sex, physical health, and mobility are important in understanding older individuals. In the last two decades there has been a considerable effort to appreciate uniqueness between people and to correct injustices done to particular groups.

The contributors to this section have focused their attention on specific issues concerning the elderly. While as a society we have recently paid more attention to critical issues such as race, sex, handicaps, and drug abuse, we have not given the same attention to these issues with the elderly. The various contributors bring to the forefront specific information on special issues relevant to the elderly. This information is necessary if counselors are to meaningfully respond to the various needs of older persons.

Miller discusses counseling with the disabled elderly from a unique framework that he labels self-environmental transactions (SETS). Miller presents counselors a model that not only focuses on the disabled elderly, but on the "self" and "environmental" transactions that are manifest in the daily life of elderly people. The author leads the counselor through a rationale and practical application of the SETS model. Miller also presents an enlightening discussion of some of the realities of being handicapped and elderly. He offers thoughtful insights into what it is like to be older and disabled.

Wolleat opens her article by stating that elderly women are twice victims, reaping the aversive consequences of "both agism and sexism." Her contention is that the milieu which has been instrumental in determining the present economic and psychological status of elderly women has differed from that of elderly men. The effects of a life history of sex role differentiation and stereotyping lead to very specific counseling issues for elderly women. Wolleat contends that counselors will not be effective with elderly women unless they are knowledgeable of their unique concerns. The author clearly outlines unique concerns for elderly women, providing recommendations for further learning for counselors interested in this topic.

Exum discusses some of the current problems and issues confronted by the elderly of various cultural groups. His emphasis is on concerns of the Black elderly. All elderly persons must contend with problems of health, income, transportation, crime, nutrition, and housing. However, the unique history of various cultural groups in American society make the later years of the culturally diverse individuals different— and often more difficult—than the later years of white persons. The counseling needs of the culturally diverse elderly are delineated by Exum and suggestions are made for counselor intervention.

Clements addresses the issues involved in pastoral counseling with the elderly. He discusses the similarities and differences between pastoral counseling and psychiatry, psychology, and social work. Clements presents a lucid description of the training, role expectations, strengths, and constraints of the pastoral counselor. The author makes a compelling argument for the centrality of the human spirit in therapeutic encounters with the elderly.

Perhaps one of the most difficult decisions facing many families of the elderly is the decision to institutionalize the elderly family member. In addition, institutionalization confronts the elderly individual with loss and change. Supiano discusses the critical issues of the institutionalized elderly. Supiano calls for individual and group counseling for older persons who are institutionalized and for their families. The process of institutionalization is often a major crisis for older persons and their families. Supiano cogently traces the various problems associated with this event and presents specific suggestions for counselor interventions.

Most people probably consider substance abuse as a problem facing "younger" people. Rosenthal and Leclair present a forceful account of widespread use and abuse of alcohol and chemicals among the elderly. While elderly substance abusers have some characteristics in common with their younger counterparts, there are also many differences. Older substance abusers have been largely ignored, in part because they keep a "low profile." The authors discuss types of legal and illegal substances abused by the elderly as well as characteristics and causes of substance abuse by the elderly. Guidelines for treatment are provided for counselors.

Counseling the Disabled Elderly

Leonard A. Miller

ABSTRACT

This chapter examines counseling with the disabled elderly using the framework of Self-Environmental Transactions (SETS). Such transactions become the focal point for the counselor's efforts and attention, to aiding the disabled elderly to function in self-fulfilling environmental transactions.

Self-Environmental Transactions (SETS) are analyzed from four viewpoints. The Self "pole" of such transactions is posited to have A Mental-Aspect as well as a Physical-Aspect. The Environmental "pole" is also broken down into these two components. The Self-Environmental Transaction is seen as an evolving locale for responding—a locale which has both self and environment as "active agents" mutually influencing each other. Common problems with the disabled elderly, both in terms of self and the environment, are discussed with possible solutions.

BEGINNING WITH AN HISTORICAL NOTE

Since 1920, when the federal government entered into partner-ship with state governments in the civilian rehabilitation of their citizens, the enduring and current emphasis in this rehabilita-tion movement has been on *vocational* rehabilitation. Entry into rehabilitation services has been through meeting three criteria of eligibility: (1) having a medically defined disability (2) which constitutes a substantial vocational handicap (3) with a reasonable expectation that available services would allow clients to become re-employed. Although employment can be rather broadly construed to include homemakers, unpaid family workers, or persons working in sheltered conditions, the net effect of such criteria has been to eliminate the elderly person (someone over the age of 65) from the rosters of state rehabilita-tion agencies.

It has not been until the 1970's that some (but not much) empha-sis has developed in the area of "independent living" goals, in which the goal of rehabilitation is to restore persons to the status of simply being able to take care of themselves and their daily needs. Such goals are typically pursued only in situations where restoring a person to independent living will release someone else in the family unit for paid employment, thus mak-ing the overall family unit more financially independent. Conse-quently, the national, state-federal rehabilitation movement may be described as *not* addressing the rehabilitation of the elderly in any concerted, organized manner. That is, with the elderly, the investment of rehabilitation funds is not seen as having any payoff in the production of a self-sustaining worker—in some sense of that word.

When one looks at the mainstream of rehabilitation literature, there is little, if any, research and/or thinking dealing with counseling the disabled elderly person. One document, for ex-ample, deals with counseling the older disabled *worker* (Muthars & Morris, 1964) but as always the emphasis is on work. In short, the national rehabilitation movement has always linked disability with work goals. Both in the generation of literature, as well as in actual practice, it has ignored that segment of the populace in which the interaction of disability with age precluded such justifiable goals.

When one looks at the mainstream of counseling literature, there is little research and/or thinking that deals with counseling the elderly, although this seems to be growing (e.g., Herr & Weakland, 1979; Schlossberg & Entine, 1977). Counseling as a general field has also had a major emphasis on the young person—someone who "faces a long life" and in need of guidance and counseling in a complex society. It has been during the past decade that counseling theorists—taking their cues perhaps from *Death and dying* (Kubler-Ross, 1974) or *Passages* (Sheehy, 1976)—noticed that counseling, like learning, might be something that is a lifelong process.

When one looks at the mainstream of literature on the elderly, generally labeled gerontology or geriatric material, (I must confess I don't like the labels) it ranges from "head-counting" psychological/sociological profiles of elderly behavior in different categories to more poignant, private accounts of what life as an elder in this country looks like (e.g., Gross, Gross & Seidman, 1978). Even the fact that 65 was set as the age at which full retirement benefits were given when the Social Security system was created in 1935, shows us how deeply cultural values enter into any discussion of the "elderly" (which is synonmous with those 65 and older). As Murphy and Florio point out (Gross, Gross & Seidman, 1978):

The fallacy of overgeneralizing about the elderly is clear from the statistics cited, whether the specific is health or education or marital status of income or living arrangements. On any given aspect of later life, one can often say "many" persons but seldom "most" and never "all" or "almost all."

To sum up this rather brief historical note on counseling the disabled elderly, let me also state that with Medicare, the recent establishment of a National Institute on Aging, the Gray Panthers, the National Council of Aging, etc., it would seem that the 1980's will be a time when the elderly will demand and receive a wider array of services and more humane consideration in our country. As in any deeply-rooted human drive to gain worthy goals for a class of people (whether ethnic minorities, women or the elderly), we *all* stand to benefit.

But what can be usefully said concerning the counseling of the disabled elderly? There seems to be three key terms that require a more in-depth consideration as I try to make at least reasonably sane, if not useful, remarks on the topic: counseling, disability, and elderly (or age). In order to do this, I must first present a "model" for counseling that will more clearly indicate how a counselor might see relationships that exist between counseling, disability and age—a model that might help us sort the trivial or merely interesting fact from those that are most useful and of import to a counselor.

COUNSELING FOR SELF-ENVIRONMENTAL TRANSACTIONS

Let me begin this section with the rather paradoxial statement that counselors do not solely have the persons they are counseling as the objects or even major reasons for their encounters (interviews). Rather, counselors place professional expertise at the service of improving the self-environmental transactions (referred to as SETS for the remainder of this chapter) which clients find themselves embedded in. In a very fundamental sense, any human life, the quality of that life, the sense of fulfillment in that life, etc., can be seen to arise from the smooth, fulfilling transactions that person is able to manifest in daily life. The Self-Environmental Transactions (SETS) which a person brings to the interview room come under examination and discussion in the counseling session. Both poles of a SET—the self pole and the environmental pole— are "active" and must be considered as contributing agents. This can be diagrammed as in Figure 1:

Figure 1
Self-Environmental Transactions (SETS)

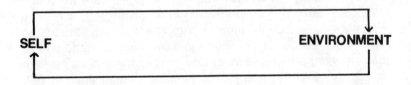

Figure 1 shows us how the person and the environment make a living dialectic or "feedback system" in which the actual, experienced life of the individual is an *evolving locale for responding. No human life is lived without a locale.* (It is also difficult to imagine a locale without someone being aware of it). For this author, an "unbalanced" counselor is someone who is hypnotized into directing all attention and effort toward only one pole of a SET. Consequently, such an unbalanced counselor might well work only with the client (self) as the source of all encountered problems, while other counselors concentrate on the environment as the chief villian. Interestingly enough, counseling theorists also reflect this essential imbalance when some stress human pathologies and/or potentials as the primary and almost exclusive source of problems or growth (e.g. Shutz, 1967) while others, often labelled "radical" theorists, since they frequently call for rather large-scale social restructuring, are hypnotized by the environment/culture (e.g., Agel, 1971; Brown, 1973).

A balanced counselor is continually sensitive to *both* poles of client SETS. For me, therefore, the essential question of counseling the disabled person translates into this question: How can the counselor improve the functioning of significant SETS for an elderly person who has a certain disability?

For purposes of discussion, each pole of SETS will be unpacked as having a mental and a physical aspect. This is only for purposes of discussion since, in truth, the mental and physical aspects of SETS are mutually influencing and comprise a *living* system, rather than just a logical one. (We might need logic to *see* but need to go beyond logic when we want the "sense" of how it works.) Ernest Becker's classic work, *Denial of Death*, is a sensitive appraisal of how our "embeddedness" in a self that inhabits a culture that is also "active" creates a matrix for our lives (Becker, 1973).

Becker also describes how mental as well as physical aspects of this embeddedness result in something that might be described as "being somewhere." So, the above question devolves into four: What can be usefully said about the Physical-Aspect of Self in the significant SETS that confront the disabled elderly? What can be usefully said about the Mental-Aspect of Self in the significant SETS that confront the disabled elderly? What can be usefully said about the Physical-Aspect of the Environment in the significant SETS that confront the disabled elderly? And, finally, what can be usefully said about the Mental-Aspect of the Environment in the significant SETS that confront the disabled elderly?

THE PHYSICAL-ASPECT OF SELF

It's in the "plumbing." Although that statement is somewhat facetious, it carries considerable truth in talking about how the body ages. The aging body, because of increased difficulty providing an adequate blood supply, is more and more prone to certain categories of disability (e.g., heart disease and cerebral vascular accidents (better known as strokes), as well as how ably the body can recover from or sustain any disabling condition. As the cardiovascular system hardens and becomes "clogged" with various materials, thereby reducing blood supply, this systemic effect of aging can turn a broken leg into a rather drawn-out affair with chronic residuals.

As further examples, collagen and bone changes, particularly in joints, result in the arthridides and problems in locomotion and manipulation. Any standard text on medical information for lay persons will graphically spell out this aging effect (e.g., Meyers, 1965; Smith & Germain, 1975). For the counselor, the optimum solution to the physical aspects of self in SETS for the disabled elderly becomes optimum solutions for maintaining locomotion, manipulation, and the ability to communicate. But solutions to these functions must be balanced by considerations related to the other three aspects of SETS: namely, Mental-Self, Physical-Environment, and MentalEnvironment.

For example, suppose a 72 year old man loses a leg due, for the most part, to a diabetic condition of a long-standing duration. Diabetes has severely impaired overall vascular functioning, resulting in the loss of a gangrenous leg. (Don't think that just because a person scrupulously watches diet and insulin intake that such conditions are necessarily avoided; the loss cannot be ascribed to personal "faults" so cavalierly.)

Whether or not to prescribe a prosthesis for this person in order to get that person walking again, must rest on several other questions: What are the chances of losing the *other* leg in the relatively near future? (Remember, *all* of the person's plumbing has been effected.) What does the person want?

Is that person willing to undertake the necessary physical therapy, ambulatory training in the use of the prosthesis, maintenance of limb-stump and prosthesis, etc.? What type of home environment is the person returning to and what is the support in that environment? (Is this person encountering a home environment where alternate solutions, i.e., wheelchair, is a poor or impossible solution?) So, we notice that even the prescription of a prosthesis must be evaluated in the total SETS this person will encounter. Where a prosthesis might be almost routinely prescribed for a young person who lost a leg in a trauma situation, it is *not* so routine with the elderly. (Training films always show *young* people jumping hurdles, dancing, and the like while wearing a prosthesis.) The "big three," as far as physical-self aspects of SETS are concerned are locomotion, manipulation, and communication. Some reasonably adequate solution to these functions must be created in order for a person to maintain an independent living status—to be at least able to care for one's needs.

Counselors of the disabled elderly, because of the interaction effect between aging and disability, will need to evaluate solutions to these problems that indicate the best *SET* functioning each person can achieve, not just the latest technological devices that are available (and are often very expensive) or the latest medical procedure that offers hope primarily to the young. But, even a fairly insensitive counselor would be impressed with this fact if the counselor takes the time to listen to the disabled, older person's "story."

MENTAL-ASPECT OF SELF

Sidney Jourard, in a book titled *The transparent self*, has a chapter on the elderly (Jourard, 1971). This chapter bears the title: "An Invitation to Die." Jourard's thesis is that the culture— on the whole—simply invited old people to die once they became useless in furthering cultural goals (mainly of an economic nature). Those who have been properly socialized promptly oblige. Invitations to die range from the more subtle ones like being ignored or not consulted to the more blatant ones of institutionalization. Jourard's remedy is to suggest that the old need new "projects" for their lives— projects that involve a feeling of dignity and worth for the individual.

In trying to develop a mutually aggreeable new project with a disabled, elderly person, the counselor comes face-to-face with the mental-aspects of self in the SETS the client is maintaining. With the beliefs, assumptions/presuppositions, and conditioning of the client, such mechanisms structure the preceived realities of the older person. In short, they produce the manner in which that person "partitions" body sensations, emotions, and thoughts so as to have an *identifiable self in a locale.*

Figure 2 illustrates the influence of the mental-aspect of self in the functioning of SETS:

Figure 2

Mental-Aspect of SETS

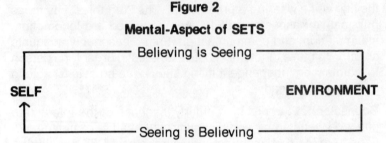

Robert Ornstein (1977), as well as several other investigators (e.g., Baker, 1967; Jourard, 1971; Weil, 1972), have presented the case for how the "models" we maintain in our awareness structure what is perceived in the environment. In my more mordant moments, I refer to the upper arrow in Figure 1 as the "Mayic Projection" (Maya being a reference to the illusory, phenomenal world Buddists posit). The lower arrow is called "The Missouri Confirmation" (after the fact that Missourians are credited with the statement: I'll only believe it if I see it!). I am *not* trying to make a case for a mentalistic philosophy in this diagram—a philosophy that maintains that "it-is-all-in-our-heads."

Actually, such a philosophy undergrids the counseling theorists whom I believe to be unbalanced toward the Self pole of SETS. These theorists believe that self-actualization and self-potential are the only things worth a counselor's attention. I'm much closer to Murray's self-envinonmental "presses" in which the self is viewed in its functional locale or site (Hall & Lindzey, 1957) or Lewin's field-theory (deRivera, 1976). My intent, however, is to get on with a useful discussion related to the manifesting in the SETS they maintain. The similarities of this position with other published positions, my intellectual ancestors, is not of major concern. I do not pretend to any great originality, but only hope for sane, useful descriptions for the person who intends to undertake counseling disabled elderly persons.

When a consideration of the mental-aspect of Self pole in SETS arises, we enter an area generally referred to in the rehabilitation literature as "psychological aspects" of disability. Other, more pretentious titles exist, such as the Psychology of Disability, but essentially the question is pursued as to how *stress* and *loss* suffered from a disability relates to the reactions a person has *after/toward* such an affliction. The essence of such thinking revolves aroung this question: When persons lose a valued dimension of their life (whether personal functioning or a relationship with someone else), are there common denominators which seem to occur in their reactions?

When an elderly person becomes disabled, this can be viewed as the *second* loss (since youth is often seen as the first). Consequently, a discussion of disability, the elderly, and the mental-aspect of self in SETS which such persons may be confronting, must be approached with "loss" or "stress" reactions having multiple sources (both age and disability). At the risk of being tedious, I would also like to remind the reader that the other three aspects of SETS (Physical-Self, Physical-Environment and Mental-Environment) are also related to any sane solutions for the personal reactions a disabled, elderly person might be having. (Sorry about those dangling participles.) Remembering that we are talking about "real" people who live, as we do, by "being somewhere" and having an evolving locale (both self and environment), Beatrice Wright, a major theorist in the area of psychological aspects of disability, presents what this author considers useful, sane descriptions of such dynamics (Wright, 1960). I do not pretend to her eloquence in print, but will describe several key concepts that are presented. These include "comparative versus asset values," the "requirement of mourning," as well as the condition of "as if." I will begin with the last concept and work my way up the list.

In the condition or state of mind where persons act "as if" they do not have a disability (somewhat more acute, usually, when the disability is not that visible and the person can "pass" for normal) we are encountering some form of denial and a refusal to entertain "pertinent" facts on the part of the client. I have put quotation marks around pertinent to indicate the status of that loaded word. I could have used reasonable, supported, credible, or appropriate as synonyms for that adjective. What is being suggested is that denial of a disability, particularly when such denial has apparent *lethal* consequences for the client or others, must be confronted by the counselor, at times, as part of the mental-aspects of the self pole.

For example, with a serious heart condition or a form of the epilepsies, a client may refuse to give up strenuous yard work or driving a car. That client prefers to operate "as if" everything is more or less as usual, with any differences ascribed to the effects of age per se.

The opposite of "as if" might be called, "Oh, My God..." in which a client overreacts to a disability, displaying an inappropriate hysteria or depression. This is sometimes due to the unwitting influence of a physician who, in the interest of getting the client to moderate behavior, mainly discusses the unsavory consequences of making a mistake with such a disability. If the older person has been looking (often unconsciously) for just such an excuse to limit behavior and become dependent on someone else, the physician's advice can be distorted or exaggerated to fit that need. This is particularly true where money payments, such as Social Security supplementation or insurance payments, are involved. Elizabeth Kubler-Ross, interestingly, also describes the stages a person typically progresses through when involved with a terminal disease or malady: denial, anger, bargaining, and finally acceptance (Kubler-Ross, 1974). Such stages also seem typical of any major loss, although often attenuated to some extent when survival is not at stake, as in the case of a non-lethal disability.

The requirement of mourning is a requirement that is laid on a disabled person by those around that person, although the individual who is disabled may well be infected with the same views and accede to the requirement. Simply stated, the requirement is this: If you don't have the faculties, capacities, talents which I have and enjoy, you should be in a state of suffering unless you are too stupid or crazy to know what you are missing—or denying how you "really" feel. In short, you should be mourning our differences (to my advantage of course).

The requirement of mourning is actually the position of a snob, who buttresses a sense of insecurity by comparing one's own vision of what a "good life" should be with the views/abilities of all those around. Since we are all socialized in a culture that innoculates us with the obvious criteria of the "good life" on TV and in other media, it is very difficult not to structure our lives along the lines of comparison with others. Consequently, the great bulk of us harbor at least subtle versions of the requirement for mourning. (One of the questions I often use in a psychological aspects of disability class is: Tell me something you know about yourself that you didn't learn through a comparison with others.)

In recommending a shift in the disabled person's perception from comparative values to asset values, Wright is recommending a shift from culturally instilled and conditioned values to values of a more personally based nature. It is, of course, patently clear that prevalent cultural values (Mental-Aspect of the Environment) have a deep and abiding influence on individual values. In a highly competitive, capitalistic society as ours, comparative values, in which judgments about our own life and position requiring almost continual comparisons, are also endemic. Regrets over not being young, beautiful, successful, and financially secure are also endemic. (So is alcoholism and the use of tranquilizers.) Asset values are based on the assumption that "being" itself, rather than "being somebody" can provide a workable framework for a highly satisfying life.

In the final phase of life, elderly persons are confronted with their own beliefs, values, and assumptions. Counselors of disabled elderly persons must confront this aspect in the functioning SETS that person is embedded in. They must realize that such mechanisms structure a great deal of the perceived reality for that person and are often linked to comparative values and a requirement for mourning. Rather, paradoxically, although elderly persons have been "socialized" longer than their younger counterparts, they are also often able to perceive the essential hollowness of values that are based on comparisons and continual exhortations to achieve. This is particularly true when their own positions, as rejected bystanders, leaves them wondering what all their rush-and-hurry had been about. For the poor, disabled elderly persons, institutionalized in a deadening locale, it certainly must occur to the great majority that they have nothing left to lose, except their life— which quite a few elect to return to the sender (Aldrich & Mendkoff, 1963.)

PHYSICAL-ASPECT OF ENVIRONMENT

For the disabled, elderly person, as for all disabled persons restricted in their mobility (locomotion solutions), America can be a very handicapping environment. It is generally true, if trite, to point out that cities and their services have been engineered for the private auto. Mass transit is often inadequate. To operate with maximum freedom, particularly for those who live in rural areas, a person needs a car. This much must be very obvious even to any grade-schooler who gets bused or driven by the mother to school in a station wagon. In allowing the disabled, elderly person to maintain reasonable mobility, the counselor is soon confronted with frustrating physical aspects of the environment.

With the passage of several federal laws (e.g., National Commission on Architectural Barriers, 1965; Architectural Barriers Act, 1968; Architectural and Transportation Barriers Compliance Board, 1973), with the continuing push of the President's Committee for the Handicapped, and with the several Governor's Committees for the Handicapped, our collective attention has been focused on physical barriers for disabled persons (Weston, 1977). Some progress has been made in ameliorating barriers in existing physical facilities, particularly when of a public nature—such as schools or courthouses. New facilities of a federal or state nature must also adhere to new standards of accessibility. But if you really want the experience of physical barriers in your community, the experience is readily available. Go to your local rental service, rent a wheelchair, and carry out your normal routine for *one* day staying in the wheelchair. (If wheelchairs don't particularly turn you on, do it with crutches.)

Counselors of the disabled, elderly person must also consider adequate housing when the SETS that person is embedded in are encountered in counseling sessions. The choice may frequently boil-down to finding physically accessible private housing, subsidized housing for the elderly that has accessibility in the design, or some form of institutionalization. Diet, help with complicated physical-health maintenance procedures (such as maintaining the good condition of a soma (the lip of the hole) after a colostemy), and modifications to housing that enable a person to function effectively (such as lower kitchen counters, light switches, etc.) also enter into consideration. I do not intend to pursue this section of the chapter any further, my goal has been to acquaint the reader with the diverse considerations that stem from the physical-aspect of environments in which the disabled elderly are embedded. Obviously, to treat such a topic in depth would require a book (as, for example, Weston, 1977).

MENTAL-ASPECT OF ENVIRONMENT

When contemplating the mental-aspect of environment, the counselor is beginning to consider optimum solutions for disabled elderly persons which include the probable reactions of stigma/prejudice toward both disability and age that others have in this culture. This is especially true when the disabled elderly client desires some type of paid employment. Who wants such a person on the payroll? Another part of this contemplation is simply finding, in league with the client, an acceptable and sustaining form of socializing—a way to have meaningful contact with other people. John Holland, a major theorist in vocational psychology, has developed a way to define vocational environments in terms of the types of people who inhabit such environments (Holland, 1973). It seems to this author that such theorizing has broader implications: one can define *any* environment by the *dominant types of people encountered*. Most people react to environments by reacting to the other persons encountered and who must be interacted with; the major component of environments are people.

In the case of a poorly operated nursing home or institution that maintains docility and proper routine by heavily sedating and "warehousing" clients who simply sit in wheelchairs or listlessly use walkers, the people involved provide one kind of mental environment. An active senior citizen's center, with a diverse program and broad interests among participants, provides a different type of environment with the most important component being *other people*. As a result, the mental-aspect of the environment pole in SETS which disabled elderly persons currently inhabit requires some thought about the collective prejudices/stereotypes of the culture as a whole, as well as the probable, ongoing reactions of individuals who comprise the particular environment of this particular client.

The documentation of cultural stereotypes and prejudices toward the disabled as well as the elderly seems convincing and fairly extensive (e.g., Gross, Gross & Seifman, 1978; Wright, 1960). I do not mean to delve into such documentation with any depth, but simply to point out that such prejudice, based on comparative values that emphasize achievement and fairly narrow definitions of the "good life," with built-in-bias, permits relatively few persons to absolutely claim that they "have arrived."

They are hardly the type of cultural values that one can turn to in order to invest the last phase of life with meaning. In addition, the deeper, unexamined assumptions of a culture are often fairly invisible, but lethal, and require patient, self-examination and contemplation in order to see their effects as well. There are assumptions, collectively generated and supported, which advertizers, teachers, and other public-opinion manipulators subtly and covertly arouse in our awareness. Such assumptions are: (1) you only live once; (2) your consciousness is solely dependent on the physico/chemical reactions of your body; without this body, you are extinct; and (3) life in general, and you in particular, are an "accident" of the universe.

Elizabeth Kubler-Ross, in a book titled *Death: The final stage of growth*, gives an excellent accounting of such deep assumptions and our reactions to such prospects (Kubler-Ross, 1975). When the counselor is working with a disabled, elderly person who has managed to construct a life-affirming and fairly satisfying set of values/assumptions that sustain self-worth in the final phase of life, well and good! For the persons who come with considerable self-hate and personal dissatisfactions with this phase of their life, classes, guided reading, etc., may well be indicated so as to provide a review of basic assumptions— assumptions that come with mother's milk and a lot of persuasive selling by people with vested interests.

PUTTING SETS TOGETHER

So where are we? Obviously, in one chapter, this author did not exhaustively examine the four major aspects of Self-Environmental Transactions (SETS), even granting that such transactions are the major focus of the counselor's expertise. This chapter assumes some sophistication on the reader's part with regard to basic counseling theory—at least with the "barebones" of putting people at ease, providing empathy, congruence in displayed responses, listening skills, etc. (e.g., Benjamin, 1969). A particular problem in regard to "protocol" might be briefly mentioned, however. In the section on Mental-Aspect of Self, I could have pointed out that *all* interpersonal exchanges are subtly under the control of "protocol regulators."

Participants in interpersonal relating continually assess, for example, the motives, the particular situation, and personal characteristics (such as race, age, sex) of each other. Such regulators determine where the interpersonal exchange is judged appropriate, and judged to be so by the participants. In interviewing an elderly person, one who doesn't believe that someone quite younger or of another sex has anything to offer, the counselors who have such characteristics may well have to work with such protocol considerations *before* any constructive counseling can be accomplished. That is, protocol must be confronted before any discussion of the SETS the client is embedded in can proceed. But any adequate discussion of ongoing techniques and problems in the counseling interview itself would provide chapters of material, and is covered by other authors writing chapters in this book as well as other sources (e.g., Patterson, 1966; Stefflre, 1965).

SUMMARY

The counselor of the disabled elderly person needs to sensitively examine and discuss with the client how information generated in each of the four aspects of Self-Environmental Transactions can help effect optimal solutions for such a person—solutions that provide greater self-fulfillment, greater other-fulfillment. Such a counselor needs knowledges in medical aspects of chronic disability, knowledge of how disabilities are linked through various systems of the body, and knowledge about legislation and programs that impact on the elderly. (Do we ever have enough knowledge?) But when everything else fails, trust in your accumulated knowledge of what people are apt to do—as well as in the Golden Rule and common sense. When that fails, TRY AGAIN.

REFERENCES

Agel, J. *The radical therapist*. New York: Ballentyne Books, 1971.

Aldrich, C., & Mendkoff, E. Relocation of the aged and disabled: A mortality study. In B. Neugarten (Ed.), *Middle age and aging*. Chicago: University of Chicago Press, 1968.

Baker, E. *Man in the trap*. New York: Macmillan, 1967.

Becker, E. *The denial of death*. New York: Free Press, 1973.

Benjamin, A. *The helping interview*. Boston: Houghton Mifflin, 1969.

Brown, P. *Radical psychology*. New York: Harper & Row, 1973.

DeRivera, J. *Field theory as human science; contributions of Lewin's Berlin group*. New York: Gardner Press, 1976.

Gross, R.: Gross, B.; B. & Seidman, S. *The new old: Struggling for decent aging*. Garden City, New York: Anchor Books, 1978.

Hall, C., & Lindsey, G. *Theories of personality*. New York: Wiley & Sons, 1957.

Herr, J., & Weakland, J. *Counseling elders and their families*. New York: Springer Pub., 1979.

Holland, J. *Making vocational choices*. Englewood Cliffs, New Jersey: Prentice-Hall, 1973.

Jourard, C. *The transparent self*. New York: D. Van Nostrand, 1971.

Kubler-Ross, E. *Death and dying*. New York: Macmillan, 1974.

Kubler-Ross, E. *Death: The final stage of growth*. Englewood Cliffs, New Jersey: Prentice-Hall, 1975.

Meyers, J. *An orientation to chronic disease and disability*. New York: Macmillan, 1965.

Muthard, J., & Morris, W. (Eds.). *Counseling the older disabled worker*. Iowa City, Institute of Gerontology, University of Iowa, 1964.

Orstein, R. *The psychology of consciousness* (2nd edition). New York: Harcourt Brace Jovanovich, 1977.

Patterson, C. *Theories of counseling and psychotherapy*. New York: Harper & Row, 1966.

Schlossberg, N., & Entine, A. *Counseling adults*. Monterey, California: Brooks/Cole, 1977.

Sheehy, G. *Passages*. New York: Dutton, 1976.

Shutz, W. *Joy: Expanding human awareness*. New York: Grove Press, 1967.

Care of the adult patient (4th edition). New York: Lippincott, 1975.

Stefflre, B. (Ed.). *Theories of counseling*. New York: McGraw-Hill, 1965.

Weil, A. *The natural mind*. Boston: Houghton Mifflin, 1973.

Weston, J. *Awareness papers, Vol. I*. Proceedings of White House Conference on Handicapped Individuals, U.S. Government Printing Office, 1977.

Wright, B. *Physical disability-a psychological approach*. New York: Harper, 1960.

Counseling for the Growing Years

Counseling
the Elderly Woman:
A Sex-Role Perspective

Patricia L. Wolleat

ABSTRACT

Elderly women are in a disfavored position in society, being victims of both agism and sexism. This chapter addresses both issues. Statistical evidence is used to show the economic plight and consequent negative psychological turmoil elderly women can expect. Comparisons are made between elderly women and elderly men. Evidence is offered that indicates that both are "victims" of society, the former to a higher degree than the latter.

Implications are discussed and guidelines are provided for counselors working with elderly women. Additional resource materials are presented.

INTRODUCTION

As groups, neither the elderly nor women occupy favored positions in our society. Twice victims, elderly women reap the aversive consequences of both agism and sexism. And if the elderly woman is also a member of a racial or ethnic minority group, her status may be even further diminished through racism.

Understanding the impact of these various forms of prejudice on clients can aid the counselor in nearly every stage of counseling with older people, from relationship-building and goal-setting, through developing intervention strategies, to evaluating outcomes.

During the last decade considerable attention has been given to the problems of sexism and agism. One of the fortuitous by-products of these national movements to reduce the various forms of bias and discrimination has been a renewed emphasis on the development of human potential. Breaking through the myths associated with aging, for example, has brought about the recognition that the elderly are not simply growing old, but that they are *growing*! This dynamic conceptualization of aging has permitted the entry of the developmentally-oriented counselor into the arena of counseling the elderly.

The counseling profession has been caught somewhat unawares in responding to developmental concerns of the older population (Ganikos & Grady, 1979). Traditionally a service offered to the young, counseling has been blind to the benefits which might accrue if it were extended to the elderly. If counselors choose to overturn this neglect, they will need to divest themselves of the myths about aging that are widely held in our society. Further, they will need to understand the milieu which helped to shape the current circumstance of older people.

A PERSPECTIVE

The model elderly person in the United States is a widowed female. In the age group 65 and over, there are only 72 males for every 100 females (Siegel, 1976). This ratio decreases as the population ages, from 79.3 in the 65-69 range to 49.5 for those 85 and over. Fifty-two percent of older females are widowed. A special focus on the elderly woman will deepen the counselor's understanding of this entire age group. In this paper I will examine the counseling-relevant attributes of elderly women *qua* women. In this approach the assumption is made that the milieu which has been instrumental in determining the current economic and pychological status of elderly females has differed in several respects from that of the elderly male. Because of the pervasiveness of sex-role distinctions in influencing personality characteristics, on an individual level, and public and legislative policy, on the social level, a special focus on the forces which have shaped elderly women's lives is essential.

It would be a mistake to assume that the psychological experience and living conditions of all elderly women would have been similar. It would be equally erroneous, however, to overlook the commonalities. In this paper, the emphasis will be on the commonalities, keeping firmly in mind the tremendous diversity in their experience, current status, and aspirations. It is also important to note that many of the common problems of elderly women, having now been recognized and identified, are currently more amenable to solution than they were in their former unrecognized state.

The damaging effects of the inferior status which accompanies having been born female and socialized into the feminine sex role are dramatically exacerbated as a woman advances in age (Janeway, 1973). These effects are both economic and psychological.

Over half of the non-married women over the age of 65 live at or below the government-defined poverty level ($2,900 annual income in 1977). Older women constitute the single poorest subgroup of individuals in the United States today (Block, Grambs, Davidson & Serock, 1978). The poverty these women experience reflects the sex discrimination in employment which is an inherent feature of our occupational structure. First, much of the work that these women have done during their lifetimes (e.g., raising children and managing a household) has not been compensated.

Second, even if a woman has worked outside the home, her salary was likely to have been only half as much as that of her male counterpart. Since social security and pension benefits are based on earnings, women necessarily receive lower monthly payments. Other policies of the Social Security Administration regarding determination of eligibility and calculating benefits work against the woman who "dropped out" to raise children and do not provide for the earlier and lengthier needs of females (Block, et al., 1978). And finally, if the older woman seeks employment for the first time or after a lengthy absence, she is likely to face both age and sex discrimination on the job market.

A recent account of one woman's plight illustrates how one set of federal employment policies adversely affect women (*People*, 1979). Jane Dubs, 57, spent 25 out of her 30 years of married life as the wife of a Foreign Service official. State Department policy for most of that period of time required wives of officials to be "teammates." In fact, their performance in this role was evaluated along with their husband's performance in their roles. Following a divorce in 1976, her husband remarried. Upon his death, the ambassador's death benefits and other insurance went to his second wife. Jane Dubs, like all exwives of federal employees, is ineligible for Social Security and other benefits, even though her role in the embassy was prescribed and evaluated by the State Department.

Undoubtedly Jane Dubs' scenario, and others more subtle, have been played out many times (perhaps with less publicity) and account for the marginal economic status of many older women.

As devastating as the economic impoverishment, are the psychological costs of being an elderly female in the latter half of the twentieth century. These psychological liabilities are associated with (a) a negative social image, which reflects a double standard of aging for females and for males (Block, et al., 1978); (b) a loss of the roles through which the female is socialized to find meaning in her life (Prock, 1975); and (c) the inadequate set of coping strategies which females have learned to use.

The double standard of aging affords the older male a much more positive image than the female. The older women in our society is stereotyped as an unattractive, passive, complaining, asexual, useless creature (Livson, 1977). This negative social image may be incorporated by some elderly women into their self images with self-crippling results (Block, et al., 1978).

As a result of the negative stereotype, the elderly female is likely to receive little affirmation of her worth from the broader society. As Jacobs (1976, p. 34) observed, a great many older American women "are underemployed, underpaid, underfinanced, underhoused, undervalued, and underloved, sometimes even by themselves." Unfortunately, the rewards the older woman may find lacking from society are also unlikely to come from herself.

The roles for which today's older women were socialized—primarily wife and mother—are inherently dependent on the presence of spouses and children and are limited in their enactment once the woman is widowed or divorced or the children are grown (Higgins, 1975). At these transition points, important aspects of the female's identity are disrupted and she may not have been prepared to easily take on new or alternative roles to forge a new identity. This type of role loss is often called "the empty nest syndrome" and has been considered to be a leading contributor to depression in older women. For those elderly women who have achieved their identity through an occupational role, the type of role loss typically associated with the male retiree may also be experienced (Cavan, 1968).

The coping strategies females learn to use constitute another problem engendered by sex-role socialization. Females are socialized to depend on males for economic and psychological support (Troll, Israel, & Israel, 1977). Because females learn to value and seek the companionship and support of males, they may undervalue other females and fail to develop supportive relationships with the very persons who are likely to be their primary source of companionship in old age. If women view their female peers as inferior conpanions (as compared to males), they may be bereft of social ties.

Bernard (1976) speculates that the decline in female homosociability (women supporting other women), noted in the twentieth century may be related to the high incidence of depression in older women. She explains that females, because of their socializaiton to be affiliative and communal, are vulnerable to the stresses of social deprivation. Males, historically, have been socialized toward separation and inexpressivity. During the nineteenth century much of the female's need for communion was met through her ties with other women, through the sharing of experiences such as childbirth.

During the twentieth century female companionship was denigrated in favor of male attention and an important source of emotional support was lost to women. This fact may be particularly crucial to the widow, since there are fewer older males and they tend to be married to younger females.

The socialization of females to be dependent on males is also related to the failure of many to learn marketable job skills and to engage in financial planning.

Another set of problems specific to the elderly female population concerns health. Although the types of problems—stress, depression, suicide, drug abuse, and alcoholism—do not differ from those found in older men, their prevalence, etiology, and modes of treatment do (Block, et al., 1978).

In general, aging in females is related to an increase in stress, unless one is financially well-off (Horrocks & Mussman, 1970). This increase in stress is precipitated by a number of conditions: (a) societal changes in value and presitge attached to femine roles; (b) changes in the woman's family relationships, e.g., death of spouse; (c) changes in financial condition; (d) changes in social network; (e) changes in health and physical condition; and (f) conflicts in identity and purpose (Block, et al, 1978). Many of these sources of stress are well within the treatment domain of counselors, especially identity conflicts.

Depression is one of the leading symptoms in women who seek psychological treatment (Weissman, 1972). Yet its prevalence is difficult to estimate since many of its milder manifestations are easily confounded with female role expectations, e.g., passivity; and in its more severe expressions it resembles senile dementia. Perhaps one of the most significant breakthroughs in female mental health is the growing acceptance of depression in older women as an emotional disturbance with social psychological roots.

Suicide in women peaks around the age of 50. Although the suicide rate is much lower among women compared to older men (1:10 over age 50), there is some evidence that women make more attempts (Garai, 1970). If all types of potentially self-destructive behaviors are considered, e.g., overeating or under-eating, smoking, delay in seeking medical treatment, drug abuse and alcoholism, life-threatening behavior is a serious mental health problem among elderly women.

The incidence of substance abuse in elderly women is difficult to determine. First, good data on incidence by sex is lacking. Secondly, there is a tendency to shield the female and/or elder alcoholic from exposure and thus the extent of the problem remains hidden. It can safely be concluded, however, that the number of female alcoholics nowhere reaches the number of males, although there is some speculation that the number of female alcoholics is likely to rise relative to males in the coming years (Block, et al., 1978).

AGISM AND SEXISM

It is not coincidental that the movements to reduce neglect of and overt discrimination toward the elderly and women have flourished contemporaneously. In fact, it might be argued that agism might not exist at all were it not for sexism. The close association between traditional concepts of the aged and of females have no doubt influenced our treatment of the elderly. Stereotypes of the older person resemble the feminine much more that the masculine stereotype. Females outnumber males in the elderly population. Thus, misogyny or "contempt of the feminine" may underlie the negative social posture toward both the elderly and females.

Much of the professional literature on the elderly overlooks the very important perspective that could be gained by viewing the elderly from a sex-role perspective. The counselor who wishes to do so will probably need to consult the women's studies' literature; the counseling literature will offer little in this regard. An analysis of the 1979 APGA publication, *Counseling the aged: A training syllabus for educators*, will illustrate this point. A complimentary copy of this publication put together by the Special Training Project on Counseling the Aged, was mailed to every counselor education program in the country with the instructions to circulate it among all faculty members (Ganikos & Grady, 1979). Thus, this work has great potential for influencing the preparation of "gerocounselors."

There are almost no references to sex differences among the elderly in the entire 320 page volume. One or two references are made in a chapter dealing with demographics (Blake & Peterson, 1979), where the point is made that the life expectancy of females being greater than that of males, the potential clientele of counselors working with the elderly will be largely female. The authors note, "The concerns of older women need special emphasis in the training of counselors and the design of service delivery. The greater number of older women make it relatively easy to obtain funding for women-oriented programs" (p. 23). They ironically, however, follow this statement with, "On the other hand, there is a considerable number of older men, and counseling as well as other service groups should guard against the neglect of these persons who might otherwise become a forgotten minority within a minority" (p. 23).

Another mention is made of females specifically in the chapter dealing with minority elderly (Solomon, 1979). This mention, however, is in a two-line quote from the U.S. Commission of Civil Rights Study on Age Discrimination, which mentions sex as one of many factors contributing to multiple discrimination against the elderly. The chapter dealing with social policies and legislation (Odell, 1979) makes no mention of sex inequities when discussing issues related to social security.

If this volume is representative of the level of awareness about sex-related issues in counseling the elderly, it is unlikely that counselors trained using these materials will be able to address the special needs of females.

I would recommend *Uncharted territory: Issues and concerns of women over 40* by Block, Davidson, Grambs, and Serock (1978), published by the Center on Aging of the University of Maryland, as an excellent, comprehensive source of information on older women. Carter and Rawlings' (1977) *Psychotherapy for women: Treatment toward equality* describes counseling and other therapeutic strategies from a female perspective.

IMPLICATIONS FOR COUNSELORS

Many of the issues and concerns of the elderly woman are well within the domain of the developmental counselor operating out of either a direct service or advocacy role. Wolff and Meyer (1979) describe a number of counseling techniques, strategies, and approaches which can be used with older people: listening; group counseling; decision-making and life-planning groups; preretirement and retirement counseling; leisure planning; employment or alternative career planning; educational planning; residential planning; support and personal growth groups; preparatory counseling for death and dying; the use of reminiscence with loss, isolation and depression; counseling for loneliness, bereavement, and widowhood; sex counseling; assertive training; residential living groups; marriage or couple counseling; intergenerational or family counseling; body and creative therapies; and techniques for working with the disoriented.

Capuzzi, Gossman, Whiston, and Surdam (1979) describe a moderately successful group counseling approach for institutionalized elderly women. What they learned from their experience, too lengthy to mention here, can be very helpful to other counselors working with this group.

There is no reason to believe that any of the above approaches would not be effective in dealing with many of the issues and concerns of older women. However, a thorough understanding of the person(s) to whom a technique is being applied is prerequisite to successful counseling with any group. Further, techniques applied in the absence of well-defined goals are like shots into the dark. They may eventually hit something, but just what, may never be known.

With these *caveats* in mind the following guidelines are offered for counseling with elderly women. They are intended to highlight the particular points to keep in mind when dealing with elderly women.

1. One of the primary deficits in the female experience is in acquiring a sense of self as a person with value. The counselor should use every opportunity to affirm the elderly woman and to help her develop a positive self-image.

2. Women during the twentieth century have been isolated from their female peers. They have not been inclined to respect and support each other. Counselors should use a variety of strategies to promote sharing with and acceptance of other women.

3. Elderly women who achieved their identity primarily through the roles of wife and mother may be threatened by current attacks being made on the traditional feminine roles. Counselors should help these women to gain confidence in their ability to choose and to implement the roles *they* desire in their older years.

4. Many elderly women are not aware of the social and political roots of agism and sexism. Counselors can help them to understand that they feel inferior because society expects them (the old and the female) to feel that way.

5. Many elderly women may have never taken themselves, their ideas, and their goals, seriously; they have been programmed by someone else. Counselors can assist these women to achieve the exhilaration which accompanies taking responsibility for one's life.

6. Many elderly women are coping with massive changes in their lives at a time when their economic resources and physical capacities may be declining. Counselors should help these women focus on the capacities they have retained and what they have to gain (Sinick, 1979).

7. Many elderly women may believe that as females they "properly" (Janeway, 1973) deserve little from life. Counselors can assist these women to accept their rights and assert themselves to obtain them.

8. Some elderly women may not have developed effective problem solving or decision-making strategies. Counselors can assist these women in learning and gaining confidence in using decision-making skills.

9. Dependence on others—especially on males—is a socialized feminine attribute. The counselor of elderly women must guard against both being contemptous of the female client's dependency needs and allowing an inappropriate dependent relationship to develop.

10. Females are socialized to look to others for the source of their goals and expectations. Counselors of elderly women should be very careful to work from a goal framework that has been explicitly negotiated with the client.

SUMMARY

Counselors of the elderly should not consider themselves sufficiently prepared until they have addressed the unique concerns of the older women. An understanding of the sex-role socialization process and how it affects both individual development and social attitudes and policy can substantially assist the counselor in dealing with the elderly.

REFERENCES

Bernard, J. Homosociality and female depression. *Journal of Social Issues,* 1976, *32,* 213-237.

Blake, R., & Peterson, D. Demographic aspects of aging: Implications for counseling. In M. Ganikos & K. Grady (Eds.), *Counseling the aged: A training syllabus for educators.* Washington, D.C.: APGA, 1979.

Block, M.; Davidson, J.; Grambs, J.; & Serock, K. *Uncharted territory: Issues and concerns of women over 40.* University of Maryland: Center on Aging, 1978.

Carter, D., & Rawlings, E. *Psychotherapy for women: Treatment toward equality.* Springfield, Illinois: Charles C. Thomas, 1977.

Capuzzi, D.; Gossman, L.; Whiston, S.; & Surdam, J. Group counseling for aged women. *Personnel and Guidance Journal,* 1979, *57,* 306-310.

Cavan, R. Self and role adjustment during old age. In J. Heis (Ed.), *Family roles and interaction.* Chicago: Rand McNally and Company, 1968.

Ganikos, M. Letter to counselor educators, March 13, 1979.

Ganikos, M., & Grady, K. *Counseling the aged: A training syllabus for educators.* Washington, D.C.: APGA, 1979.

Garai, J.C. Sex differences in mental health. *Genetic Psychology Monographs,* 1970, *81,* 123-142.

Higgins, D.H. *Female "neslitis:" Self-concept, role flexibility and achievement.* Paper presented at 28th Annual Scientific Meeting of the Gerontological Society, Louisville, Kentucky, October, 1975.

Horrocks, J.E., & Mussman, M.C. Middlescence: Age-related stress *Genetic Psychology Monographs,* 1970, *82,* 49.

Jocobs, R.H. A typology of older American women. *Social Policy,* 1976, *7,* 34039.

Janeway, E. Breaking the age barrier. *Ms.,* 1973, *1,* 50-53.

Livson, F.B. *Cultural faces of Eve: Images of women.* Paper presented at annual meeting of the American Psychological Association, San Francisco, August, 1977.

Odell, C.E. Aging-relevant issues, policies, and legislation: What the counselor should know. In M. Ganikos & K. Grady (Eds.), *Counseling the aged: A training syllabus for educators.* Washington, D.C.: APGA, 1979.

People, May 28, 1979, *11,* 39-40.

Prock, V.N. The middle years: The mid-stage women. *American Journal of Nursing,* 1975, *75,* 1019-1021.

Siegel, J.S. Demographic aspects of aging and the older population in the United States. *Current Population Reports,* Series P-23, No. 59. Washington, D.C.: GPO, 1976.

Sinick, D. Adult development changes and counseling challenges. In M. Ganikos & K. Grady (Eds.), *Counseling the aged: A training syllabus for educators.* Washington, D.C.: APGA, 1979.

Solomon, C. Elderly non-whites: Unique situations and concerns. In M. Ganikos & K. Grady (Eds.), *Counseling the aged: A training syllabus for educators.* Washington, D.C.: APGA, 1979.

Troll, L.E.; Israel, J.; & Israel, L. *Looking ahead: A women's guide to the problems and joys of growing older.* Englewood Cliffs, New Jersey: Prentice-Hall, 1977.

Weissman, M.M. The depressed woman: Recent research. *Social Work,* 1972, *17,* 19-25.

Wolff, A.R., & Meyer, G.W. Counseling older adults: Suggested approaches. In M. Ganikos & K. Grady (Eds.), *Counseling the aged: A training syllabus for educators.* Washington, D.C.: APGA, 1979.

Culturally Diverse Elderly: An Overview of the Issues

Herbert A. Exum

ABSTRACT

In this chapter some of the current problems and issues faced by elderly members of Asian, Black, Hispanic, and Native American communities are reviewed. While some of the problems faced by culturally diverse elderly are shared by the majority of elderly Americans, there are also some unique and often misinterpreted problems experienced by this group. This chapter attempts to highlight these problems for counselors.

The chapter is divided into three sections. The first section addresses issues related to the physical welfare of culturally diverse elderly. Issues such as crime, housing, and transportation are presented. The second section focuses on social and mental health issues. Here, the importance of the church, community, and family are emphasized. The final section points out steps counselors may take to enhance the quality of life of culturally diverse elderly. The goal of this chapter is to give counselors insight into particular needs of culturally diverse elderly and various skills and roles counselors need to help them.

INTRODUCTION

Problems and issues which impinge upon the quality of life of older culturally diverse people are discussed in this chapter. While the central focus is on life styles of older Black people, many of their problems are shared by older members of cultural and ethnic configurations that exist outside the white middle class mainstream. The term culturally diverse will refer to Asians, Blacks, Hispanics, and Native-Americans collectively.

These four groups were selected because the needs of their ethnic communities are frequently either unknown or misinterpreted by counselors. The major similarity among these culturally diverse elderly is their limited access to money, power, and institutional support in the American society. They also share the historical, cultural, and psychological effects of overt discrimination. Beyond these points, the variations in life style experienced by these elderly are great.

STEREOTYPING AND AGE DISCRIMINATION

Dancy (1977) suggests that the youth-oriented American life style is afflicted with a "no deposit no return" syndrome. In this system, once an individual has made a youthful contribution to society, it is assumed that that person's "bottle" is empty and valueless. The elderly are seen as empty bottles ready to be discarded. Rosenfelt (1971) describes a similar attitude called the elderly mystique. The mystique essentially posits becoming old as an unmitigated misfortune.

Participants in the elderly mystique know society finds it difficult to accept or forgive the existence of old people. Ironically, the perceptions of this insidious mystique are currently shared by many elderly persons. The older person expects derogation, stigma, and rejection. The consequence of the belief system is fulfillment of these negative expectations. As Rosenfelt states, believers in the system accept a very limited view of the possibilities available to them and are deformed into conformity. The believers become as warped and limited as the mystique would have them become.

Both the "no deposit no return" syndrome and the elderly mystique support viewing the elderly not from the perspective of their positive untapped potential, but from the considerations that must be weighed in order to accommodate and care for them (Dancy, 1977).

The problems of the culturally diverse elderly in general and the Black elderly in particular are compounded when racism is combined with agism. Most of this society's policies toward the elderly still are based on the circumstances of the white elderly. These policies do not respect or account for the variety of life styles and situations or the various cultural and ethnic groups of elderly citizens of this country (Hill, 1977). Ironically, in one respect the culturally diverse elderly have received "equality" in American society. They, and other elderly, are perceived to be equally worthless.

THE EFFECTIVE COUNSELOR

The pitfalls of stereotypic and ageist attitudes will seriously hamper, if not render completely ineffective, counselors working with the culturally diverse elderly.

The issue to be faced is not a difference of human needs, but a difference in the availability of social support for the non-privileged (Hispanic, Native-American, Black or Asian) living in triple jeopardy (Dancy, 1977). Effective counselors must first examine their attitudes toward the culturally diverse elderly for negative influences of stereotyping and generalization. Effective counseling starts with an examination of self. Effective counselors must also work within the reality of elderly Asian, Black, Native-American, or Hispanic clients. Sensitivity to the problems and issues faced by these groups is essential. A short review of some of the major problems and issues may be helpful toward this end.

FACTORS AFFECTING PHYSICAL WELL BEING

The Michigan Comprehensive Plan on Aging (1974) reported the results of a survey to determine what older citizens considered to be the major problems of aging. Elderly Black people listed six major difficulties: income, health, crime, nutrition, transportation, and housing. Though the survey was conducted in just one state, the problems listed by the participants accurately reflect problems culturally diverse elderly face nationally.

Income

Jackson (1977) states the greatest problem of Black elderly is level of income. Fifty percent of Black elderly are living below the poverty level (Dancy, 1977; Jackson, 1977) compared to only 23% of their white counterparts. There are proportionately four times as many Blacks in poverty among the 55 to 59 age group. For elderly Native-Americans the situation is also dismal. Regardless of the environmental setting (urban, rural, or reservation) in which elderly Native-Americans live, their standard of living is quite low. By whatever standard one chooses to employ, elderly Native-Americans constitute one of the most deprived segments of American society. The sole source of income for most elderly Native-Americans is welfare. Few benefit from social security, veterans benefits, pensions or other retirement funds because they do not know of their right to these funds (Essandoh, 1977). The true extent of poverty among elderly Native-Americans is not known. One indication, however, is an unemployment rate of 80% in most Native-American communities (Essandoh, 1977).

Sue (1977) contends that the incidence of poverty for elderly Asian-Americans is much higher than that of elderly Blacks or Latinos. In San Francisco's Chinatown, nearly 90% of elderly Asians are living well below poverty level (Solomon, 1979). Solomon notes many elderly residents have been found living on between 25 and 60 dollars a month.

The myth that Asian-Americans are a "model minority," having no problems and completely able to care for themselves, is partially responsible for their present plight. The notion that Chinatowns and "Little Tokyos" are pleasant insular communities is far from reality. Suzuki (1975) suggests they are overcrowded, impoverished, and segregated. Solomon (1979) notes that 90% of the elderly Asians in San Francisco's Chinatown are living in extreme poverty. Kim (1973) indicates many of the Asian-Americans elderly languish in poverty and poor health.

The perceptions of Hispanic-Americans often fall at the other extreme. These elderly receive little attention because the general population of Hispanic-Americans have so many serious problems (Moore, 1971). Solomon states that income leads the list of problems for HispanicAmerican elderly. Most Hispanic-American elderly have not been able to save for retirement, do not receive adequate pension and social security benefits, and do not receive public assistance. Accordingly, it is apparent why income in such a priority.

Because low income is such a pervasive problem, all other life needs are made proportionately worse. The culturally diverse elderly are denied access to an adequate food supply, adequate housing, and transportation due to poverty. Income is perhaps the major issue for the elderly culturally diverse person.

Health

Very frequently the elderly culturally diverse person lacks sufficient income to pay the deductibles and premiums required for Medicare. Furthermore, the culturally diverse elderly are often victims of poor services from professionals harboring agist and/or racist attitudes. Asian-Americans and Hispanic-Americans often do not receive services due to language barriers. The culturally diverse elderly in urban settings are often forced to seek medical assistance some distance from home since few physicians work in the central city (Dancy, 1977). Public transportation is poor in most cases and nonexistent in some. Insufficient income makes other sources of transportation unavailable. Hence many elderly culturally diverse citizens seldom see a physician. Solomon (1979) notes only 34% of the Asian-American and elderly studied have ever had a physical and dental examination.

Because of these conditions, health care for the culturally diverse elderly is frequently self-help and folk remedies. Blake (1977), Fujii (1976), and Solomon (1979) suggest the lack of transportation or means to pay for travel to medical centers, the high cost of prescription drugs, the fear of hospitals, and the distrust of white physicians as reasons for the persistence of beliefs in folk remedies and their continued use among the culturally diverse elderly. There are also cultural and historical reasons for the use of folk remedies among culturally diverse elderly. Blake (1977) notes in rural populations:

> The elderly are often involved with the natural elements and participate in nature in ways that are little understood in urban communities. To them, there are many natural processes which they understand very well, and guide their lives in meaningful ways. We see their attitudes toward health care as an extension of these attitudes. . . . Natural processes that the elderly consider normal. . . are understood in. . . urban. . . situations. The professional approach to health care alters or interupts what is natural (p. 56).

Drug misuse, another health issue for older persons, occurs when they unwittingly misuse medicines prescribed for specific ailments. Over-the-counter drugs are especially subject to misuse (Primm, 1977). Elderly culturally diverse people seldom know of dangerous interactions that can occur when drugs are mixed. More is not always better. Primm (1977) states that both pharmacists and physicians must take the time to educate the elderly in the appropriate use of medication. Unfortunately, drug misuse persists because suitable health care facilities and supportive agencies are often unavailable in the community (Dancy, 1977).

For elderly Native-Americans, preventive health care is nonexistent (Essandoh, 1977). They typically seek medical assistance on a crisis basis which is due primarily to difficulties in receiving transportation to health care facilities (Solomon, 1979). Bell, Kassachau, and Zellman (1976) note that many Native-Americans are often not identified because BIA (Bureau of Indian Affairs) criteria are inappropriate. The authors state that Native-Americans in Texas are sometimes assumed to be Chicano because of Spanish surnames. The Native-Americans who qualify for Indian Health Services (IHS) typically find these facilities not accessible to their communities and lacking dedicated professional staff (Essandoh, 1977).

Health is the critical issue for the Native-American elderly. The average life expectancy for Native-Americans is 46 years (Essandoh, 1977). This is substantially lower than the expectancy for Asians, Blacks, and Hispanics. Minimum age requirements for services to the elderly prevent most Native-Americans from ever receiving them. This problem is so serious that Montana altered its state plan for the elderly so that Native-Americans could be considered "old" at age 45 (Solomon, 1979).

As previously noted, the culturally diverse elderly share the common problem of lack of access to health care facilities. Asian and Hispanics also share problems associated with language. Bilingual services for the culturally diverse elderly are practically nonexistent.

Because the culturally diverse elderly are poor, the state hospital is the fate of those needing constant supervision due to physical conditions. This experience of dependency on state resources can strip away the old person's sense of self-worth and subsequently lead to deterioration in the person's condition (Dancy, 1977). Health remains a critical issue for the culturally diverse elderly.

Crime

Considerably more Black elderly (62%) than white (28%) are worried about crime in their communities (Dancy, 1977). Elderly culturally diverse people are so likely to be victims of criminal assault because they are frail and because they live in the city's oldest and most declined neighborhoods. Again, because of low income, the culturally diverse elderly are not able to move to areas with lower crime rates. The protection once afforded by the extended family disappeared in a large measure as did the extended family.

Crime, expecially in urban areas, is a problem for old people regardless of their ethnic or cultural group. At present, there seems to be no way to effectively stop it. Old people may take preventive measures by traveling in groups, or with an escort, by doing banking by mail, and by doing grocery shopping on different days to avoid establishing a routine. Regardless of the reasons for criminal assault on the elderly, living in fear for one's safety severely limits the quality of life of the culturally diverse elderly person.

Transportation

Most culturally diverse old people do not own their own means of transportation. The high cost of fuel and maintenance make car ownership unrealistic. The cost of using taxis and even buses also eats away at the limited and already low income of old people. This problem is further compounded by the fact that the culturally diverse elderly often live in poorer neighborhoods which lack efficient and safe mass transit (Dancy, 1977; Essandoh, 1977). Asian and Hispanic elderly often cannot read schedules and rates printed in English. Nor can they communicate with the English-speaking bus drivers. Reservation and rural elderly Native-Americans have no access to public transportation. They are almost totally dependent on relatives or neighbors who themselves have limited access to reliable means of transportation (Essandoh, 1977).

Nutrition

Problems associated with nutrition are of two general categories: getting enough to eat and eating proper foods. Getting
enough to eat is not as severe a problem as it might be because
elderly Asians, Blacks, Hispanics, and Native-Americans are
accustomed to subsistent living. Traditional diets are high in fat
and carbohydrates which tend to "fill up" the person. Nonethe-
less, inadequate diets and limited information about proper eating habits are two major problems for the culturally diverse
elderly.

Diet modification is a special issue for the elderly Black person.
Elderly Black people are affected in great numbers by hypertension. A major part of the treatment plan is reduction in caloric
intake, decreased consumption of polysaturated fats, and
lowered sodium intake (Lewis, 1977). For most elderly Blacks,
however, the treatment plan itself causes cultural conflict. Compliance with dietary modification is difficult sometimes because
elderly Blacks are reluctant to give up traditional foodstuffs, but
more often because they cannot afford to buy other types of
food. The use of traditional foods such as hot sauce, barbeque
sauce, bacon drippings, ham, hot links, fried chicken, and fried
fish has to be closely monitored and sometimes omitted
altogether.

One of the serious inadequacies of present programs is that
nutritionists are generally unfamiliar with the eating habits and
dietary preferences of the culturally diverse elderly. Elderly Native-Americans, for example, depend almost totally on government food commodities. These foodstuffs are often lacking in
necessary vitamins and have been known to be injurious to the
health of elderly Native-Americans (Essandoh, 1977). Edlerly
Native-Americans' traditional diet, according to Essandoh, consisted of fresh fish, ham, meat, fruits, and vegetables. The traditional diet is well beyond the means of the majority of
Native-American elderly.

Solomon (1979) reports that federally funded nutrition programs
fail to include special dietary preferences of older Asian-Americans. Basic foodstuffs such as rice and tea are often not included on menus.

Inadequate nutrition affects many of the culturally diverse
elderly. This problem is compounded by low income. The in-

titial cost of foodstamps makes even their acquisition too expensive.

Housing

The percentage of Black elderly people in homes for the aged is much less than the percentage of white elderly. This should not be necessarily perceived as a strength when it is noted that elderly Blacks tend to live alone in substandard housing. Also, older Black people pay a much higher portion of their income compared to white elderly— up to 40%—for inferior housing (Hill, 1977).

In addition, the small proportion of elderly Black in residences for the elderly is not solely a matter of choice. This lack of access is due to both low income and racial discrimination (Dancy, 1977; Jackson, 1977). Ironically, notes Jackson, the church-related homes are particularly guilty of refusing services to their Black members.

Low-cost housing projects for Native-American elderly have consistently failed because elderly Native-Americans have incomes which are so low that they are unable to pay monthly rent and utilities. In addition, little (and more often no consideration) is given to the desires of elderly Native-Americans regarding style, location, or building construction. Cultural values related to housing are ignored (Essandoh, 1977).

The notion of the extended family is seen as a strength of culturally diverse life style. Filial piety is seen as one of the most important virtues in the Asian value system (Chang, 1977; Sue, 1977). The kinship family system is supposed to support all its members. The multigeneration extended family is well known. The Hispanic person is oriented toward receiving help from the family (Trinidad, 1977). However, as Jackson (1977) notes, this "strength" is used to deny services when services actually are needed. It is in error to automatically assume that older culturally diverse people are being loved, honored, respected, and "taken care of" by their families. While some families are able to care for their elderly, most cannot. Older culturally diverse people are entitled to their share of social security benefits which they contributed to during their working years. The mythology surrounding the culturally diverse extended family often interferes with this.

In this discussion of the factors affecting the physical well-being of the culturally diverse elderly, the importance of adequate income was underscored. Adequate income is the key to the quality of life for culturally diverse old people. It is the key because adequate income equals adequate housing, transportation, health care, and nutrition.

While adequate income will solve most problems related to basic life needs, it does not solve high level needs (as described by Maslow, 1968). Income cannot guarantee self-esteem, mental health, or social well-being. In the following section, some of the pertinent issues relative to the mental health and social well-being of the culturally diverse elderly are discussed.

FACTORS INFLUENCING MENTAL HEALTH AND SOCIAL WELL-BEING

Approaches to the study of mental health of culturally diverse elderly vary greatly. Two basic topics seem to be the focus of most studies, however. These topics are self-esteem and the effects of internal and external stressors on social and psychological behavior (Henry, 1977). The key to mental health among culturally diverse elderly seems to be a sense of belonging or a feeling of "wellness;" optimism or faith; and continued responsible activity.

The normal decreased social interaction and natural withdrawal (by society and the older person) posited by Disengagement Theory (Cumming & Henry, 1961) is not characteristic of successful aging in culturally diverse people. Disengagement is imposed. It is not a developmental process as the theory would suggest, and it does not produce psychological well-being. Psychological well-being does seem to be correlated with meaningful activity within the family and community. Activity theory which suggests older people have similar psychosocial needs vis-a-vis middle-aged people (Brine, 1979) seems to more accurately describe successful aging for culturally diverse elderly. The two traditional sources of meaningful activity for culturally diverse elderly have been the extended family and the church.

The Extended Family

Perhaps the most noted characteristic of ethnic community social structure is the extended family. The extended family pattern provides ethnic communities with a balanced division of tasks and workers. It also provides roles for individuals of all ages. All members of the family have a function to perform and they know that when they reach old age they will still have a function to perform (Maldonado, 1975). The extended family promotes a sense of group identity and interdependence. It also maintains respect for the aged.

Older people are perceived as valued family members, not just appendages. Older people are appreciated for their experience and expecially for the role they play in child rearing. The elderly are the link with the past and the bearers of tradition. One of their key functions is the transmission of culture to the young.

Extended families have always functioned for the mutual benefit of family members. Because culturally diverse people have had limited access to supportive social services, the elderly have relied on the supportive resources of their families. Dancy (1977) and Henry (1977) suggest that the kind of support the elderly want most from their families is emotional rather than strictly financial. Unfortunately, most culturally diverse people do not live in large extended families. Jackson (1976) notes that the majority of Black families with elderly heads (65 or older) contained only two persons in 1970. Maldonado (1975) suggests the Hispanic extended family seems to be gradually becoming a nuclear family. Chang (1977) indicated that the value of filial piety has dissipated within the younger Asian-American community, and that they no longer feel compelled to support their elders. Hsu (1971) and Kalish and Moriwaki (1973) report similar findings in Asian-American communities. Solomon (1979) also notes the breakdown of the extended family relationship among Native-Americans.

The principle reasons for this shift in family structure seem to be economic and social. Maldonado suggests that as Hispanics participate more in the urbanized industrial life style of American society, these are greater social and economic pressures to accept and adopt a different family structure. Hsu notes the basic root differentiating American and Chinese value systems is the individualistic orientation of the former and the interdependent family orientation of the latter. This is also the basic difference between African (Black) and American value systems. Kalish and Moriwaki indicate that this value conflict is a deep source of concern for elderly Asian-Americans. Almost all culturally diverse elderly face death in a cultural milieu different than they had known or imagined. The care and respect they had expected from family and community are often absent. The influence of American values and social structure has forced many younger culturally diverse people to move against traditional values.

The result of this disruption of social structure ranges from disappointment, to loneliness, and to mental illness on the part of culturally diverse elderly. Solomon indicates the physchological well-being of Hispanic elderly stems from a system composed of the family, traditional healers, and the church. When this system fails to offer psychological support, alcoholism and other mental disturbances occur. Sue (1977) suggests the true magnitude of the impact of shifting social structure is hard to gage since the prevalence of mental illness is consistently underestimated in Asian-American populations. Fujii (1976) cites the suicide rate for Asian-American elderly is three times the national average. Alcoholism and drug abuse are documented (Graves, 1971; Pascarelli, 1974) among both Native-American and Black elders. Loss of emotional support from extended family relationships is perhaps a contributing factor.

These findings suggest that all culturally diverse elderly are not as psychologically adjusted as counselors may have believed. The findings also suggest that successful aging for culturally diverse elderly has been made more difficult due to loss of meaningful activity, status in the family, and self-esteem. Perhaps the most painful realization for the elderly is that they had no control over the events which led to their present situation. Beard (1977) and Peterson (1977) note that a sense of independence and self-determination is crucial for the culturally diverse elderly to experience personal efficacy.

Discussion still continues regarding whether the rise of the nuclear family has in fact destroyed the extended family. The important issue is not whether the multigeneration extended family actually still exists physically. The issue is whether culturally diverse elderly still have the feeling of family—the feeling of active participation in an on-going tradition in which they have a significant role. These findings indicate that counselors cannot automatically assume that clients have these feelings.

The Church

The second major source of psychological well-being and meaningful activity for culturally diverse elderly is the church. It has been found that members of church affiliated groups tend to have higher psychological well-being than non-church affiliated groups (Henry, 1977). Spirituality is a source of great psychological strength for culturally diverse elderly. Cutler (1976) found that membership in church affiliated groups alone was a significant predictor of life satisfaction and happiness in elderly people. Historically, religion and the institution of the church have played a vital role in the survival and advancement of culturally diverse people. The church is usually the one cultural institution which remains relatively free from white authority. Churches have provided a place where culturally diverse elderly can feel important.

The religious experience of the culturally diverse elderly, especially those from low-income groups, helps them to value life (Dancy, 1977). They do not fear death (in a religious sense) because of the hope for life after death. Through the church, culturally diverse elderly are reminded that they possess dignity and that such dignity will endure (Dancy, 1977). The church is also a place where the elderly may exercise leadership, engage in problem-solving activities, and experience feelings of mastery and achievement. Presently, the church as a cultural institution seems relatively intact. While younger members of ethnic communities may not conserve traditional religious beliefs, the elderly remain steadfast. Hence, the church remains a power source of affirmation for culturally diverse elderly.

RECOMMENDATIONS FOR COUNSELORS

The Counselor as Advocate

Factors which impinge upon the quality of culturally diverse elderly are of such magnitude that counselors must seriously consider roles as advocates. Due to their decreased capacity for stress, elders occasionally need advocates (Macione, 1979).

As advocates, counselors use all means at their disposal to represent the client's best interests (Gunnings & Simpkins, 1972). Counselors could help most in this role by influencing public attitude toward culturally diverse elderly in such a manner that at least the four following steps are completed:

1. Culturally diverse elderly must have a guaranteed annual income above the poverty level. Presently, the Supplemental Security Income Program of 1974 has two serious limitations. First, the income floor that was established was not supplemented to the extent that it should have been by the states. This, combined with rising inflation, has made the original income floor much too low. Secondly, the program has always been clouded with confusion over the issues of implementation and coverage. Consequently, there are approximately half a million Black persons who are entitled to benefits under this Supplemental Security Income Program that still are unaware of their eligibility. Many Hispanics do not seek these benefits because they cannot prove legal residence. Many elderly Asian-Americans are not aware of their eligibility (Solomon, 1979).

2. Comprehensive geriatric centers in ethnic communities must be developed. Presently many old culturally diverse people are not in homes for the aged. They live either in the inner cities of in rural areas and they generally live both alone and in substandard housing. Title VI under the Civil Rights Act should be enforced with reference to the institutional facilities for culturally diverse aged (Jackson, 1977).

3. The dignity, prestige, and status of older culturally diverse people must be preserved. The main issue is to get culturally diverse elderly involved in programs for themselves. Most social policies toward the elderly are based primarily on circumstances and situations of white elderly and not appropriate to the needs of culturally diverse elderly in this country (Hill, 1977). Also as Lindsay (1977) notes, older people need to build on the strengths which many of them have. Fields (1977) states that it should be the obligation of agencies to recruit and train Black elderly at all levels of participation. Seldom do funding agencies make a concerted effort to involve

Black elderly groups. Since traditional white American announcement methods, e.g., the Federal Register, do not reach the Black community, funding agencies should announce through traditional Black groups and organizations, e.g., Black churches and Black newspapers (Fields, 1977). Fields' statements hold true for not only Black elders but for culturally diverse elderly in general.

4. The number of young Asian, Black, Hispanic, and NativeAmerican people in the area of gerontology must be increased. While Fields argues neither for short-term nor long-term training, he does feel that there should be long-term training in order to increase the number of Black, Asian, Hispanic, and Native-American counselors and health professionals in the field. His major concern was that training be academically based. Fields also states that the curriculum should include how policies are formed; what policies exist; how they affect the lives of elderly non-whites; who influences policy; and specifics of particular groups.

The Counselor as Therapist: Counseling Style

Programs in gerontological counseling typically utilize both remedial and preventive components to help older persons contend with stress in the environment. This form of counseling uses structured techniques that allow clients to explore options and to discuss problems associated with growing old (O'Brien, Johnson, and Miller, 1979).

This style of counseling seeks to facilitate behavior change through reflecting feelings and through focusing on positive aspects of self. Structured introspection techniques are the basic methods through which this goal is accomplished.

The basic inappropriateness of a model like this is that it ignores the fact that elderly culturally diverse people distrust this style of interaction. Furthermore, it does not actively assist the culturally diverse elderly client to maintain or regain dignity, prestige, and/or status within the person's own cultural milieu. The model does not allow the elderly to use their strengths. It is not developmental. It does little to actively promote self-determination. Smith (1977) suggests more nontraditional styles are more appropriate for culturally diverse clients. Gunnings (1971) clearly indicates action-oriented approaches are more effective with non-white clients. Clients have more favorable responses to counseling when they see counselors are able to give direct service in resolving problems (Riker, 1979).

Communication

Clear communication between counselor and client is essential to counseling. Many culturally diverse elderly, however, are not able to either read or speak English. Unless the counselor is bilingual, counseling cannot begin. If bilingual counselors are not available, the English speaking counselor may contact a family member or community resource person who is billingual to assist in the counseling process.

Even when the counselor and client speak the same language, some modifications may need to be made in the counselor's communication style. Macione (1979) lists several suggestions for enhancing the effectiveness of communication with elderly clients:

1. When clients have impaired hearing, speak clearly and directly into their good ear.
2. Face clients directly when speaking.
3. Do not cover your mouth when speaking thus allowing clients to lip read.
4. Do not smoke or chew gum when speaking to clients who have hearing impairments.
5. Keep counseling areas free from extraneous noise.
6. Speak slowly using simple phrases, and provide ample time for replies to questions.
7. When persons are completely deaf, use written communication, writing clearly in large letters (p.56).

Counseling Setting

Transportation, as previously noted, is a problem for the culturally diverse elderly. Many potential clients may not be able to get to the counselor's office. Others who have transportation options may not be willing to come to the counselor's office. Accordingly, the counselor must be prepared to go to the client. Counseling may take place in rehabilitation settings, churches, and/or the elderly person's home. Home visits provide the counselor with information regarding the culturally diverse person's life style, values, and family resources. While all culturally diverse elderly persons will not desire or need home visits, the counselor's willingness to make the visit will be interpreted as a sign of deference. The counselor will be held in higher esteem.

Macione (1979) offers the following suggestions which may be helpful in modifying counselors' offices for elderly clients:

1. Avoid highly polished floors which may be slippery. Avoid scatter rugs which are not tacked down.

2. Have large readable clocks and calendars in the office to help provide orientation.

3. Have an office setting with a minimum of stairs.

4. Provide a firm chair with a straight back for clients. Soft, deep chairs are not as comfortable for clients with back pain. Deepseated chairs are difficult for many older clients to get in and out of because of decreased muscular strength.

5. Allow clients with rheumatoid disease freedom to move about frequently. Sitting in one position for long periods may be uncomfortable if not painful.

6. Keep room temperatures that are well within the comfort zone for warmth. Elderly people are more prone to feel cold due to decreased fat beneath the skin or reduced circulation (p.55).

Referrals

Macione (1979) suggests that counselors learn names and specializations of local physicians; especially those who are accommodating to elderly culturally diverse people. Generally, counselors need to be familiar with support services available for the elderly in their communities. Counselors need to be aware of the availability of services such as meals-on-wheels, companionship services, foster care, volunteer visitors, public health nurses, hot-lines, and homemaker and health aid services. Counselors should also become familiar with the basic eligibility requirements for social security and public assistance benefits. Ideally, counselors should establish good rapport with intake workers at special social service and specialized care agencies which serve their clients. In this way counselors will be able to keep abreast of policy changes affecting their clients.

Follow-up is an essential part of referral. Counselors who work with culturally diverse elderly should check to make sure their clients arrive at appropriate agencies and receive appropriate services. Counselors should not tolerate their clients receiving inferior or substandard services due to their age, color, or ethnic heritage.

COUNSELOR BURN-OUT

Counselor burn-out occurs when counselors internalize responsibility for resolution of their clients' problems. White counselors working with culturally diverse elderly may be susceptible to burn-out for several reasons. First, culturally diverse elderly generally have multiple chronic problems. Solving any of the problems may be difficult and solving all of them impossible. Counselors will be overwhelmed if they attempt to do the impossible. Second, counselors may try to resolve their guilt feelings related to racist and/or agist attitudes through their hard work. Third, some counselors may push themselves too hard to try to "make ammends" to culturally diverse elderly persons for all the years of race and age inequity, prejudice, and discrimination they have experienced.

Fourth, counselors may encourage dependency among their clients because it both fits their stereotype of elderly people and because it enhances their own egos. Finally, counselors may not be able to negotiate feelings related to expectations of their clients' deaths. Not all counselors are effective in the presence of death and dying, yet they frequently exhaust their personal resources in trying to deal with this issue.

SUMMARY

All counselors will not be able to work effectively with culturally diverse elderly because of language, cultural, personal, or educational variables. This need not necessarily be interpreted as personal inadequacy. Counselors who do not feel they are working effectively have other alternatives to burn-out, i.e., referral, co-counseling, or peer counseling.

REFERENCES

Beard, V. Health status of a successful black aged population related to life satisfaction and self concept. In W. Watson, et al. (Eds.), *Health and the black aged*. Washington, D.C.: The National Center on Black Aged, Inc., 1977.

Bell, D.; Kassachau, P.; & Zellman, G. *Delivering services to elderly members of minority groups: A critical review of the literature*. Santa Monica, California: Rand Corporation, 1976.

Blake, H. "Doctor can't do me no good:" Social concomitants of health care attitudes and practices among elderly black in isolated rural populations. In W. Watson, et al., (Eds.), *Health and the black aged*. Washington, D.C.: The National Center on Black Aged, Inc., 1977.

Brine, J. Psycho-social aspects of aging: An overview. In M. Ganikos & K. Grady (Eds.), *Counseling the aged: A training syllabus for educators*. Washington, D.C.: APGA, 1979.

Chang, P. Working with the elderly Asian. In N. Newsome (Ed.), *Insights on the minority elderly*. Washington, D.C.: The National Center on Black Aged, Inc., 1977.

Cumming, E., & Henry, W. *Growing old: The process of disengagement*. New York: Basic Books, 1961.

Cutler, S.J. Membership in different types of voluntary associations and psychological well-being. *Gerontologist*, 1976, *16*, 335-339.

Dancy, J. *The black elderly, a guide for practitioners*. Ann Arbor, Michigan: The Institute of Gerontology, The University of Michigan - Wayne State University, 1977.

Essandoh, R. Major concerns of the elderly native American In B. Newsome (Ed.), *Insights on the minority elderly*. Washington, D.C.: The National Center on Black Aged, Inc., 1977.

Fields, C. The black elderly: A collection of concepts and ideas. In B. Newsome (Ed.), *Insights on the minority elderly*. Washington, D.C.: The National Center on Black Aged, Inc., 1977.

Fujii, S. Older Asian-Americans. *Civil Rights Digest,* 1976, *9*, 22-29.

Graves, T.G. Drinking and drunkenness among urban Indians. In J.O. Waddell & O.M. Watson (Eds.), *The American Indian in urban society*. Boston: Little, Brown, 1971.

Gunnings, T.S. Preparing the new counselor. *Counseling Psychologist*, 1971, *2*, 101-102.

Gunnings, T.S., & Simpkins, G. A systematic approach to counseling disadvantaged youth. *Journal of Non-white Concerns in Personnel and Guidance*, 1972, *I*, 4-8.

Henry, M. Perceived health status of the black elderly in an urban area: Findings of a survey research project. In W. Watson, et al., (Eds.), *Health and the black aged*. Washington, D.C.: The National Center on Black Aged, Inc., 1977.

Hill, R. A conversation among noted black gerontologists. In B. Newsome (Ed.), *Insights on the minority elderly*. Washington, D.C.: The National Center for Black Aged, Inc., 1977.

Hsu, F.L. *Psychological anthropology: Approaches to culture and personality*. Homewood, Illinois: Dorsey Press, 1971.

Jackson, H. A conversation among noted black gerontologists. In B. Newsome (Ed.), *Insights on the minority elderly*. Washington, D.C.: The National Center on Black Aged, Inc., 1977.

Jackson, J.J. The black aging: A demographic overview. In R.S. Kalish (Ed.), *The later years: Social applications of gerontology*. Monterey, California: Brooks/Cole Publishing Co., 1977.

Kalish, R., & Moriwaki, S. The world of the elderly Asian American. *Journal of Social Issues*, 1973, *29*, 187-209.

Kim, B.L. Asian-Americans: No model minority. *Social Work*, 1973, *18*, 43-57.

Lewis, J. A study of hypertension compliance in a group of elderly third world patients. In W. Watson, et al., (Eds.), *Health and the black aged*. Washington, D.C.: The National Center on Black Aged, Inc., 1977.

Lindsay, I. A conversation among noted black gerontologists. In B. Newsome (Ed.), *Insights on the minority elderly*. Washington, D.C.: The National Center of Black Aged, Inc., 1977.

Macione, A. Physiological changes and common health problems of aging. In M. Ganikos & K. Grady (Eds.), *Counseling the aged: A training syllabus for educators*. APGA, 1979.

Maldonado, D. The Chicano aged. *Social Work*, 1975, *20(2)*, 213-216.

Maslow, A. *Toward a psychology of being*. New York: Nostrand, 1968.

Moore, T.W. Mexican-Americans. *Gerontologist*, 1971, *11*, 30-35.

O'Brien, C.; Johnson, J.; & Miller, B. Counseling the aging: Some practical considerations. *Personnel and Guidance Journal*, 1979, *56(6)*, 288-291.

Pascarelli, E.F. Drug dependence: An age-old problem compounded by old age. *Geriatrics*, 1974, *29(12)*, 109-115.

Peterson, J. The social psychology of black aging: The effects of self-esteem and perceived control on the adjustments of older black adults. In W. Watson, et al., (Eds.), *Health and the black aged*. Washington, D.C.: The National Center on Black Aged, Inc., 1977.

Primm, B. Poverty, folk remedies and drug misuse among the black elderly. In W. Watson, et al. (Eds.), *Health and the black aged*. Washington, D.C.: The National Center on Black Aged, Inc., 1977.

Riker, H. Potential crises situation for older persons: Preretirement, retirement, leisure, relocation, housing. In M. Ganikos (Eds.), *Counseling the aged: A training syllabus for educators*. Washington, D.C.: APGA, 1979.

Rosenfelt, R.H. The elderly mystique. In McNeil (Ed.), *Readings in human socialization*. Belmont, California: Brooks/Cole Publishing Company, 1971.

Smith, E.J. Counseling black individuals: Some stereotypes. *Personnel and Guidance Journal*, 1977, *55,* 390-396.

Solomon, C. Elderly non-whites: Unique situations and concerns. In M. Ganikos & K. Grady (Eds.), *Counseling the aged: A training syllabus for educators*. Washington, D.C.: APGA, 1979.

Sue, S. Psychological theory and implications for Asian-Americans. *Personnel and Guidance Journal*, 1977, *55*, 381-384.

Suzuki, P.T. *Minority group aged in America: A comprehensive bibliography of recent publications on Black, Mexican-Americans, Chinese, and Japanese.* Monticello, Illinois: Council of Planning Librarians, 1975.

Trinidad, L. The Spanish-speaking elderly. In B. Newsome (Ed.), *Insights on the minority elderly*. Washington, D.C.: The National Center on Black Aging, Inc., 1977.

Counseling for the Growing Years

Pastoral Counseling

William M. Clements

ABSTRACT

Pastoral counseling is first defined as an activity for both the specialist practitioner and the parish minister. Elements which distinguish pastoral counseling from psychiatry, psychology, and social work are presented along with elements which are held in common among all the pcychotherapeutic professions. Limitations to the parish-based minister as pastoral counselor are discussed: limited education in counseling; time constraint; and role expectations. Strengths of the minister are also discussed: trust; continuity in relationships; accessability to the public; and low cost of services for the consumer.

For work with aging persons, the pastoral counselor seeks growth as a major goal of the activity. This growthful process is facilitated by a focus on the parishoner's personal and environmental assets. The losses of aging are noted but not dwelled upon. The emphasis is on what can be accomplished and is worthy of effort with the time and energy which are available. The pastoral counselor remains aware of the central core of the human spirit throughout the counseling process and sees this spirit as the most significant asset which can be experienced by the counselor and the parishoner.

INTRODUCTION

Pastoral counseling has been defined in a variety of ways over the centuries by church bodies, theologians, and practitioners. For the broadest definition, an understanding of the meaning of *ordination* provides the key to interpret the place and significance of counseling within the pastoral office. In some ordination services, for example, the ordinand is charged with the responsibility to teach, preach, administer the sacraments, heal, counsel, and seek out the needy among those entrusted to the care of the church. Within this rubric, pastoral counseling is best understood as one of several interrelated functions of ministry which are engaged in during the course of pastoral activities.

What Is Pastoral Counseling?

In other, perhaps more specific, definitions the content of the counseling session would determine whether or not pastoral counseling took place. Thus, persons who, in the office of the counselor, vocalize profound concerns or raise issues which surround ultimate meanings to which the faith speaks, would have a different content in their sessions, presumably, than persons seeking relief from an embarrassing tic, such as an eyeblink that might be distracting and interfere in interpersonal communication, yet does not directly call into question the meaning of existence. In the first example the significance and directivity of human existence might be an explicit part of the conversation, while in the latter example, the counselor's only concern might be the extinguishing of objectionable behavior, whose meaning is extraneous to the discrete goal of modifying behavior in a particular direction.

Specialist practitioners of pastoral counseling in the early days of the modern movement often reported that much of what went on in the psychotherapeutic encounter was preparation for a mature spiritual quest, which took place once the influence of neurotic distortions had been limited through therapy. First there was therapy which cleared the way, then there was a spiritual pursuit with the pilgrim freed from the necessity of repetitive or false starts and more open to the newness of emerging experience.

Cutting across virtually all these definitions would be the notion that the provision of pastoral counseling for persons in need is at least an act of *diakonia*, the implementation of the faith in loving service to humanity, regardless of whether or not the service was directly interpreted in theological language. Such acts of *diakonia* are engaged in without regard to the faith stance of those persons seeking the service, though for persons who have meaningfully participated in the religious community the encounter might have powerful symbolic meanings, as well.

> Pastoral relationships are rich in symbolic meaning. Our cultural emphasis on analytic reason fails to grasp the power of metaphor and symbolic action in human life. Technological reason develops procedures, not purposes. Pragmatic reason formulates explanations; it does not envision sacred meaning. In this situation the Christian tradition helpfully reminds us that the actions of pastors, though not extraordinary, have symbolic meaning. A telephone call that inquires into how one is doing since coming home from the hospital can be a reminder to the sick of God's presence, even though the pastor does not talk about God. Pastors' actions and manners tend to speak at a level of communication not always articulated in words (Underwood, 1979, p.9).

The late theologian Daniel Day Williams developed the idea of "linkage" as a means of understanding the interrelationships found in ordinary human experience. With this insight the polarities of expression such as body-soul, secular-religious, event-symbol, are linked to each other in human experiences so that the neat categorizations found in our language are, at best, simplifications of a much more complex reality.

> What has to be recognized is the significance of the fact that every part of being and experience is linked actually or potentially with every other part. There is no happening in the history of the body or mind which may not involve the whole person at the spiritual center of existence (Williams, 1961, p. 27).

This sort of conceptualization has tended to blur previous distinctions between the religious and the profane as operative categories, since human experience is a continuous stream of consciousness taking place in a responsible searching self in which:

> There is no way of knowing without living through the problem with the person just what it means to him and to his relationship with God. The very process of working the problem through may create new connections. And the process of working it through may transform its meaning (Williams, 1961, p. 28).

Modern pastoral counseling is, therefore, at a point in its self-understanding and development where human wholeness and human experience are not divided between secular and religious categories, with the pastoral counselor assuming responsibility for the latter and referring the former. This position contradicts the common understanding of personal existence. Pastoral counseling still concerns itself with religious symbols, values and meaning. However, it is not restricted to this "stained glass ghetto."

The spiritual dimension of existence is not thought of as if it existed in an air-tight compartment sealed off from the remainder of personal experience. The human spirit interpenetrates all of personal existence and is, in turn, interpenetrated by the other facets, or dimensions, of existence. What seems to be a trivial event, might, in fact, link up with other events in such a way that the individual's ultimate destiny in life is affected. Pastoral counseling is concerned with the personal meanings and experiences attached to these points of linkage and to the explication of how they relate the individual to transcendant reality.

Professional Similarities

Large areas of overlap exist between professions such as psychiatry, pastoral counseling, psychology, and clinical social work, in terms of what transpires during a therapy session. Perhaps as an experiment we could record a large number of psychotherapeutic sessions conducted by equivalently trained private practitioners from each of the above groups. We might envision a very sophisticated experiment in which patients would all be randomly assigned to therapists after being matched for presenting problems, age, sex, socio-economic, and ethnic factors.

Then we might play back all of the recordings for a panel of judges, asking them only two basic questions: (a) What is the professional identity of each therapist? and (b) What are the manifest differences between the professional groups which you have chosen based on the contents of the recorded sessions? Perhaps the panel of judges would conclude: (a) the task was impossible; (b) the task was possible, but unfortunately meaningless; or (c) the task was inconclusive since greater differences were found to exist within groups than between groups, etc.

Personally I think the experimental task would be difficult, if not impossible, since individual variables related to the personality of the therapist are so important (in distinction from professional variables), and the professions overlap in so many areas. If this conclusion is correct, then perhaps those distinctions associated with each professional group (testing psychology, medicine-psychiatry, religion-pastoral counseling, environment-social work) are not significant enough to obscure the similarities between groups.

In other words, distinctions between groups are not as important as is often assumed, and no professional group is exclusively concerned with its own distinctives to the exclusions of those areas of common expertise shared with other professional groups. While psychologists don't prescribe medicine, psychiatrists don't absolve people from sin, and pastoral counselors don't construct sophisticated psychological tests, each group does deal with family and interpersonal relationships, persons in distress and intrapsychic realities.

DISTINCTIVE ASPECTS OF PASTORAL COUNSELING

While pastoral counseling is similar in many respects to other professions practicing psychotherapy, it does have certain distinctive aspects—some quite obvious, others more subtle. An awareness of these distinguishing characteristics will be a means of locating pastoral counseling among the helping professions in psychotherapy.

Pastoral counseling is a sub-specialty of the ordained ministry. It has a long and distinguished tradition within the evolution of the pastoral ministry. Gregory the Great wrote a most influential treatise entitled *Pastoral care* in 590 A.D., on the occasion of his becoming Bishop of Rome. Each succeeding generation has added to and expanded the body of literature dealing with the cure of souls within the traditions of Christian theology and practice. Tertullian, Cyprian, John Chrysostom, Bernard of Clairvaux, Francis of Assisi, Luther, Calvin, Ignatius, Bunyan, Knox, Weslay, and William James have all made their contributions to the modern movement, as have secular thinkers such as Rogers, Frankl, Freud, Jung, and others. Contemporary pastoral counseling draws upon these rich traditions, stretching back in time almost 2,000 years, while at the same time appropriating the insights of modern theorists and practitioners.

Pastoral counseling has traditionally been concerned about the whole person more than it has about any one attribute or characteristic of personhood. The "healing, sustaining, guiding and reconciling of troubled persons whose troubles arise in the context of ultimate meanings and concerns," has been the focal point of pastoral counseling throughout history (Clebsch & Jaekle, 1964, p.4). At its best, pastoral counseling concerns itself with the intersection between the spiritual, emotional, and rational dimensions of human existence as expressed in thought, affect, behavior, and belief in the counseling session. Frequently, this involves adjustment, change or support within these four areas to the extent that they are distorted or dysfunctional for the social networks within which an individual chooses to exist and seek meaning.

Ideally, all pastoral counselors are trained in theology, psychotherapy, and personality theory, having received clinical training and supervision adequate for the level at which they function. The American Association of Pastoral Counselors (AAPC), for example, has approximately 1,500 members, from over 60 different denominations, distributed into the three membership categories of Member, Fellow, and Diplomate.

Persons who are Members are most often parish-based ministers who function as pastoral counselors under the direct supervision of a Fellow or Diplomate. Fellows are frequently specialist practitioners of pastoral counseling whose ministry is largely one of psychotherapy. Diplomates, on the other hand, are not only practitioners, but are also highly skilled in the supervisory processes involved in the teaching of pastoral counseling. Together, the association intends for the membership to function collegially so that individuals do not engage in pastoral counseling in isolation from peer review or consultation. With over 270,000 ordained clergy in the United States, the members of the AAPC form an elite of interested and adequately trained pastoral counselors.

What about the remaining 268,500 clergy who are not affiliated with this professional association? Some, of course, would be highly trained and certified as psychologists, psychiatrists, or social workers. Persons so certified would not normally be found in the local parish setting as the pastor of a congregation. In pratical terms this means that traditions which utilize an educated clergy for religious leadership have pastors who are college graduates, most often educated in the liberal arts, who then attend a seminary for professional training. At the seminary these persons are exposed to a wide variety of theoretical and practical subjects, such as biblical studies, historical studies, doctrinal development, contemporary theology, and a variety or practical studies such as liturgics, counseling, administration and homelitics. Education after college lasts between 3-5 years and culminates in the M.Div. (Master of Divinity) degree. Following several years of postgraduate practical experience in a parish or other applied setting, the minister is then elegible for 1-2 more years of academic work leading to the degree of D.Min. (Doctor of Ministry).

LIMITATIONS OF THE MINISTER
AS PASTORAL COUNSELORS

Education

Most pastors educated since 1960 have successfully completed between 3 and 15 hours of academic course work in pastoral care and counseling. This course work normally includes exposure to major theories of emotional and spiritual development across the entire life span from infancy to old age and death. Aging and the elderly are one of the focal points for discussions as are readings about developmental crises encountered in the pastor's work with persons from various ages.

Like other "front-line" workers, such as family physicians and school teachers, the pastor's major preparation is for work and leadership with normal people who are experiencing the expected crises of living (marriage, birth, adolescence, moving into a new community, sickness, retirement, divorce, and losing a job). Preparation does not normally include sufficient background for extended individual, marriage, or group psychotherapy, but does provide solid grounding in the theory and practice of individual counseling for growth and in small group supportive and growth-enhancing opportunities for persons in the context of the religious fellowship. Thus, the average pastor who counsels is well versed in normalcy and the expected life crises which punctuate human development.

Time

The pastor's effectiveness is, or course, reduced by a limited amount of time available to be spent with any one person in counseling activities. The role of pastor includes leadership in educational activities, worship, fund raising, public speaking, calling on new people in the community, visiting sick people, and those who are confined to their homes because of various disabilities, in addition to weddings, funerals, and all of the informal counseling time spent in conjunction with each of these responsibilities. The effective minister has skill in the areas of short-term and referral counseling activites which demand less of an ongoing time committment than that which is involved in long-term psychotherapy.

Role

There are certain values which religious institutions have attempted to maintain and support through pronouncements and pastoral acts. Sometimes guilt-ridden people tend to project a condemnatory image on the person of the pastor because of past experiences with other religious leaders or their fear of judgment which they feel might be warranted by behavior which does not measure up to the ideals espoused by their religious group. Because a pastor knows one's parishoners in a variety of ways—as teacher or friend, for example—some persons experience a certain embarrassment which prevents their seeking pastoral counseling from one whom they encounter in numerous non-counseling situations. Of course, the pastor who is secure and communicates acceptance and warm caring in interpersonal relationships can help to minimize the limitations which accrue from being a representative of a highly developed system of ethics which is never fully actualized in the lives of human beings.

STRENGTHS OF THE MINISTER

Trust

The minister, priest, or rabbi is one of the most trusted professionals in our society. All across the country the religious counselor has access to persons because of this trust which has frequently been built up over the course of a lifetime of interactions between people in happy as well as sad occasions. This element of trust enables pastoral initiative to be exercised in times of crisis without a specific "cry for help" being a necessary prerequisite for contact. Millions of pastoral visits have taken place when elderly persons are hospitalized or placed in an extended care facility. A very large percentage of these visits take place without an overt request for contact. When the pastor learns of the crisis a visit is made. At that point, in the home or hospital, a joint determination is made in respect to the suitability of future supportive or counseling contact between the individual or family constellation. Along with the physician, the pastor knows and interacts with people at their best and at their worst. Trust enables and facilitates depth communication to emerge.

Contintuity

Population surveys indicate that a surprisingly high percentage of persons who identify themselves as religious attended worship services in the immediate past. As a result of the occasions of worship and social activities found in a typical parish, persons and families have a continuous relationship with their religious leaders. Such continuity enables much preliminary "get acquainted" talk to be sidestepped because the persons seeking contact are likely to already be known by their pastor through the parish softball team, attendance at religious education classes, or participation in church governance meetings. Contact is not limited just to those moments of crisis either, such as sickness, birth, marriage, and death, but extends to the whole range of life experiences found in the typical community of faith.

Accessability

The average religious leader is accessible to parishoners and the public at large. Persons in serious distress don't speculate whether their pastor is accessible, or how long they might have to wait for an appointment. The assumption is that a telephone call or a knock on the door is all that is needed. More often than not, this accessability is simply taken for granted and utilized (Clineball, 1966, pp. 52-56).

Cost

Persons seeking counseling from a parish-based minister normally do not expect the cost to be prohibitive, if there is any charge at all. Even when a non-member seeks counseling, the minister is not likely to consider the client's ability or willingness to pay a fee as part of the screening criteria for scheduling an appointment.

Limitations to the minister as counselor arising from prior educational deficits, time constraints, and a negative transference role are real; however, these limitations are probably more than balanced by the strengths arising from trust, continuity, accessability, and cost. Besides, what other professional group in contemporary American society still makes housecalls?

PASTORAL COUNSELING AND THE NORMAL ELDERLY PERSON

Pastoral counseling activities for personal growth among normal elderly people represents an exciting new development. It draws on the basic strengths of the minister mentioned above, while minimizing those weaknesses inherent in the minister's role and education. This is accomplished by a simple shift in perspective from a deficit-oriented focus on pathology to a strength-oriented focus on growth as the normal human condition in old age. With this approach the pastoral counselor assesses a person's strengths and matches them up with their desires, opportunities, and needs in such a way that growthful goals are accomplished.

Consider, for example, the case of Thomas J., who suffered a disabling stroke and was confined to a nursing home and spent much of each day in a wheel chair. Thomas had an extremely limited income which barely met necessities under these new circumstances. Since his wife died a few years ago, shortly after they had moved to a milder climate, Thomas did not have a large number of friends from work or the church on which he could rely. With adult children living hundreds of miles away, he was experiencing significant feelings of isolation and loneliness.

Here the pastor was confronted with an impoverished, lonely, disabled man who longed for contact with his family, specifically with his pre-teen grandchildren. What strengths did he possibly have? Thomas was a goal-setter first of all. He reported success at setting and meeting proximate goals for himself during his younger years. In the past few years, however, this behavior had more or less atrophied from disuse, much as his muscles were now withering away. Secondly, a major strength was the personal flexibility which emerged in the course of the first few conversations. And thirdly, Thomas knew that he was lonely. Furthermore, he knew who he wanted to talk with—his grandchildren. In a sense, this unmet need for contact with his family was an asset instead of a liability in that it provided some degree of motivation for new behavior.

If you were the pastoral counselor, what would you have done? Counsel him to become more content with his isolation? Provide a place for him in the choir so that he could get to know more people in the nursing home? Suggest that he call his grandchildren on the telephone collect? (Thomas could not write because of the stroke.)

In fact, the counselor didn't focus on Thomas's increasing dependency needs. He didn't discuss human finitude and the nearness of approaching death. Instead, the counselor observed Thomas carefully, making sure that he "dropped by" during a meal so that the manual dexterity of Thomas's good left hand could be noted. Then the pastor interceded with the administrator of the home so that Thomas could gain access to an unused electric typewriter a couple of hours a week. The next thing anybody knew Thomas was writing one or two letters a week on the electric machine—hunting and pecking with a strong index finger.

A few weeks later a letter arrived from his eight-year-old grand-daughter; then one came from a twelve-year-old "little leaguer" talking about his team, etc. Thomas was still poor, he was still disabled, he was still more lonely than he liked; but, now he had contact in a very meaningful way with his grandchildren, which was a real plus. In addition, he was beginning to ask himself if there existed other alternative means for him to accomplish his goals, such as flower gardening. (He bought some large flower pots and placed them on a table so that he could reach them.)

Thomas had many losses which might have been assumed incorrectly to have been overwhelming to him. His wife was now dead, he had moved into a nursing home a great distance from old friends and familiar surroundings, and he had experienced a disabling stroke. Altogether his case appears rather bleak if these losses are taken out of the context of his total life situation which includes strengths and assets and needs capable of being met constructively. Without a focus on growth and an assessment of strengths, the pastoral counselor in this situation certainly would not have been as helpful to Thomas as he was.

On the other hand, the losses of old age should not be denied or ignored in work with elderly people. They need to be accurately perceived in terms of their effect on the client's resources. The focus is on mobilization and constructive utilization of what is present, not a mere cataloging of what can no longer be done. Thomas's losses constituted a serious challenge to the core of his existence, the spiritual center of his awareness, and his will. They could not be denied, yet Thomas was enabled to again experience himself as capable of making decisions and effective in reaching out to persons he loved.

Thomas is in stark contrast to another person named Lucy, whose life and spirit have been of continuing importance to me in work with other elderly persons who also happen to be disabled. After talking with Lucy for 45 minutes one day, I knew that something was terribly wrong and I didn't know what it was. I could feel the obvious sadness which filled the room. It was almost beyond sadness and bordered on horror. In that moment I was confused. Was it Lucy's horror or something she had touched in the deep recesses of my psyche? Whatever was happening in that room had not been talked about between us.

> I reached out to hold her hand: "Lucy, do things seem sort of hopeless for you?" Slowly the tears flowed down her cheeks as she looked at me and nodded her head. Her deep sobbing said to me, "You can never know how hopeless I feel." Gradually the words began to emerge, half-coherent because of her emotions, and I thought I heard her say, "They keep putting syrup on my cornbread, and I have asked them so many times not to do that, but it is still there every night."

What that meant for this woman in her eighties bolted into my awareness like a freight train! Lucy, who had been able to make major decisions all her life, now was not allowed even to decide what went in her mouth! How much more could her decisional environment shrink? No wonder Lucy was feeling helpless, angry, and ineffective. In the face of such present reality, she was now effectively making her last decision—to die (Clements, 1979, pp. 4-5).

In thinking about Lucy it has seemed to me that her tears were also hot-protesting to the very end what was being done. It was as though she found herself in the middle of a lake and couldn't swim, but kept coming up for air again and again as she flailed about and tried to scream out in desperation, knowing that the end was near yet not ready to allow her spirit to be trampled or crushed. Those desperate moments in Lucy's room gave evidence that her spirit was indeed alive and well, demanding that a major change take place. She would no longer tolerate being caught in the spider web of uncaring, routinized institutional attention. She would move toward life, or she would die. No one could deny Lucy room for her spirit.

The human spirit, the core of existence as present in conscious experience and perception, does not get lost despite insults to the body or the fracture of life-long relationships through death. While the spirit is in and of the body, it is not the body. A person's spirit is never totally identified with the body, as Lucy so movingly communicated. For the pastoral counselor, this human spirit is any person's ultimate asset, although it is not property which is possessed or owned by the individual.

SUMMARY

The central task for pastoral counselors in our work with the elderly, therefore, is to enable an awareness of personal spirit to emerge into consciousness. This emergence is always an act of creative growth—reaching out to the future unknown, leaping across the chasm separating what is from what could be. It is never an easy task for the client. It is intense for the counselor as well. To leap willingly from the known to the unknown is never without risk. It is an act of faith that calls into question the central affirmation of human existence.

This leap is never completely divorced from material corporeal existence either. Real palpable issues which can be touched, even tasted, are always present. Cornbread and syrup or an electric typewriter and one good finger are always involved— never *just* an idea in the mind. Real symbols have real referents.

As you go about the exciting task of working with the aging, I hope you can catch glimpses of the human spirit which touches and is touched by all of existence. In these moments of awareness you receive a gift from the supposed client, for to be present at the emergence of new life is truly a gift.

REFERENCES

Clebsch, W.A., & Jaekle, C.R. *Pastoral care in historic perspective: An essay with exhibits.* Englewood Cliffs, New Jersey: Prentice-Hall, Inc., 1964.

Clements, W.M. *Care and counseling of the aging.* Philadelphia: Fortress Press, 1979.

Clinebell, H.J., Jr. *Basic types of pastoral counseling.* Nashville, Tennessee: Abingdon Press, 1966.

Williams, D.D. *The minister and the care of souls.* New York: Harper and Row, 1961.

Underwood, R.L. *Pastoral care and the office of the pastor.* Austin Seminary Bulletin, Faculty Edition, May, 1979, pp. 5-12.

The Counseling Needs of Elderly Nursing Home Residents

Katherine Perry Supiano

ABSTRACT

The institutionalized elderly are confronted with numerous losses and life changes which may necessitate involvement in counseling. Relocation to a nursing home has been shown to be a major life transition, often reaching crisis proportions. Once settled in the home, the elderly individual must adjust to a variety of new demands at a time when one is especially vulnerable. The counselor may be called upon to accurately assess the client's mental, social, and emotional status, assist in placement decisions, and make necessary referrals. Counseling issues include both problems specific to the home's environment and to the client's personal concerns. Loss is a recurrent theme in counseling with nursing home residents, and the counselor should be prepared to respond to expression of it Short-term, realistic goals aimed at achieving the client's maximum potential are most desirable.

In addition to individual counseling strategies, family counseling and group counseling are discussed. Families should be utilized with nursing home residents whenever possible. This enables families to participate fully in decisions regarding older members, maintains the client's ties to the outside world, and may be more appropriate for some clients than group counseling.

Group counseling is a widely expanding therapeutic tool in nursing homes. Group counseling in nursing homes is distinguished by its emphasis on process versus content, by the more active role of the leader, and by the special considerations made for members.

INTRODUCTION

The process of becoming a nursing home resident constitutes a major crisis in the lives of most older people and their families. Transfer of an elderly person from home or hospital to a nursing home frequently takes place at a time when the individual is especially vulnerable to the impact of change. The elderly are confronted with a multitude of losses: death of a spouse, physical and mental decline, loss of occupational status, decreased economic independence—many of which occur simultaneously. With the advent of institutionalization, older people may find themselves in need of counseling services. It is hoped that this chapter will provide insight into the special needs of elderly persons residing in or preparing to move into a nursing home.

THE IMPACT OF INSTITUTIONALIZATION

Most elderly people share a negative view of nursing homes. This attitude is a result of many factors: a desire to continue living independently, to remain in a familiar environment, and to be close to family and friends. Often, a move to a nursing home signifies imminent death to the older person. These attitudes are not without some justification, and they have a profound impact on adjustment to nursing home placement. As Brody (1975) points out, "The image of the institution in the eyes of the community and the treatment accorded the residents affects the mental health of all old people who live daily with the knowledge that they too may some day need congregate care." (p. 4).

Relocation of the aged individual to a nursing home involves what many authors describe as the "institutionalization syndrome." This response typically includes depression, fear, passivity, decreased life satisfaction, and higher mortality rates. Using a battery of psychological tests, Shrut (1965) found even healthy institutionalized residents to be more fearful, less socially alert, less productive, less cooperative, and more preoccupied with death than a matched sample of apartment dwellers.

Wolk and Telleen (1976) found a significantly lower measure of life satisfaction and activity level among instituuionalized elderly as compared to a parallel sample of retirement village residents. In a compilation of case studies, Menninger (1963) noted a high incidence of depression and passivity in long term institutional residents. Most importantly, institutionalization has been associated with heightened mortality rates in the elderly.

Aldrich and Mendkoff (1963) used the records of a nursing home for the ten years prior to its closing to examine this effect in that home's entire population. In comparing age corrected anticipated death rates to actual survival rates, they found that the actual death rate was "substantially and significantly higher than the anticipated rate" (p. 189).

The major portion of this increase occurred in the first three months following admission, during which it was three times greater than the expected rate. Similar findings have been reported by Killian (1970), Lieberman (1961, 1969), Markus *et al.* (1971b), and Marlowe (1974). Recent work by Borup, Gallego, and Heffernan(1979) has questioned the validity of these mortality findings. It remains unclear whether these effects are due to pre-existing characteristics of the individuals which contributed to the original need for placement or are causally related to relocation per se.

Recent studies suggest that the essentially negative impact of institutionalization may be explained according to Seligman's Learned Helplessness Model (Seligman, 1976). Briefly, learned helplessness refers to a psychological state in which persons' view (not necessarily in a conscious manner) their behaviors as having little impact on their environment. Seligman asserts that in cases where one's responses cannot control the outcome of those responses, it is possible and probable that the individual will learn to be helpless. Furthermore, this hypothesis is not limited to cases of actual control, but is extended to perceived control as well. The individual's perceived powers of prediction and control in potentially stressful situations are thought to be mediating variables in the state of learned helplessness.

The earliest research that dealt with this topic was performed by Ferrari (1963), in which two populations of elderly were compared—one institutionalized by necessity, the other by choice. Ferrari's results are striking; within three months of admission, 94% of the involuntary group died, in contrast to 2.6% of the voluntary group. While this study is riddled with methodoligcal problems, the trend has been continually substantiated in studies of involuntary relocation. One of the most convincing was carried out by Blenker (1967). Blenker randomly assigned independently living elderly persons to one of three types of supportive care services: minimal, consisting of informational and emotional support; moderate, providing intermediate care; and maximal, giving direct extensive aid. At six-month follow-up, maximal care recipients were found to have the highest mortality rates, while those in the minimal care group had the lowest.

In a study by Langer and Rodin (1976), nursing home residents in the experimental condition were given a communication from the administrator which emphasized their responsibility for themselves, whereas the control condition was given a communication stressing the staff's responsibility for their welfare. To further strengthen the effect, the experimental group was given the opportunity to care for a plant, rather than have the staff care for a plant, as was done in the control group. Ratings by self-support, staff-report, and behavioral measures revealed that the experimental group was significantly more alert, more participative, and enjoyed a markedly improved sense of well being, as compared to the control group. In their conclusion, the authors state that, "Mechanisms can and should be established for changing situational factors that reduce real and perceived responsibility in the elderly. . . . It suggests that some of the negative consequences of aging may be retarded, reversed, or possibly prevented by returning to the aged the right to make decisions and a feeling of competence" (Langer & Rodin, 1976, p. 197).

Schulz and Brenner (1977), in evaluating these findings, hypothesized that, holding other variables constant, (1) the greater the individual's choice in relocation, the more positive the outcome of relocation; (2) the more predictable the new environment, the easier the adaptation; (3) the extent to which the relocation reflects a net decline in controlability will affect the adaptability of the individual to the new environment; and 4) the individual's enduring characteristics also play some role in adaptive success.

Implications for Counseling

It has been estimated that approximately five percent of the elderly, well over a million people, live in nursing homes at any one time. Most nursing home residents are in their mid-seventies, are female, and are Caucasian (Butler & Lewis, 1977). More than half have three or more chronic physical conditions and nearly this many suffer from at least one mental disorder (NCHS, 1972). Clearly, the institutionalized elderly constitute a specific population with a unique set of needs. As with all people, however, elderly clients will present their own individualized problems and concerns to the counselor. For this reason, counseling should begin with a quality assessment of the client's unique situation.

Initial assessment should ensue after rapport has been established and the client is certain that confidentiality will be maintained (this latter point is critical with the aged, where disdain for professional help is common). It is imperative that this initial assessment include an evaluation of the client's total situation: physical functioning, mental status, social and economic situation, and availability of familial/peer supports. Several assessment tools exist to serve this purpose, of which the Geriatric Functional Rating Scale (Grauer & Birnbom, 1975), the Older American Resources and Services Methodology (Pfieffer, 1975), and Butler's Personal Mental Health Data Form for Older Persons (Butler & Lewis, 1977) are good examples. Having this awareness of the client's background and current needs, the counselor can ease the transition to nursing home life by maximizing continuity from the client's previous lifestyle to this setting.

When counselors are involved in decisions regarding placement, they should be operating from an accurate knowledge base that aids the client and family in selecting the appropriate level of care. Ideally, placement decisions are made in an interdisciplinary format with input provided by physician, nursing staff, social worker, as well as counselor. The final decision is optimally made by client and family with informational guidance from professionals. An interdisciplinary approach is preferable in all helping encounters with the elderly, as their problems are multiple, complex, and tend to mask each other. When this is not possible, counselors need to be aware of the limits of their expertise and make any necessary referrals.

From the onset of the counseling relationship, it is important to communicate to the client a willingness to explore every alternative to nursing home placement. There are, however, many clients for whom no viable alternatives exist. When these other possibilities have been depleted, the counselor's role becomes one of facilitating the client's acceptance of placement. Here the counselor's objectives are to help clients accept the inevitable and concentrate their energies in changing the alterable. The counselor should encourage clients to verbalize whatever apprehensions they may be feeling. In doing so, the counselor allows individuals to participate fully in decisions regarding relocation and new lifestyles.

Research has continually indicated that individuals who are encouraged to become actively involved in decisions concerning the relocation process fare better in their new environment (Schulz & Brenner, 1977). Similarily, involving family members in counseling from the beginning elicits their cooperation and encourages their continued participation in the care of their aged member. These efforts by the counselor enhance the client's sense of control and feelings of self-esteem.

Once in the nursing home, the older individual is required to make several adjustments in lifestyle. Many of these are inherent in the nature of the institution, such as inflexible routines, repetitive menus, lack of privacy, inability to retain one's own possessions, and an abundance of unfilled time. Many are the result of staff attitudes and behavior, including impersonalization, desexualization, and infantalization. Some are due to the elderly residents themselves, and include any number of physical, mental, social, and emotional reasons. None of these factors constitutes an inevitable part of institutional life. In the better facilities, these detriments to quality care are prevented to a great extent. Yet even in the finest homes, problems develop which indicate counselor intervention.

The majority of counseling with nursing home residents probably takes place within the home. Whenever possible, clients should be allowed to attend sessions outside of the home, if this conforms to their wishes. The "change of scenery" can go a long way in facilitating independence. Counselors should be aware of the many Medicare restrictions which prohibit many residents from leaving the home. A check with the home to insure the client's ability to leave is called for prior to discussing this possibility with the client. Holding sessions within the home provides the counselor with an opportunity to obtain accurate perceptions of the client's environment and insight into attitudes toward it. When sessions are conducted in the home,

Counseling for the Growing Years

every attempt should be made to insure the client's privacy. A separate room for counseling is preferable, but the client's room is suitable if undisturbed.

The counselor should be aware of and compensate for whatever handicaps are present. Acknowledgement of special needs in a tactful way indicates empathy on the part of the counselor. Accommodate sensory losses by sitting close to the client, maintaining eye contact, and speaking slowly and clearly. Arrange for easy access to the room where counseling takes place and allow for wheelchair space when necessary. Whenever possible, hold sessions in a warm, draft-free, well-lighted room. Providing for the comfort of clients goes beyond common courtesy and may have a marked influence on the efficacy of counseling.

Problems addressed in counseling may involve issues specific to the client's life in the home, or may involve more global personal concerns. With this population, loss is a predominant theme and can be anticipated in counseling. Losses should be acknowledged with all the seriousness clients accord them. In early sessions, discussion of seemingly small losses may be a means of testing the counselor's willingness to explore these areas. Further, the cumulative effect of losses should not be underestimated. The losses experienced by aged clients exact a great price from them in terms of energy expended in grief and adaptation. The counselor should be supportive in this period of vulnerability; encourage verbalization, exploration, and insight into feelings; and facilitate restoration to optimal functioning.

One final issue which warrants consideration is the establishment of counseling goals. It is essential that goals be well thought out and realistic. Returning home is the dream of many clients for whom it is not feasible. When such expectations are not met, the client plunges into despair. False hope helps no one and can only thwart the therapeutic process. Instead, goals aimed at achieving the client's genuine potential are the objectives of choice.

As Brody (1975) has observed, "For the (institutionalized) aged, therapeutic gain must be defined in terms of small goals. The more global expectations which are indices of improvement with other groups, such as discharge from institution to community, re-employment, or reconstruction of family relationships, are not always applicable. When the aged person moves from wheelchair to walker, from apathy to minimal level of social participation, from total disregard to performance of simple grooming tasks, if decline is forestalled or retarded, these too are legitimate therapautic achievements" (p. 96).

SPECIFIC INTERVENTION STRATEGIES

In addition to work with individual elderly nursing home residents, two other counseling strategies suggest themselves: counseling in a family context, and counseling with groups of nursing home residents.

Counseling with Families of Nursing Home Residents

Families should, if possible, be included in counseling sessions involving an institutionalized client. This has practical value, in that the family typically makes the final decisions concerning its elderly members (Cath, 1972). Secondly, most families wish to be involved in decisions regarding older members. Contrary to society's view, few families abandon their elderly on the nursing home doorstep. Recent work has indicated that the majority of families are concerned about the welfare of their aged, and find placement of elderly members an extremely difficult decision (Butler & Lewis, 1977). Thirdly, family counseling may be more appropriate for clients unwilling to participate in nursing home group therapy. Family sessions are more acceptable to many older clients, in that the family constitutes a "natural" unit and is less threatening. Finally, involvement of the family is not often in the best interests of the client. As has been mentioned earlier, it is important to maintain as many of the client's ties to previous lifestyle as is possible.

Family counseling involving an aged institutionalized member presents the counselor with several unique concerns. Essentially, the counselor is dealing with an expansion of typical family dynamics. A dual generation gap may be evidenced in middle aged children torn between the needs of their parents and the demands of their own children. Counselors need to be sensitive to the often unspoken feelings of other family members. Feelings of guilt, abandonment, unresolved-past conflicts, and a confrontation with one's own imminent aging are recurrent themes. The counselor's acknowledgement of these feelings frees up members to deal with immediate issues.

It is imperative to accurately define the problem to be addressed. Often, the older member is so readily labeled "patient," that it is difficult for the family to accept collective ownership of any problems. In keeping with the systems model of family counseling, problems need to be defined in the context of the entire family, instead of focused on specific individuals. Toward this goal, issues presented by family members are reflected to clarify content, then refocused in a systems framework. Eventually, the family assumes this responsibility of refocusing its comments.

Obtaining full family attendance in this type of family counseling is often difficult. Rather than pursuing distant (geographically and/or emotionally) members to participate in a full session, it is appropriate to first ascertain which family members have easy access to the home and assess their willingness to participate. The approach to families is crucial and is most effective if presented in a non-threatening, positive way. Elicit the older client's feelings on who to include; stronger relationships exist with siblings than with children for many aged persons. To accurately represent the entire dynamic of the family, involve as many members as is possible, but be prepared for infrequent attendance on the part of some family members.

A major issue in this type of family counseling is goal setting. Once goals are precisely specified and agreed upon, communication is greatly enhanced. This has a mobilizing effect on the family, as they derive a sense of movement toward objectives. The importance of setting realistic goals cannot be overemphasized. While the counselor should communicate an attitude of hope to the family, unjustified optimism can only damage the process. Unrestrained optimism invalidates the feelings of family members, sets counseling up for failure, and serves as a crutch to the counselor (Herr & Weakland, 1978). Setting realistic goals, with full participation of family members, avoids this patronizing approach; it recognizes the ability and responsibility of the family to respond constructively to solving its problems.

Another issue that may arise is side-taking. The counselor who has been working with an elderly client in a nursing home may slip into an inappropriate "advocacy" role, "defending" the older member against the family. Working against the family is counterproductive to both the needs of the older client and the family as a whole. The goal to be remembered is working with the family; side-taking and arguments only circumvent this process and provide a poor model of meaningful communication.

In summary, the family unit provides a dynamic medium for constructive change. In it counselors and families find a powerful avenue for problem restitution and personal growth. Family counseling in an institutional setting retains the family's participation in the care of its older member, provides continuity to the older member, and may offer younger members insight into the aging process.

Group Counseling with Nursing Home Residents

The development of group work with the institutionalized elderly represents a positive trend in the care provision of nursing homes. Originally viewed as a way to fill the residents' empty hours, group programs have come to be regarded as an effective tool in maximizing the social, physical, and emotional potential of participants. As Cohen and Hammerman (1975) have noted, "Such programs help to insure the resident's satisfactory life and good adjustment and offer opportunities for growth and continuing development. Programs which provide opportunities for the residents' participation are to be preferred to those of a more passive nature that stress 'doing for'" (p. 123).

Groups in long term care facilities are diverse and range from task oriented groups (reading and music appreciation) to process oriented socialization groups. Burnside (1978) has outlined four levels of group work in nursing homes: (1) Reality Orientation, (2) Remotivation, ((3) Reminiscence Groups, and (4) Therapy Groups. Reality orientation groups have found wide acceptance in programming for elderly diagnosed as having Chronic Brain Syndromes. The approach is one of continual reality testing for disoriented residents. Remotivation groups focus on aspects of daily living and resocialization. Such groups are very structured and have a clear member/leader dichotomy.

Reminiscence groups are designed to help members review their lives and share memories. Therapy groups are conducted within specific theoretical psychotherapy frameworks, and are typically confined to age psychotic clients. In addition to the group types Burnside has outlined, Euster (1971) has described orientation groups to ease entrance to the institution, and "living and learning" groups to provide a therapeutic milieu within the nursing home environment. Some of the most common types of nursing home groups are topic-specific groups. These address subjects popular with members: Hennessey's (1976) Music Therapy groups, and Koch's (1978) novel approach to poetry writing in groups are good examples.

Group counseling in a nursing home setting has many features which distinguish it from other group work with the elderly. The major distinction in nursing home group counseling is an emphasis in process versus outcome. The ongoing special interaction is seen as more valuable to the needs of the members than is attainment of goals.

Nursing home groups are optimally smaller than the traditional eight to twelve. This allows members to sit closer and alleviates many communication problems that result from visual and auditory losses. It also allows the wheelchair bound participant full access to the circle and makes physical contact readily available.

Groups in a nursing home environment optimally have smaller goals of shorter range. This allows for earlier goal attainment, enabling all members to feel a degree of success. The pace of the groups tends to be slower, compensating for physical and mental deficits and encouraging full participation from all members. In keeping with the physical needs of nursing home residents, the leader should attempt to hold sessions in a warm, well-lighted room, free from distractions. It is advisable to keep the regimen of the nursing home in mind; scheduling sessions during meals, bath or nap time will only result in low attendance. The role of the leader in nursing home groups is also different from that of other leaders. This type of group generally requires a more active, directive approach. More information giving and self-disclosure are often necessary and the leader may need to provide more support and encouragement than is required elsewhere. Furthermore, confrontation is usually an inappropriate method for this kind of group, especially at the beginning.

In selecting members for this group, the ultimate decision remains with the leader (Burnside, 1978). Merely accepting referrals from other sources is an inappropriate selection strategy and may lead to a poor composition of participants. Burnside (1978) suggests that a variety of personalities provides the best combination, with a balance of quiet and talkative members and a mix of men and women. She proposes that the group should be homogeneous with respect to mental intactness, as a mix of alert and disoriented members may lead to confusing expectations of the group. This latter suggestion should be considered in light of specific group goals. Many reality orientation groups specifically provide for such a mixture to enhance modeling for the more confused and peer support by more alert members.

Regardless of the format of the group, several general objectives for group work with nursing home residents emerge: (1) to involve residents in a positive group experience, (2) to facilitate the development of interpersonal relationships, (3) to enhance personal growth and development, (4) to provide an avenue for socialization, and (5) to involve residents in programmatic aspects of group activity.

SUMMARY

It has been demonstrated that the institutionalized elderly constitutes a specific population with a unique set of needs. Counseling nursing home residents and their families requires considerable patience on the part of the counselor. Change comes slowly and gains often appear small. Yet, potential for positive growth and change exists in the institutionalized elderly. To tap this potential and fully actualize it, counselors must understand, accept, and enhance the personal strengths of their clients through the provision of an enriching therapeutic encounter. In doing so, counselors can aid clients in accepting losses, defining new goals, and achieving mastery to the fullest extent.

REFERENCES

Aldrich, C.K., & Mendkoff, E. Relocation of the aged and disabled: A mortality study. *Journal of the American Geriatrics Society*, 1963, *11*, 185-194.

Blenker, M. Environmental change and the aging individual. *Gerontologist*, 1967, *7*, 101-105.

Borup, J.H.; Gallego, D.T.; & Heffernan, P.G. Relocation and its effect on mortality. *Gerontologist*, 1979, *19(2)*, 135-140.

Brody, E.M. *A social work guide for long-term care facilities.* Rockville, Maryland: National Institute of Mental Health, DHEW Publication No. (Adm) 75-177, 1975.

Burnside, I.M. (Ed.). *Working with the elderly: Group processes and techniques.* North Scituate, Massachusetts: Buxbury Press, 1978.

Butler, R.N., & Lewis, M.I. *Aging and mental health: Positive psychosocial approaches.* Saint Louis,: C.V. Mosby, 1977.

Cath, S.H. The geriatric patient and his family: The institutionalization of a parent-a nadir of life. *Journal of Geriatric Psychiatry*, 1972, *5*, (1), 25-46.

Cohen, S.Z., & Hammerman, J.H. Social work with groups. In E.M. Brody, *A social work guide for long-term care facilities.* Rockville, Maryland: National Institute of Mental Health, DHEW Publications No. (Adm) 75-177, 1975, 123-124.

Euster, G.L. A system of groups in institutions for the aged. *Social Casework*, 1971, (Oct.), 523-529.

Ferrari, N.A. Freedom of Choice. *Social Work*, 1963, 8, 104-106.

A geriatric functional rating scale to determine the need for institutional care. *Journal of the American Geriatrics Society*, 1975, 23, 472-476.

Hennessey, M.J. Music and group work with the aged. In I.M. Burnside (Ed.), *Nursing and the aged.* New York: McGraw-Hill, 1976, 255-269.

Herr, J.H., & Weakland, J.H. The family as a group. In I.M. Burnside (Ed.), *Working with the elderly: Group processes and techniques.* North Scituate, Massachusetts: Duxbury Press, 1978, 320-339.

Killian, E.C. Effects of geriatric transfers on mortality rates. *Social Work*, 1970, 15, 19-26.

Koch, K. *I never told anybody: Teaching poetry writing in a nursing home.* New York: Vintage Books, 1978.

Langer, E., & Rodin, J. Effects of choice and enhanced personal responsibility for the aged: A field experiment in a nursing home setting. *Journal of Personality and Social Psychology,* 1976, 34, 191-198.

Lieberman, M.A. Relationship of mortality rates to entrance to a home for the aged. *Geriatrics,* 1961, 16, 515-519.

Lieberman, M.A. Institutionalization of the aged: Effects on behavior. *Journal of Gerontology,* 1969, 24, 330-340.

Markus, E.; Blenker, M.; Bloom, M.; & Downs, T. Some factors and their association with post-relocation mortality among institutionalization aged persons. *Journal of Gerontology,* 1971, 26, 537-541.

Marlowe, R.E. When they closed the doors at Modesto. Unpublished paper presented at NIMH Conference, 1974; As cited in R. Schulz and G. Brenner, Relocation of the aged: Review and theoretical analysis. *Journal of Gerontology,* 1977, 32, 323-333.

Menninger, K. *The vital balance: The life process in mental health and illness.* New York: Viking Press, 1963.

National Center for Health Statistics (DHEW). Unpublished data from 1969 survey of institutions, Washington, D.C., the Center, 1972.

Pfeiffer, E. (Ed.). *Multidimensional functional assessment: The OARS methodology.* Durham, North Carolina: Duke Univerisity Press, 1975.

Schulz, R., & Brenner, G. Relocation of the aged: Review and theoretical analysis. *Journal of Gerontology,* 1977, 32, 323-333.

Seligman, M.E.P. *Helplessness: On depression, development, and death.* San Francisco: W.H. Freeman, 1976.

Shrut, S.D. Attitudes toward old age and death. In R. Fulton (Ed.), *Death and identity.* New York: Wiley and Sons, 1965, 161-169.

Wolk, S., & Telleen, S. Psychological and social correlates of life satisfaction as a function or residential constraint. *Journal of Gerontology,* 1976, *31,* 89-98.

Substance Use and Abuse Among the Elderly

David M. Rosenthal
Steven W. LeClair

ABSTRACT

The use and abuse of chemicals by an edlerly population has rarely been examined. Evidence suggests that the elderly are increasingly using and abusing legal and illicit substances. Reasons for the abuse of prescribed drugs are many and responsibility must be shared by older people, physicians, pharmaceutical companies, and training institutes. Previous literature also indicates an increasing number of elderly street addicts and methadone patients. Older addicts tend to maintain a low profile in an attempt to survive in their environments. Evidence also suggests that many older alcoholics start drinking at fifty-five due to feelings of depression. Counseling strategies are discussed to facilitate treatment of this hidden and often ignored population.

INTRODUCTION

Few people see old age as a time for potential growth and development. In American society the emphasis has been placed on remaining young while fearing and ignoring the aging process in ourselves and others. It becomes easier to avoid what one fears most! The myths and errors related to aging have created the stereotypic senior citizen as being "invalid, irascible, mentally deficient, unloved, and unloving—an economic and emotional burden on the young and middle-aged" (Weg, 1978, p. 103). In spite of contradictory data these stereotypes still exist (Weg, 1978). This fear and prejudice often result in society ignoring a potential problem, and in this case, one finds few studies, programs, and/or medical school courses which examine the elderly substance user.

The purpose of this chapter is not to argue against the use of drugs. No one can deny the need and value of some medications in the lives of the elderly. However, one must be concerned about drug misuse and the reasons for that misuse. Solutions must be generated if this preventable situation is to be stopped.

The literature on substance use and misuse by the elderly can be divided into three main categories. These broad categories examine the use of legal drugs, illegal drugs, and alcohol. In this article, the authors examine the literature in the same manner, beginning with legal drug usage followed by examination of illegal drugs and then alcohol. These sections are followed by a discussion of possible intervention strategies useful for counselors working with elderly individuals.

Legal Drugs

There are large numbers of elderly individuals receiving a variety of legally prescribed psychoactive drugs. The past decade has shown an increase in use of prescribed drugs by the elderly with persons over 55 becoming the largest consumers of legal drugs (*The Journal*, 1974). The task force on Prescription Drugs (1969) also noted that persons over 65 acquired about three times as many prescribed drugs as those under 65. While individuals over 65 comprise a small percentage of our population (approximately 10%) they purchase approximately 25 percent of all prescription drugs (Cheung, 1975). These statistics certainly indicate that elderly individuals, for whatever purpose, are being exposed to a large number of substances which leads researchers to feel that they are an "at risk" population (Peterson & Whittington, 1977). Contact with a great number of drugs can only serve to enhance the likelihood of the problem.

Etiology of Elderly Misuse

While the need and value of medication in the lives of older people cannot be denied, one must be concerned with the potential for misuse. With the changes inherent in advancing age, medical aid becomes more frequently sought and needed. For many elderly who are concerned with personal health, drugs provide a tangible and frequent reassurance about their health. It must be made clear that as individuals grow older they become more concerned with death and their own ability to function.

Oftentimes this concern can become a preoccupation leading a person to search for the proverbial "fountain of youth." In these cases, the individual, with issues of health foremost in mind, manifests a ritualistic dependence on certain drugs that have eased certain pains. Oftentimes, they ask for prescriptions to be refilled long after a rational need for a drug has disappeared (Brady, 1978). Many also attempt to diagnose their own ailments, then treat the ailments with assorted vitamins, health foods, and over-the-counter remedies which have been advertised as providing relief for a great variety of difficulties.

This search for a slowing down of the aging process only makes the elderly person more susceptible to advertising by an industry which has responded by presenting vitamins and other remedies as solutions to many of the elderly's concerns. Lofholm (1978) argues that vitamins should only be considered if an individual's diet is poor or meals are irregular. Others point out that "far too much nonsense clutters up our advertising media about the safety of patent remedies, their specificity, and the need for them by anyone and everyone" (Brady, 1978, p. 6).

One finds that money is being spent by elderly individuals on low or fixed incomes for medications which are not helpful and often only serve to complicate medical problems. Spending money on unnecessary drugs can also result in not being able to afford needed drugs when they are prescribed for specific ailments.

Another frequently occurring problem related to self-medication is that of omission (Schwartz, Wang, Zeitz, & Goss, 1962). In these cases elderly individuals have either forgotten to take their medication or have decided to discontinue use of a prescribed drug which has produced unpleasant side effects. Other examples of omission include those individuals who (a) are too sick to remember to take their medication, (b) do not feel like shopping for a prescription at a particular time, or (c) decide a certain drug is expensive and one they can do without. One possible remedy would be for physicians to attempt to get by on a single dosage a day when appropriate and carefully explain the necessity of the medication to all patients. Hopefully, this will help patients understand the importance of the medication as well as minimize the possibility that the patient will forget.

Other medication errors are related to (a) improper timing and sequencing of doses, (b) the high incidence of inaccurate or even total lack of knowledge possessed by the individual as to why a specific drug was prescribed, (c) trading of drugs between neighbors, friends, and relatives, and (d) retaining unused prescriptions and self-administering them at a later date. These concerns could be alleviated by physicians spending time with patients to explain the reasons for specific drugs while also giving clear and concise directions. The formation of a patient-doctor relationship might help alleviate some of the causes of abuse.

In many of these cases, the elderly themselves were responsible for the drug misuse. While many senior citizens seemed to feel that the medication was critical to their survival and did resist withdrawal, others seemed to feel that they could choose which drugs to take and under what conditions.

Professional Errors

While elderly individuals are responsible for their own drug misuse, that responsibility must be shared by professionals and the institutions which train them. Many professionals report that among the major reasons for drug misuse by the edlerly is over-prescription of drugs by physicians and a concurrent lack of interest shown in elderly patients by their doctors (Carroll, 1975). As noted earlier, treating older people may stimulate fear and conflict in health care providers. These individuals have been trained to heal the sick, not maintain people until they die. Physicians must examine their own feelings about life and death if they are going to work effectively with an elderly population (Mauksch, 1975).

There are many other causes of professionally related misuse that appear to be a result of apathy and non-caring. It is interesting to note that fewer drugs are prescribed for older people who suffer from organic mental impairment than for mentally intact patients who have the cognitive resources to press their physician for drugs (Brody, 1975). Basically, what appears to happen is that physicians may be prescribing drugs to those who complain rather than on sound medical judgment. Other examples of similar inconsistent behaviors would include (a) telephone prescriptions being given to individuals who argue that they cannot make it to the office, (b) instructing patients to take a prescription as needed without taking time to explain possible effects of a drug, (c) permitting unrestricted refill of a drug and/-or (d) prescribing a drug to minimize undesirable patient behavior.

Medical Training

If treatment is going to be effective, research and additional course work related to the elderly must be in our training institutes. There is a definite lack of knowledge about drugs suitable for the elderly. Most medications used for these patients have been evaluated primarily with younger subjects who are less prone to side effects and may need different drug dosage levels than their elderly counterparts. According to Pfeiffer (1978), textbooks of psychiatry, internal medicine, and pharmacology make no specific mention of modifications which may be necessary for a physician when prescribing medication for an elderly person. He further argues that health care providers receive little instruction in working with an elderly population. It has also been noted that the *Physicians desk reference* (1974) contains little information about dosages suitable for the elderly. The lack of information and course work cannot be minimized when one considers the growing percentage of people in our population who are defined as "elderly."

Misuse of Illegal Drugs

Existing literature on the aging addict is also scarce and inconclusive (Heller & Wynne, 1974). It is generally felt that the greatest number of drug addicts are young adults (Heller & Wynne, 1974) and that long term addicts either died or matured out of their addiction by simply stopping. This view has been questioned by Capel et al. (1972), Pascarelli (1972), and Pascarelli & Fischer (1974). Capel et al. (1972), investigating the narcotics addict in New Orleans, discovered a substantial number of addicts between the ages of 45 and 75. It appeared that many of these older addicts had not died but had succeeded in changing their lifesytles and camouflaging their habits through a variety of adaptive techniques.

Pascarelli (1972) noted an increase in the number of people maintained on methadone in their late thirties and forties. In a later review, Pascarelli and Fischer (1974), as did Capel, et al.(1972), noted a change in pattern of drug use and a modification of addict lifestyle. They argued that the older addict maintained a low profile by avoiding harassment, arrest, and public attention. This was often done by entering methadone programs, using drugs that were easier to find, or by adjusting to a decreased daily intake. Older addicts often learn to adapt to rapidly changing situations. They are able to substitute drugs and avoid getting "strung out," while keeping a job or some other form of steady income. Basically, they learn to survive in their environment while obtaining drugs for euphoric purposes (Heller & Wynne, 1974).

Age may force older addicts into methadone treatment and/or cause chemically dependent people to look to other more accessible drugs as substitutes. As a result, practitioners may begin to find an increase in the number of people suffering from the side and interactive effects of drugs (Heller & Wynne, 1974).

Alcohol and the Elderly

While alcohol use and misuse among the elderly could be included in the section concerning "legal drugs," the pervasiveness, complexity, and seriousness of the problems associated with this topic warrant a special discussion. Many people in our society have been exposed to alcoholism in one form or another, and it has caused great concern and confusion. Although alcoholism manifests severe medical complications in a relatively short amount of time, it continues to be a major problem among many individuals in their later years. It is estimated that as many as 15% of all people over the age 65 have drinking problems (Zimberg, 1974a).

Zimberg (1974a) has defined alcoholism in terms of alcohol-related problems with one's family, physical, or mental health, employment, finances, or with the law. This is opposed to looking at it in terms of amount or frequency of alcohol consumption. While the above problems may be easily diagnosed, they are often masked because of the probable medical and social problems confronted during the aging process itself. Research has suggested that the incidence of alcoholism peaks between the ages of 35-50 and declines with increasing age (Bateman and Peterson, 1971, 1972; Gorwitz, et. al., 1970; Locke, et. al., 1960; and Malzberg, 1947) so it is easy to see why it is sometimes overlooked as a potential cause of problems among the edlerly.

There exists, in fact, two groups of elderly problem drinkers (Zimberg, 1974a). The first group, chronic alcoholics, have had a long history of abuse and have somehow managed to survive in spite of the self-limiting quality of the condition.

These individuals frequently show one or more of the many symptoms of chronic heavy drinking—seizures, chronic brain syndrome, cardio-pulmonary disorders, gastrointestinal problems, and cirrhosis of the liver—yet they remarkably continue to function. The second group of elderly problem drinkers that Zimberg identified are the situational alcoholics. These people started their problem drinking at a later period of life, most often in a reaction to the stresses and problems experienced as a result ot the aging process. They typically do not exhibit the serious medical sequelae that are apparent with chronic alcoholics but do experience the same or similar problems with their family, finances, and the law.

Depression is a relatively common symptom among both groups of elderly individuals and some quite often turn to alcohol in an attempt to assist themselves through life. There probably aren't too many poorer choices of anti-depressants because the physiological function of alcohol is exactly the opposite of the desired goal; it only tends to make the depressed individual more depressed. What has been shown to be effective in lifting the depression and helping individuals deal with the stresses in life are socialization programs sometimes with the assistance of true anti-depressant medications. In fact, another similarity between the two groups of elderly problem drinkers is the fact that individuals in both groups seem to respond readily to a therapeutic environment, i.e., where they can find someone to listen to them and help them realize that someone cares about them (Zimberg, 1974b).

COUNSELING STRATEGIES AND IMPLICATIONS

It has been mentioned that attempts to escape from the depression caused by life adjustments, losses, and the physical symptoms of aging along with attempts to retain as much youthful vitality as possible are among the major motivators and reinforcers among elderly substance abusers. It has also been mentioned that socialization programs where individuals can find companionship are very successful in helping people with their concerns. Although these points are widely accepted, the authors are not aware of any systematic research undertakings studying types of treatment regimens believed to be effective. For this reason, the authors will elaborate on what a socialization program is and how it can be developed for use with the elderly substance abuser population.

The first step that must be taken is to identify individuals who are having substance abuse problems. Counselors must acknowledge the social influences operating on elderly individuals and educate other professionals who work with the elderly. Among the most effective "outreach" activities are the following: discussions with physicians to help locate patients; working with pharmacists to identify long-term users, creating targeted public education campaigns at focal points for the elderly; working with individuals to identify friends and family members with problems; and lobbying local medical associations to facilitate physician re-education programs and in setting up referral networks (Heller & Wynne, 1974; LaJambe, 1978). As we stated earlier, identification of the elderly substance abuser may be made more difficult by the masking of apparent symptoms by physiological processes associated with growing older.

Once substance abusers have been identified, the task becomes one of getting them involved and interested in a treatment program. This is often difficult due to the stigma attached

with being labeled "alcoholic" or "drug addict." Total acceptance of individuals should be made on their terms to satisfy
their need for control of this situation. This acceptance should
be shown in terms of warmth and caring on the part of the counselor with communication of positive regard and respect
towards the individual. Realization, on the part of the client, that
a problem does exist and that someone else cares enough to
help with their problem is the beginning of the therapeutic process.

Once the substance abuser has entered treatment, the immediate goal is to deal with physical symptoms that may be associated with the problem. If the individual has developed a dependence upon one or more substances, the initial treatment involves a detoxification or "drying out" period supplemented by
vitamins, meals, fluids, rest, and general medical care. Chronic
abusers are not the only clients whose physical side may need
attending to, but they are often the ones who have this need as a
higher priority.

Physical symptoms and sequelae of substance abuse are
usually the first priority, but the mental and emotional conditions that have previously been reinforced must be reduced at
the same time. It is the social system of the abuser that has often
times made a significant contribution to the development of the
abuse problem. All factors must be taken into account when
treatment is planned. It is imperative for the counselor to identify specific problem areas that have been reinforcing the abuse
in each individual. Each individual develops and maintains
one's own problem a little differently. To gain this information
the counselor must help clients self-disclose and discuss their
problems and pain. In this way one has established a positive
relationship while gaining necessary information.

One of the best methods for the counselor to reach someone
who has become a substance abuser is to show genuineness
and compassion (Wandres, 1976). Elderly individuals are
especially receptive to these expressions of caring and will respond with an exploration of concerns, thus facilitating the
treatment process.

Many alcoholics have difficulty relating to other persons and
suffer from loneliness and a lack of self-esteem. These
behaviors generally allow for a maintenance of isolation rather
than contact with other individuals. Therapy programs de-

signed to help elderly alcoholics form interpersonal relationships while receiving peer support can facilitate reduction in alcohol-related behavior. Elderly alcoholics do respond positively to treatment and counseling when services meet their needs.

Zimberg (1974a) also argues that allowing elderly substance abusers to open their feelings to someone in a caring and safe relationship may be sufficient treatment. Some, however, may need more involved therapies involving a variety of techniques and styles. One treatment technique that has been proposed is group counseling. Such groups consist of counselors and other substance abusers who are experiencing similar difficulties. The group should be very supportive, establishing a solid environment, within which abusers can be confronted with their problems and in which they can respond openly. Similar types of groups can involve families and/or social units of abusers so a more systematic problem-solving approach can be utilized. Again, for people depressed due to social isolation, contact with others appears to be therepeutic.

The teaching of alternative behaviors by counselors has also become a popular and effective treatment tool. Assertiveness training (developing the ability to appropriately express personal rights and feelings in the presence of others), relaxation training (learning alternative responses to anxiety provoking events), and self-control training (guiding these features of one's own behavior that might lead to positive consequences) are all innovative techniques which can be useful for elderly substance abusers.

Finally, one point that needs to be mentioned concerning problem-solving approaches to elderly substance abuse is this: It is entirely possible that problem-solving systems used may be different from those utilized with younger abusers. It is important for counselors to be knowledgeable of problems of aging (which are often induced by society, i.e., retirement). It is also important for counselors to realize that everyone needs to experience self-dignity and worth and that methods for achieving this are often different for the elderly.

SUMMARY

Substance abuse is a problem that crosses racial, economic, and generational lines. The elderly use and abuse substances much like younger people—to alleviate boredom and loneliness; to cope with problems and stresses of everyday life; and to try to prolong feelings of youth and vitality.

Substance abuse is a problem of society and social systems and many people regard use of drugs as commonplace, expected, and without risk (Brady, 1978). While our knowledge of the physical effects of drugs is increasing multifold, knowledge of, and attendance to, mental and emotional dependence is not maintaining that pace. The elderly are "easy marks" for substance abuse because of society-induced and reinforced problems of dependence, lack of self-dignity, and feelings of minimized self-worth. What must be done is to reach out to elderly substance abusers helping them realize that someone cares and will take time to listen.

In this chapter we have discussed ways to identify individuals who are in need of assistance and methods of involving them in treatment programs. It has been shown that if elderly people are motivated to change and do avail themselves of counseling, then the chances of their "recovery" are excellent. The authors feel that the professional community must come to realize that drug abuse and alcoholism are problems among the elderly and that with outreach, re-education, care, and respect these problems can be resolved.

REFERENCES

Bateman, W.J., & Peterson, D.M. Variables related to outcome of treatment for hospitalized alcoholics. *International Journal of Addiction*, 1971, 6(2), 215-224.

Bateman, N.J., & Peterson, D.M. Factors related to outcome of treatment for hospitalized white male and female alcoholics. *Journal of Drug Issues*, 1972, 2(1), 66-74.

Brady, E.S. Drugs and the elderly. In R.C. Kayne (Ed.), *Drugs and the elderly*, Los Angeles: U.S.C. Press, 1978.

Brody, E. In O.T. Carrol (Ed.), *N.I.D.A. services research: Drug use and the elderly: Perspective and issues.* U.S. Department of H.E.W., Alcohol, Drug Abuse, and Mental Health Administration, 1975.

Capel, W.C.; Goldsmith, B.M.; Waddell, K.J.; & Stewart, A.T. The aging narcotic addict: An increasing problem for the next decades. *Journal of Gerontology*, 1972, 27(1), 102-106.

Caranasos, G.T.; Stewart, R.B.; & Cluff, L.E. Drug-induced illness leading to hospitalization. *Journal of the American Medical Association*, 1974, 228(6), 713-717.

Carroll, L.T. (Ed.). *N.I.D.A. services research: Drug use and the edlerly: Perspectives and issues.* U.S. Department of H.E.W., Public Health Service, Alcohol, Drug Abuse and Mental Health Administration, 1975.

Cheung, A. In L.T. Carroll (Ed.), *N.I.D.A. services research: Drug use and the elderly: Perspectives and issues.* U.S. Department of H.E.W., Public Health Service, Alcohol, Drug Abuse and Mental Health Administration, 1975.

Drug programs ignoring the aged. *The Journal*, Toronto, 3(1, 2), January, 1974.

Drug use in America: Problem in perspective. Second report of the National Commission on Marijuana and Drug Abuse. Washington, D.C., U.S. Government Printing Office, March, 1973.

Extum-Smith, A.N., & Windsor, A.C.M. Principals of drug treatment in the aged. In I. Rossman, (Ed.), *Clinical Geriatrics.* Philadelphia: J.B. Lippincott, 1971.

Freeman, J.T. (Ed.), Clinical principles and drugs in aging. Springfield, Ill.: Charles C. Thomas, 1963.

Gorwitz, K.; Buhn, A.; Warthen, F.J.; & Cooper, M. Some epidemiological data on alcoholism in Maryland. *Quarterly Journal of Studies on Alcoholism*, 1970, 31, 423-443.

Heller, F.J. & Wynne, R. Drug misuse by the elderly: Indications and treatment suggestions. In S. Senay, V. Shorty, & H. Alksne (Eds.), *Developments in the field of drug abuse.* Cambridge, Massachusetts: Schenkman, 1974.

Kayne, R. Drugs and the aged. In I. Barnside, (Ed.),*Nursing and the aged.* New York: McGraw-Hill, 1976.

LaJambe, P. Outreach is key in program for older drinkers. *NIAAA Information, Feature Service,* March 3, 1978.

Locke, B.Z.; Krama, M.,; & Pasamanick, B. Alcoholic psychoses among first admissions to public mental hospitals in Ohio. *Quarterly Studies,* 1960, 21, 457-474.

Lofholm, P. Self medication by the elderly. In R.C. Kayne (Ed.), *Drugs and the elderly,* Los Angeles: U.S.C. Press, 1978.

Malzberg, B. A study of first admissions with alcoholic psychoses in New York State, 1943-1944. *Quarterly Studies,* 1947, 8, 272-295.

Mauksch, H.D. The organizational context of dying. In E. Kubler-Ross (Ed.), *Death: The final stage of growth,* New Jersey: Prentice Hall, 1975.

Pascarelli, E.F. Alcoholism and drug addiction in the elderly. *Geriatric Focus,* 1972, 11(5), 4-5.

Pascarelli, E.F., & Fischer, W. Drug dependence in the elderly. *International Journal of Aging and Human Development,* 1974, 5(4), 347-356.

Pascarelli, E.F. Drug dependence: An age-old problem compounded by old age. *Geriatrics,* 1974. 29(12, 109-115.

Peterson, D.M., & Whittington, F.J. Drug use among the elderly: A review. *Journal of Pyschedelic Drugs,* 1977, 9(1), 25-37.

Pfeiffer, E. Use of drugs which influence behavior in the elderly: Promises, pitfalls, and perspectives. In R.C. Kayne (Ed.), *Drugs and the elderly.* Los Angeles: U.S.C. Press, 1978.

Physicians desk reference. New Jersey: Medical Economic Incorporated, 1974.

Schwartz, D.; Wang, M.; Zeitz, L.; & Goss, M.E.W. Medication errors made by elderly chronically ill patients. *American Journal of Public Health,* 1962, 52, 2018-2029.

Shropshire, R.W. The hidden faces of alcoholism. *Geriatrics.* 1975, 30(3) 99-102.

Task Force on Prescription Drugs Final Report. Office of the Secretary, U.S. Department of H.E.W., February, 1969.

Task Force on Prescription Drugs. Department of Health, Education and Welfare. The drug users and the drug prescribers. Washington, D.C.: U.S. Government Printing Office, 1971.

Wandres, J. Problem drinking and retirement. *Retirement Living*, February, 1976.

Weg, R.B. Drug interaction with the changing physiology of the aged: Practice and potential. In R.C. Kayne (Ed.), *Drugs and the elderly*. Los Angeles: U.S.C. Press, 1978.

Wiersum, J. Psychotropic drugs in addiction. *Journal of the American Medical Association,* 1974, 227(1), 1979.

Zimberg, S. Two types of problem drinkers: Both can be managed. *Geriatrics*, August 1974a, 135-138.

Zimberg, S. The elderly alcoholic. *Gerontologist*, June 1974b, 14, 221-224. 221-224.

Section IV

Counselor Training and Practice

The sign in the photo reads:

1. Learn to spell your words.
2. Spell with a partner.
   ...you put your words in alpha-
   ...order?
   ...try to find your words
   ...onary.
   ...d antonyms and syn-
   ...your words?
   ...to divide them into

Counseling for the Growing Years

AN OVERVIEW

The training of counselors to work with the elderly cannot be left to chance. Yet, when one examines the counseling literature, very little can be found which points to specific rationale or training procedures for counselors who are to work with an elderly population. It is partially because of this paucity of material that this book has been written. Materials in this section are a beginning in providing needed information. Hopefully, works presented here will stimulate others to develop and share ideas for counselor training and practice which can be specifically aimed at working with the elderly.

Farwell provides an overview of counselor training. He emphasizes the human environmental interaction that is basic to all counseling. Using this concept as a stepping stone, Farwell discusses counselor characteristics, counselor education, and counselor preparation experiences both of a general and specific nature. The major contribution of this paper is the order it provides for the educational process and the detail it outlines. Upon reading this paper one is left with the idea that all counselors need some common training, but that certain specialists, working with the elderly for instance, require additional skills and competencies.

Maynard takes a more pointed approach and focuses specifically on the use of group approaches in counseling the elderly. His paper reveals the lack of information in counseling literature pertinent to the use of group approaches with an elderly population. Maynard goes beyond the counseling literature and presents a rationale for use of psychotherapeutic group counseling approaches. He pays particular attention to reality orientation, remotivation, reminiscing groups, and group psychotherapy. He provides the reader with a *broad* perspective from which to view group counseling with the elderly while providing *specific* information on a number of group strategies.

Smith contributes to the development of counselor training and practice by overlaying the needs and concerns of the elderly on existing counseling theories. Her work provides information about specific counseling approaches and tests each in relation to a specific population. The end result is a clearer understanding of the transition from theory to practice. A secondary result of her work should be to stimulate further research which, in turn, will continue to improve training and practice.

Katz and Libbee present a training program for individuals who are going to work with minority elderly. Their work is significant on two fronts. First, the workshop model they describe can be used as a prototype for a number of other counseling concerns. Second, this paper demonstrates that educating counselors to work with the elderly can occur in a number of ways, some formal— others less formal. In either case, results can be beneficial to participants.

Counselor Preparation for Work with the Elderly

Gail F. Farwell

ABSTRACT

The preparation of a counselor for working with the 65 and over population has commonalities with the preparation of any counselor. However, there also are unique aspects to that preparation. To a point, the knowledge, skills, and attitudes of all counselors are common.

Respect for the dignity and worth of each individual is an essential attitude for any counselor. An understanding of the developmental processes of life, how growth and change take place, and the relationship between a human's system and the environmental system in which growth and behavior are nurtured are essentials for all counselors. Knowledge and skill in interpersonal relationships, communication, a range of intervention, assessment, and evaluation skills are also required.

On the other hand a counselor working with a 65 and over population is in need of some special knowledge. In-depth study of later age psychological and physical characteristics are essential. There are many sociological factors such as agencies, legal parameters, and social expectancies that need consideration. Major changes in life style occur as one advances in age. Counselors need to be in tune with these elements. The counselor function of advocacy will be a special characteristic needing attention.

Characteristic of the preparation of counselors is having the practical side of education under close scrutiny and supervision. The counselor candidate needs to anticipate the demands of having the professional delivery system carefully evaluated and have a readiness for the encounter, confrontation, and growth that accrues from the supervisory process.

INTRODUCTION

The purpose of this essay is to identify aspects of preparation for the professional counselor working with the elderly. Initially I am going to offer a definition of counseling as it is being used in this chapter. I see this as desirable because it is from the definition of counseling that the role model for professional counselors results. In turn, this assists in delineating the scope of preparation for the professional counselor working with all age groups. It has equal application to specialized work.

As utilized in this chapter, counseling is a professional relationship and process between a counselor and a counselee directed toward specific goals negotiated between two parties that moves the target person toward self-competency. SELF-COMPETENCY is that phenemenon of development that includes a personal awareness of what one is, what one stands for, and what one is becoming. This definition implies the developmental notion that modification of one's current status is always a reality. Situational variables, over which we may or may not have control but which are inevitably present, must be confronted and integrated toward the goal of functional self-competence. To me, counseling is the unique intervention employed on behalf of a target person or population. Attendant to comprehensive counselor role and functioning are six major intervention forms, some are direct (first order) interventions with a counselee and some are indirect (second order) interventions on behalf of a counselee or counselee population.

To be identified as a *first order intervention* there must be the direct involvement of the counselee; counseling, group work and instruction are first order intervention forms. A second order intervention form is for the benefit of the counselee, but that individual's direct in-person involvement isn't necessary for accomplishing the identified desired outcome; consultation, programming (program development and management), and evaluation—accountability are second order interventions. Acceptance of these intervention forms as means for assisting counselees to achieve self-competence sets the stage for offering ideas about the scope of professional counselor preparation.

WHO SHOULD BE A COUNSELOR?

This question has been baffling counselor educators for a long period of time. It baffles others, too. Some argue that a counselor must be indigenous to the client population— teen agers for teen agers, blacks for blacks, males for males, and facetiously, maybe even psychopaths for psychopaths. I believe this concept to be ridiculous because if we want to really get down to cases, no one could ever counsel another because no two people are alike; even identical twins originating from the same sperm and ovum have been shown to be quite ideosyncratic and are truly unique.

On the other hand, I am the first to argue that the more familiarity the counselor can have about individual development, societal impact on development of the individual about mores, morals and standards that chacterizes a culture or a segment of the culture, and about life conditions that determine decisions and accommodations, the more likely the counselor will be acceptable to the counselee. Too, it follows that not only acceptance will be attainable but that necessary and desirable knowledge will be present for the counselor to make some sense out of the experience and needs of the counselee and to assist that counselee toward growth and change specified by agreed upon goals.

First, I believe that the effective counselor must have a reasonably "open system." This doesn't mean that there are no values or biases present. If a counselor is going to be amenable to a population spread, (and I believe *all counselors must be* because of the uniqueness of people, the variety of societies, cultures, and sub-cultures, and the characteristics of institutions), then the counselor's system must be of substantial breadth to accommodate a broad range of experiences, needs, and values. The reasonably open system is desirable for being able to accept a broad range of persons, for being able to empathize with the individual ideosyncraticness presented, by beings that are met through relationships with others. Herein, it is my intent not to minimize other forms of help, but rather to elucidate on the knowledge, skill, and experience desirable for implementing the professional counselor role in general, and then more specifically the essentials for working with the aged.

Second, the effective counselor should possess a reasonable amount of academic intelligence and proficiency. There is a body of knowledge about people; about behavior and behavior development; about instrumentation and interventions; about cultures, societies, and institutions; and about research methods and outcomes that should be part and parcel of the professional counselor's arsenal.

Third, there should be a readiness and willingness on the part of the prospective counselor to put one's own personal demonstration of knowledge, skills, and values on the line for observation, review, and refinement. This is what supervision is all about. The hallmark of a profession is a willingness to prepare, to review, and to evaluate the adequacy and proficiency of its membership.

Selection of oneself for possible entry into a profession should be on the basis of a proclivity for the dimensions of the profession as well as a reasonable knowledge of what the profession expects and demands of its members (Farwell, et al., 1974). The reader should remember that earlier I defined counseling as a *professional relationship and process*. There are many relationships that are helpful and there are many needs of human beings that are met only through relationships with others. Herein, it is my intent not to minimize other forms of help, but rather to elucidate on the knowledge, skill, and experience desirable for implementing the professional counselor role in general, and then more specifically the essentials for working with the aged.

Fourth, I believe there should be a determination of criteria by the preparing institution and a thorough selection process that identifies those persons believed to most likely engage successfully in and profit from the counselor education sequence.

WHAT IS COUNSELOR EDUCATION?

Counselor education or preparation, whichever you prefer, is the process of selecting, instructing, supervising and evaluating individuals who are motivated to become professional counselors and who possess both the personal characteristics and energy to fulfill the learning demands derived by the profession. Too, the candidate should come into the field realizing that the educational process is never terminated and the clientele, the profession, and licensure-certification boards have a right to expect (and most likely will require) the practicing counselor to engage in a continuing education program for the upgrading of knowledge and skills.

This fact of continuing education has not always been true in this or other professions. However, in this late twentieth century continuing education is a reality. There are several good reasons for its existence and continuation. There is an information explosion; professions have engaged in research; and there is much seminal theorizing that brings about change in knowledge and method. The professional counselor needs to keep on top of new developments as well as continuing to harness the "tried and true" that stands the test of time and experience. The potent social movement of consumer advocacy has had an effect on services as well as products and the argument is presented that adequate professional service cannot be provided if the persons delivering the service stagnate.

The preparation of counselors is the province of several organizational structures in higher education. In some cases counselor preparation is administratively an independent department with varying titles such as Department of Counseling and Guidance, Department of Counselor Education, Department of Counseling Psychology, or Department of Counseling and Personnel Services. Sometimes counselor preparation is a sub-unit of a Department of Educational Psychology, a Department of Psychology, or a Department of Human Development. Another alternative offered on some campuses is to find counselor education in a Department of Education or a Department of Administrative (Educational Administration) Services. Counselor preparation is a graduate program of studies.

Personally, I think it makes little difference where the unit is organizationally and administratively delivered. I do think it makes a big difference in how the counselor education faculty defines its program, the commitment the faculty has to the learning sequence, and the institutional support given.

In answering the question, what is counselor education, the reader should be alerted to the fact that specialization of counselor preparation, while being a graduate program of studies, places reliance on social science learnings of undergraduate programs in such areas as psychology, sociology, education, anthropology, and the humanities. However, anyone aspiring to be a professional counselor should realize that at least a master's degree, and in some instances a doctoral degree, is required for an entry position; and that this same requirement may exist for licensure or certification. Individuals aspiring to be professional counselors who do not possess undergraduate education in the social sciences and humanities can usually find a program that will consider them for admission with deficiency, expecting that the necessary foundations will be developed while in graduate student status.

There has been a developmental history regarding job entry. As characterizes many pursuits, the accumulation of experience and research data has nurtured changes in expectancies and requirements. At the time of this writing (1979) there is a big thrust for licensure of individuals and accreditation of both preparation programs and service agencies. At the same time there are forces at work for regulation, represented by accreditation and licensure, there are social and political forces raising a "hue and cry" about over-regulation. There are a potpouri of forces at play—interests of professional associations (American Personnel and Guidance Association, Association for Counselor Education and Supervision, American Association of Marriage and Family Counselors, American Psychological Association), the power of the dollar through third party payments (Medicaid, Medicare, insurance companies), the concern of government (licensure legislation, government sponsored social services), and legal battles (malpractice suits, and other forms of litigation)—that are influencing expectations and practice in counselor education.

Counselor preparation is a didactic-experiential learning situation that stresses competent application of knowledge and skills. The counselor candidate can expect to be observed and supervised in individual and group interactions. The candidate should realize that there will be considerable monitoring of one's behavior in both laboratory and field settings and that selective retention in a program is a combination of both intellectual academic competence and positive evidence of constructive interface with counselees and other professionals when delivering one's self in counseling, group work, instruction, consultation, programming, and evaluation.

THE COUNSELOR PREPARATION EXPERIENCE

General

For me the following assumptions lie behind professional preparation for the counselor: (1) The candidate is academically
competent to pursue graduate level work; (2) The candidate's
personal structure is such that one can expect positive, constructive interpersonal relationships; (3) The candidate is motivated toward an occupation of service to other humans; and (4)
The candidate has been informed, understands, and accepts
the detailed learnings and experiences needed to move toward
professionalism.

There are additional assumptions that apply to the preparation
program: (1) There is a competent faculty and reasonable stu-
dent-faculty ratio for effective advisement, and evaluation; (2)
There are adequate fiscal resources to support the program and
an institutional commitment for continued support; (3) There
are adequate physical accoutrements in the form of
classrooms, learning laboratories, and specially adapted space
for counselor interventions, library resources, audiovisual hard-
ware and software, and research tools (computer access,
calculators, etc.); and (4) Adequate arrangements for field experience have been demonstrated and are available.

Accepting the above assumptions as valid, I argue for both the
generalist and specialist aspects of preparation for those working with the elderly. The arguments I make are predicated on
my knowledge of existing standards proposed by professional
associations—primarily those of the American Personnel and
Guidance Association and the American Psychological Association—my experience as a counselor and counselor educator,
and the anticipatory development that one can reasonably expect a range of 65 year old plus users to experience.

The first tool any counselor utilizes is the self. How well does
the individual know one's own person? What are the strengths
and limitations? What values and mores are held that give
direction to action? Can the person acknowledge both success
and failure? Is the candidate open to new ideas and experiences? Can the person field challenge, observation, and
supervision? One of the goals in counselor education is personal encounter, confrontation, and growth. There should be a
guarantee of experiences for the candidate where a continued

integration of the self will be promoted and made possible. This will be accomplished through advisement, instructional groups of a variety of dimensions— large to small, supervision, and quite possibly counseling. The academic learning, skills, and tools of the trade are all an overlay to the basic characteristics of personhood.

There is a body of social science literature that appears helpful to anyone who might be a counselor. All counseling theories— and there are many—have a grounding in conceptions of the human being and how the person grows and develops. Too, we are dealing with the human condition—its strengths and frailities. Most of the behaviors we are contending with are learned behaviors—likes, dislikes, attitudes, values, feelings, mores, disappointments, expectations, skills, and competencies. Thus, we need to understand the learning process.

A review of these behaviors will result in the realization that these learnings do not occur in a vacuum but in a social context of cultures and institutions. Counselors need a firm knowledge base in personality development, human growth and development, and learning. There are advantages in a good understanding of perception and motivation. Because development and learning are in a context, counselors should be informed about cultures and their impact on the maturing of humankind. Such areas as social stratification, collective behavior, minority groups, group dynamics, and social psychology are helpful areas of knowledge. Information about the political and economic systems at work are essential background as counselees help users make viable decisions and accommodate the circumstances of life. I would argue that the above identified areas are a common springboard for persons in the helping professions.

In the special field of counseling, the candidate needs gounding in counseling theory and application, group processes, case study procedures, consultation models and delivery systems, life style development with particular emphasis on vocational development, assessment foundations and skills, and evaluation procedures. From these formulations, there needs to be a carefully thought through role and function based both on implications from theoretical models and the pragmatics of the work environment. There are both legal and ethical considerations that must be acknowledged and understood.

Parallel to and intertwined with these learnings should be the opportunity to practice the knowledge and skills under supervision in multi-practicums or in a combined practicum internship experience. Emphasis is placed on the "under supervision" variable because it is here that the candidate has the opportunity to "try one's wings" in a controlled support environment. Generally speaking, a candidate begins this experience in a structured controlled laboratory situation with gradual movement toward more and more independence and responsibility in field settings.

Special

In the former section I've presented the framework for the general background of anyone seeking to be a professional counselor. I believe there are some special areas of inquiry and experience needed by counselors working with those in the latter stages of life-style development. There should be a grounding in the psycho-social characteristics of aging. What are the changing conditions that indicate a change in the accommodation processes for the counselee? New relationships with family, with friends, with employers, and with recreational partners are dimensions that must be considered. A good understanding of changing physical expectations as people advance in years is needed. Bodily changes influence attitudes, feelings, and activities. Help in coping with these natural changes, as well as "crisis" changes that might occur, are subject matters that might confront a counselor.

There are many societal factors that require cognizance by the counselor working with those in the growing years beyond 65. There are special laws—federal, state and local—that impinge on these lives. The counselee may have informational deficits regarding these laws. There are specially designated agencies and services for assisting senior citizens. The counselor cannot hope to have expertise in all areas, but it is desirable to be well informed for both consultation and referral. It behooves the counselor to be in a position to know some of this and to know other "helpers" who can be brought into the picture to work as a team member in the facilitation process.

What are the work rights of the senior worker? What are the community attitudes, as well as individual attitudes, toward retirement from gainful employment? Has the counselee engaged in prior planning for the later years? How does the elderly person accommodate the loss of a wife or husband of many, many years? What are the issues associated with self-identity and self-concept as an older person? Are there any recreational interests and how does the individual feel about leisure pursuits? Do the existing relationships with children, grandchildren, and friends have a positive and rewarding structure? Has the individual been successful in negotiating the maze of life with a reserve of fiscal resources? Does the counselee have retirement income, social security, support from family? What are the feelings and attitudes possessed regarding these matters? Where is the person regarding continuing citizen responsibilities such as voting, running for office, and maintaining activism in community affairs? Physical death is an inevitable event; what are the counselee's feelings about demise?

These are just a few of the the developmental phenomena, questions, issues, problems, feelings, and attitudes that can be subject matter for counseling sessions, group involvement, and/or consultation contacts. Some of the characteristics of these contacts would be similar for any human being regardless of age, but many of them have unique dimensions because the counselee is in the later years of life.

The counselor candidate should have some first-hand experience under supervision in attending to and facilitating processes that are directed toward such interests, attitudes, needs, and crises. Practicum and internships that involve candidates with age 65 and over counselees should be part of the professional preparation.

Field Experiences

Special attention needs to be paid at the time of practica and/or internship for the counselor working with the aged. There is some literature from counseling, social work, and psychiatry in working with older counselees. Much of this work can be viewed as crisis intervention. The thesis within this manuscript emphasizes proactive intervention, advocacy, and development.

First, it is quite likely that the counselor will be younger than the target person. There is no way that the counselor can have "shared experiences"—the older person has done, seen, and lived through more. The time in history for the older person was different; there are special implications for the counselor to understand the older person's frame of reference. As people become older they are likely to experience less mobility, and thus, a much more restricted sphere of operation. This can impose a range of attitudes that must receive considerate attention.

Second, in the past much field experience has been gained in settings where the helping has been directed toward students and career-seekers. Thus, the settings have been schools, colleges, employment agencies, and business/industrial environments. Older clientele will be seen in retirement complexes, nursing homes, senior citizen centers, congregate nutrition sites, or recreation facilities. Setting differences become obvious; the student counselor will need to grasp these new parameters because it is within these contexts that help will be offered. With this aspect of counseling being so relatively recent in development, it is quite likely that on-site supervision can be delivered by personnel not necessarily "counselor-prepared." There are special implications for the "field placement contract" to be negotiated among the student counselor, the counselor educator, and the field placement supervisor. This is desirable so that all parties concerned can have a role in specifying expectations and goals, experiences needed, services to be delivered, and evaluation procedures to be implemented.

Third, because of the unique needs of older citizens and the splintered character of service delivery, the student counselor will have great need to become familiar with federal, state, and local legislation and agencies that serve the older citizen. What is public policy concerning aging and the aged? What are the referral agencies available to and the procedures employed by the field experience site? How does one operate the advocacy-proactive role and what political, social action, and educational resources can be utilized for this purpose? Advocacy means a commitment to seeing that the counselee's needs (as mutually perceived within the context of counseling, group work, and consultation) are met as quickly and completely as possible.

This advocacy role should be included within the broader context of program management and implementation. As an advocate the counselor must be prepared to followup and follow through on behalf of the target individual or target group to see that positive action is implemented or forthcoming. The counselor will find it necessary to learn the "tools" of broader-based political and social action and how to gain access to sources of power and support. Fourth, dimensions of supervision should be clearly outlined. What is the responsibility of each of the three members of the triad—the counselor candidate, the counselor educator, and the field supervisor? What experiences are expected by the counselor preparation program? Is there differentiation between the expectations of a first-time practicum student and a more experienced practicum student or intern? What will be the nature of feedback to the counselor in preparation? Who has the responsibility for evaluation? What about audio and video taping, case studies and case reports, and case conferences and programmatic and ethical issues. These should be carefully considered and subject to a statement of educational policy between the agency and the counselor preparation program. The purpose of supervision is to assist the candidate in integrating the personal, the didactic, and the experiential. It is a time for final determination of the proper choice of speciality, adequacy, competency, and professional entry.

SUMMARY

The professional education of a competent counselor to work with the elderly is a complex task. It is a varied mixture of personal integration and strength, good relationship qualities, and a knowledge base about elderly people and how to help them. To be a professional counselor requires commitment and dedication; also, it demands of the person capability in dealing equally well with ambiguity and structure. Lastly, the education of the counselor is never completed. The variability and uniqueness of the human being, one's own potential for initiation and creativity, and the constantly changing social situation place stress on the professional counselor for continued search for new ideas, new ways of doing things, and continual refinement of those ideas and skills that stand the test of time.

REFERENCES

Farwell, G.F.; Gamsky, N.R.; & Mathieu-Coughlan, P. (Eds.). *The counselor's handbook*. New York: Intext, 1974.

Rogers, C.R. The necessary and sufficient conditions of therapeutic personality change. *Journal of Consulting Psychology*, 1957, 22, 95-103.

*The following sources were also used in development of this chapter.

Ganikos, M., & Grady, K. (Eds.). Counseling the aged: A training syllabus for educators. Washington, D.C.: APGA, 1979.

Standards for the preparation of counseling and other personnel service specialists. Washington, D.C.: Association for Counselor Education and Supervision, American Personnel and Guidance Association, 1973. (Note: Adopted by the APGA Executive Council in December, 1977.)

Gentry, W.D. (Ed.). *Geropsychology: A model of training and clinical service*. Boston: Ballinger, 1977.

Harris, L., & associates. *The myth and reality of aging in America*. Washington, D.C.: National Council on Aging, 1975.

Hollis, J.W., & Wantz, R.P. *Counselor education directory*. Muncie, Indiana: Accelerated Development, Inc., Publications Division, P.O. Box 667, 1978. (Note: This publication is revised periodically.)

Kagan, N.R. Presidential address, division 17. *Counseling Psychologist*, 1977, 7 (2), 4-7.

Krauskopf, C.S.; Thorsen, R.W.; & McAleer, C.A. Counseling psychology: The who, what, and where of our profession. *Journal of Counseling Psychology*, 1973, 20, 370-374.

Verwoerdt, A. Training in geropsychiatry. In E.S. Busse & E. Pfeiffer (Eds.), *Behavior and adaption in later life* (2nd edition). New York: Little, Brown, 1977.

Weinrach, S., & Bamboa, T. Caveat emptor: A guide to graduate study in counselor education. *Personnel and Guidance Journal*, 1977, 54 (4), 216-218.

Counselling for... ...g years

Group Counseling
with the Elderly:
Training and Practice

Peter E. Maynard

ABSTRACT

As at other stages in the life span, group work with the elderly has proven to be an effective tool. Most group methods for working with the elderly were developed by nursing or social work personnel. Their professional literature reflects this tradition. Counselors only recently began working in Gerontology and few counselor training programs emphasize gerontological counseling. Several widely used group methods with the elderly—Reality Orientation, Remotivation Threapy, Reminiscing groups, Group psychotherapy—are discussed and implications for counselor training are delineated. Ever emerging forms of group work, family group counseling, preretirement groups, and other preventative methods are outlined.

INTRODUCTION

As of June, 1976, everyday in the United States 1600 more Americans turn 65 (Blackman, 1976). This number will continue to grow and by the year 2000—when the post World War II baby boom passes age 65—there will be an estimated 43 million older Americans or twice as many as there are at present. Today about one in every ten Americans is over 65, by 2020 it will be one in six and could go higher depending on medical advancements. These population trends towards an older citizenry provide a mandate for counselor preparation programs to attend to this area of gerontological counseling, both on a pre-service and in-service basis. Many of the counselors-in-training will find that there will be job opportunities for counselors with aged clients in various settings. Counselors already operating in other areas of counseling will find that they will have the opportunity—or even may be required to change their orientation away from younger populations— to counseling the elderly.

As with other populations from elementary aged children (Warner, Niland & Maynard, 1971), adolescents (Maynard, Warner & Lazzaro, 1969), and the middle aged adults (Rogers, 1970), group counseling is an effective method to offer treatment. More recently group work with the elderly has been found to be very effective (Burnside, 1978). Group work with the elderly has been used in various settings as a mode of treatment or as a vehicle for promoting growth, learning new skills, or developing new coping mechanisms. Rotenberg (1976) states that the elderly suffer many losses.

Health problems affect normal social functioning. Poor eye sight, loss of hearing, and inability to walk are common among the elderly. But elderly also have a tremendous ability to recover, move ahead, and grow. Group work with the elderly can play a special role by providing older adults with an experience of positive social interaction, an expectation of health, and an enhancement of social functioning. Konopka (1963) in speaking of social group work stated that social group work "is a method of social work which helps individuals to enhance their social functioning through purposeful group experiences and to cope more effectively with their personal, group, or community problems" (p. 163.)

Group work with the elderly takes place in various settings, both inpatient—state hospitals, private hospitals, nursing homes, residential homes for the elderly and group homes—and outpatient—community mental health clinics, health maintainence organizations, senior citizen centers, day care centers for the aged, churches, and in private practice. Terminology describing types of group work offered varies. At one end of the continuum are many references to group psychotherapy in which the primary goals of the group include establishing therapeutic alliances between leaders and members. At the other end of the continuum are activity groups wherein the learning of new skills in arts and crafts and current event discussions are used to stimulate the elderly to keep them active and aware. Some limited group techniques are used to get members working together and sharing although this may not be a primary goal.

Toward a Definition

As usual, the waters get muddied when one tries to distinguish between group psychotherapy and group counseling. Patterson (1974), when speaking of individual psychotherapy and counseling, notes that counseling and psychotherapy are on a continuum, with counseling "concerned with the essentially normal individual" while psychotherapy is "concerned with the abnormal or seriously disturbed individual." However, he felt that this is really no distinction at all. Do psychotherapists see abnormally disturbed persons and when they become less disturbed, hand them over to a counselor? Are counselors not able to help abnormally disturbed clients make decisions about normal problems of living?

Super (1955) states that counseling deals with the normalities even of abnormal persons in that it helps to locate and develop personal and social resources. Some of the confusion in terminology comes from the fact that various professional disciplines are engaged in group work with the elderly. Most professionals who pioneered in this work were from the medical field—psychiatrists and psychiatric nurses—or were closely allied to a medical model—social workers. These professionals tended to label most groups regardless of the goals of the group as therapy. Counselors are very recent entrants. Rather than drawing fine lines of distinction, this chapter will address areas exemplified by remedial-rehabilitative, preventative-educative, growth, family, and activity group work.

This chapter will first examine the state of the art of group counseling with the elderly. There will be a discussion of various types of group work, some of which were designed for use with elderly exclusively by nurses and social workers to meet specific needs. Group psychotherapy is discussed as it applies to the aged. Newer emerging forms of group counseling are also included. At the end of each section, training for group leaders is included.

STATE OF THE ART

Gerontology is not an exact science and in fact is not usually seen even as a specific discipline. Genontologists come from various backgrounds and diciplines and include practitioners as well as researchers. Many never work directly with older persons, but work in the biological sciences in laboratories. Compared to other professional groups that have been historically involved with the elderly, counselors are newcomers. This is even more so in group counseling than in individual counseling.

Although group work with the elderly has not been publicized frequently, there has been a growing awareness since World War II of the efficacy and economy of working with the elderly in groups. Adrian Verwoerdt (1976) noted that "Supportive psychotherapy with aged patients is best carried out in a group context. The experience in the group enhances a sense of belonging, an appreciation for the value of external sources of satisfaciton, and the effectiveness of reality testing" (p. 138). According to Burnside (1978), group work with the aged is conducted by very diverse professional groups including psychiatrists, nurses, and administrators of skilled nursing facilities. Counselors are conspicuous by their absence from this list.

The publications on group work with the elderly are widely scattered throughout the periodical literature addressed to psychiatrists, psychiatric nurses, social workers, nursing home administrators, and to some extent to psychologists. Counselors looking for information on group work with the elderly will find themselves plowing through journals such as the *Journal of the National Association of Private Psychiatric Hospitals, Journal of Geriatric Psychiatry, Journal of Gerontological Nursing, The*

Gerontologist, and the *American Journal of Occupational Therapy.*

These journals, of course, are not the standard journals for counselor educators and trainees. It probably would be safe to say that unless a university or college had a medical school, a college of nursing, and a school of social work, a counselor education major would not be able to locate these journals to do research or background reading on group work with the elderly. Some articles on group pcyhotherapy with the elderly have appeared in *Group Psychotherapy,* and the *International Journal of Group Psychotherapy,* but most of the writing on this topic has appeared in periodicals which are outside the mainstream of materials that most graduate counseling students encounter during their training or while practicing their profession.

Some of the concerns expressed by Robert Blake in the *Personnel and Guidance Journal* in 1975 are still applicable; the counseling profession has moved quite slowly in the direction of gerontological counseling. Blake's (1975) article was one of the first articles wherein the counseling needs of the elderly and techniques one would employ in counseling an elderly person were specifically discussed. Blake noted that by his count only eight articles appeared in the *Personnel and Guidance Journal* up to 1975. This journal is the main publication of the American Personnel and Guidance Association, the major professional association for counselors in the United States.

Of the articles Blake mentioned, he found that only four of these were directly related to counseling the aged and the others were only indirectly or tangentially related. Blake cited several examples of times when special features have been produced on the counseling needs of special populations, while counseling needs of the elderly were not addressed. In 1973 the *Personnel and Guidance Journal* had a special feature entitled "Outlook for the counseling specialist." Blake said that although articles in this issue dealt with areas of adult counseling, little was said about the range of human problems associated with aging and being old.

More recently the *Personnel and Guidance Journal* (November, 1976) in a special issue on "Counseling over the life span" included several articles on counseling the elderly. These articles answered some of Blake's (1975) concerns and demonstrated that there were counseling professionals who were not only concerned about counseling needs of the elderly but who had become actively involved in aiding the elderly. Two very recent articles have appeared in the *Personnel and Guidance Journal* which further emphasize the counseling needs of the elderly. O'Brien, Johnson, and Miller (1979) outline problems of multiple losses that the elderly experience. They suggest a number of strategies for counseling aged persons to help them realize their continuing potential and residual personal strengths.

A review of the last seven volumes of the *Journal of Counseling Psychology* revealed that this journal also has had very few articles on counseling needs of the aged. No articles on group counseling with the aged were found. Similar reviews of *Counselor Education and Supervision*, a journal which is mostly concerned with the training of counselors, yielded similar results. The *Journal of Specialists in Group Work*, which is now in its fifth volume has yet to publish an article about group work with the elderly or on training group counselors to work with aged persons.

A review of the major texts on group counseling that are traditionally used in counselor education and counseling psychology programs disclosed that only Corey and Corey (1977) have included a chapter on group counseling with the elderly. The major texts in group psychotherapy can be similarly criticized. Even Yalom's text, *The theory and practice of group psychotherapy,* (1975), which is considered by many professionals to be the leading text in this area, does not address itself to issues for working with elderly persons.

Group counseling activities have certainly expanded in the last several years. One begins to wonder why group counseling activities and training have remained centered at the beginning and middle portions of the life span. Group counselors seem to have been unable to initiate an expansion of counseling services to the elderly. Counselor educators especially need to attend to the potential for establishing training programs of an interdisciplinary nature to prepare counselors for work with the aged. Counselors have focused on the school and vocational areas, placed some emphasis on rehabilitation, and recently have shown interest in marriage and family.

With shifting of the population from a predominance of young persons to an increasing number of retired and very old persons, priorities in counselor education must be re-examined. The inclusion of the new division of the Association of Mental Health Counselors should facilitate the growth of training opportunities in gerontological counseling. Hopefully, counselors increasingly will become qualified to do group counseling in settings where the elderly are now treated.

Very few counselors are now employed in Health Maintenance Organizations (HMO), Community Mental Health Clinics (CMHC), or even in senior citizens centers, in which the elderly seek aid on an outpatient basis. Still fewer counselors are employed in state hospitals, private hospitals, nursing homes, or residential homes for the aged. Traditionally, the group work that has been done in these settings has been done by medical personnel, psychiatrists, nurses, or by social workers.

TRADITIONAL GROUP APPROACHES

Burnside (1978) in her book, *Working with the elderly: Group processes and techniques*, outlines different levels of group work with the aged. These levels also indicate the knowledge base, skills, and practice needed for the leader. The four levels are:

1. Reality Orientation
2. Remotivation
3. Reminiscing: music, art, poetry, creative movement, scribotherapy, and current events
4. Group psychotherapy; family therapy

Burnside is by profession a nurse and has had wide clinical experience with the aged. The first three levels that she mentions are probably rather new to most counselors, especially those who have had no prior experience with the elderly. It would seem that most group counselors coming out of traditional master's level counselor preparation programs are not well equipped to enter into group counseling with the elderly without additional course work, training, and/or supervised experience.

In this section of the chapter I will examine various types of group work with the elderly and discuss some of the settings in which these various types of groups are employed. Comments on the training needs of counselors are included.

Reality Orientation

Reality orientation was devised as a first step in treating confusion in the elderly. It was originated in a Veterans Administration Hospital by a nurse supervisor who noticed that confused patients appeared to respond somewhat better when they were told who they were, where they were, and why they were there (Taulbee & Folsom, 1966). These groups are designed for persons who are very disoriented —sometimes to the point of just staring at the walls.

Reality orientation groups are a non-threatening way to stimulate persons so that they begin to respond to outside stimuli and take responsibility for their own identity. Older persons who have been placed in nursing homes or other facilities choose to tune out the world. This is a defense against the hurt, anger, and confusion they feel. The counselor must begin treatment by helping the elderly regain a sense of who they are, where they are, and to become aware of other basic reality factors.

For elderly patients to get confused and tuned out in an institutionalized setting is not unusual (Cohen & Spence, 1976). Spence conducted a project within a state mental hospital to reorient the hospitalized elderly. Even younger persons institutionalized for periods over 20 years were classified as geriatric patients because of their similarity to elderly confused persons. Reality orientation groups were intitiated to begin to prepare these persons for re-entry into the community.

Treatment is usually carried out in a classroom setting with a chalkboard and other materials readily available. It employs some very simple techniques and is well received by many persons who admit to needing "some help with memory." At first, very simple instructional materials such as clocks, calendars, bulletin boards, and other educational materials are used—but always in an adult manner. The elderly respond with hostility if they feel they are being talked down to or are being treated in a childish or juvenile manner. It is as important to facilitate the retention of dignity and worth and a feeling of control for the elderly as it is for any other client.

The maximum number of persons to be included in a basic reality orientation group is four, especially if the persons to be included are highly confused. Through a trial and error basis it was learned that thirty minutes was the optimal time span for the group to meet (Taulbee, 1978). To facilitate the reality orientation process, group metings are best scheduled at the same time each day and in the same place. Any change of time or place will add to the confusion of elderly clients. Identical instructors should be used over the entire length of the group. Usually a minimum of two weeks in the group is needed to obtain desired effects.

After about a month in a basic reality orientation group, most aged persons are ready to move to an advanced group. In the advanced group, eight or ten persons can be accommodated. In these groups memory games that are not too complicated but require concentration and stimulated recall ability are used to vary group sessions (Taulbee, 1976).

In the reality orientation groups described by Taulbee (1978), nursing assistants were trained to conduct these groups. Very little group process was involved in these groups and mostly "one to one" teaching methods were used. The major consideration in establishing these groups is staff attitude. Since leaders of these groups are often para-professionals, the counselor, social worker, or nurse-supervisor must establish program philosophy and standards. Health care personnel must realize that giving care extends beyond the physical needs of the elderly and includes adequate psychological attending. Counselors, or others in charge of delivery of services, need to initiate group counseling with the staff concerning values and attitudes. Taulbee (1978) suggests that a reality orientation program for the elderly should include these basic principles:

1. Do not hurry the elderly.

2. Explain all procedures before asking them to perform. Face them when speaking; speak distinctly but not too loud.

3. Talk to them as though you expect them to understand, even those who are disoriented or confused.

4. Treat them with dignity and respect. Do not talk down to them or treat them like children.

5. Encourage them to take care for themselves as much as possible.

6. Use social reinforcement; compliment successes and do not emphasize failures.

7. Use the positive approach by looking first for abilities, then for disabilities.

8. Establish a climate of caring and genuine concern for each individual.

After the counselor-trainer has established a positive values orientation and has determined that the health care workers are able to work positively with the elderly, then training can begin. It is presupposed that counselors, social workers, or nurse-supervisors conducting training will have attended to their own attitudes toward working with the elderly. Taulbee (1976) has a packet of material available that could be used in training staff personnel. Role playing and video taped feedback sessions are valuable training techniques to be used in preparation of leaders for reality orientation.

Reality orientation was designed primarily for use in inpatient settings. In these settings, it is suggested that all staff members be trained in this treatment modality so that it might be offered on a 24 hour basis. It has proven to be most effective when applied consistently by everyone who comes in contact with confused clients. However, some use of reality orientation as a group technique has been tried in outpatient settings. To be most effective in these settings, counselors will need to train families to apply reality orientation with the elderly person at home.

The counselor's role in reality reorientation groups could be as leader or co-leader. However, it is likely that the counselor's role will be one or trainer/consultant since these groups are usually conducted by paraprofessionals in inpatient and outpatient settings and by family members in the home. Group counselors need to use their group skills when conducting preliminary sessions for values clarification about the elderly which should precede training of reality orientation teachers.

Remotivation Therapy Games

Remotivation therapy was originally designed for hospital patients but has been adopted for use with elderly persons as well. It can be used as a follow-up technique to reality orientation groups. Remotivation therapy can be employed in outpatient as well as inpatient settings although it is primarily used with institutionalized populations. As with reality orientation, kits for training and conducting remotivation therapy groups are available through the American Psychiatric Association. Separate kits are available for use in either hospital settings or nursing homes.

Remotivation therapy (RT) is a group technique for stimulating and revitalizing individuals who are no longer interested and involved in either the present or the future. The technique is a structured program of discussion based on reality that uses objective materials to which individuals are encouraged to respond (Dennis, 1976).

Remotivation therapy sessions are usually held once or twice a week for twelve weeks. Dennis (1978) suggests that a more intensive schedule is preferable, such as, three times a week for four weeks. Groups can consist of a maximum of fifteen members. Burnside (1978) has suggested that ideally persons should have some ability to interact with others and not be totally regressed. For repressed persons therapy should begin with reality orientation, move into remotivational therapy, and be followed up by reminiscing therapy (Barnes, Sack, & Shore, 1973).

Since many facilities that treat the elderly are small or understaffed, a full range of mental health treatment is not always available. This may mean that an elderly person who is not an ideal candidate for inclusion in remotivation therapy will be invited to join such a group. Dennis (1976) suggested that minimally, to be selected for a remotivation therapy group, a person should have a willingness to join the group, an ability to hear and speak, and lack preoccupation with hallucinations.

The remotivation group leader must see the group as a chance for the older person to start anew and to leave behind labels of "sick" and "uncooperative." The remotivation leader must recruit members for the group by offering a chance to change and improve and an opportunity to learn new things. Different topics that will appeal to the interest of group members are introduced at each session. The leader must present topics that appeal to diverse backgrounds, experiences, and interests of older persons. Sensual stimuli are important to the success of such a group and numerous and varied visual, auditory, tactile, and olefactory stimuli should be included. Visual aids and use of appropriate objects can be helpful in maintaining a high level of attention, interest, and reaction.

Dennis (1978) described the use of remotivation technique with elderly at a state hospital. The group consisted of 12 geriatric patients hospitalized for an average of five years with a mean age of 73.1 years. The following twelve topics were introduced to the group: vacations, gardening, sports, rocks, pets, art, the sea, transportation, holidays, weather, hobbies, and animals and their by-products. Discussion of these topics was always accompanied by objects as stimuli to encourage the use of as many senses as possible.

In remotivation groups, the leader should seek certain specific behaviors from group members and be able to reinforce these. According to Dennis (1978), behaviors most desired during the sessions are: (a) attentiveness to the leaders and others, (b) participation in the discussion, (c) responsiveness to material presented, (d) appearance of enjoying the experience, (e) realism in discussion, and (f) communication with others.

The skills needed to design and conduct remotivation therapy groups are more complex than those needed in reality reorientation. Counselors wishing to lead such a group must choose topics which will stimulate group discussion and interaction. Since group interaction and communications is a stated goal of remotivation therapy, certain group dynamics will be present. Counselors, or other professionals wishing to conduct this type of group, need to have some experience in group leadership.

Of the groups reported in the literature that were built upon the remotivation therapy techniques, all took place in institutions or inpatient settings. As has been mentioned, counselors are less likely to be employed in such settings. Conceivably, remotivation therapy groups could be used in outpatient settings particularly in elderly day care centers and Community Mental Health Clinics.

Reminiscing Groups

It is usually very difficult for an older person not to reminisce. All older persons have interesting memories and events to share. Not only can this be an extremely interesting form of reaction, but it can prove to be a beneficial therapeutic experience for older persons. Reminiscing groups have been found to be feasible and adaptable in various settings with aged persons (Ebersole, 1978).

The major goals for establishing a reminiscing group have been identified by Ebersole (1978) as producing a cohort effect, socialization, avoiding interactional deprivation, stimulating memory, gaining respect from the group because of clarity in expression, reducing generation gaps, recreating, sharing one's life review, setting the climate for other types of groups, and learning self actualizing behavior. Some of these goals are self explanatory but for most counselors some of these need expansion or explanation.

A cohort is a sociological term referring to the grouping of persons who fall in a specific age group for research purposes. By narrowing the cohort to 10 years, for instance those born between 1900 and 1910, a group who experienced identical historical events and similar developmental states when certain events occurred is created.

> In a reminiscing group of age peers, individuals can slowly begin to identify their accomplishments, tribulations, and shared viewpoints. It is necessary for them to define their unique chronological position, elaborate on it, and embrace it before the legacy they have produced as a group becomes apparent (Ebersole, 1978, p. 237).

Reducing the generation gap is often as rewarding an experience for the group leader as it is for the elderly.

Butler (1963) introduced the concept of life review and included it as a possible technique that could be employed in a reminescing group. The life review is a process through which each group member is encouraged to come to terms with the totality of the life experience and to fashion a meaning acceptable to oneself. This is essential for mental health since most people need to view disappointments, regrets, shame, and guilt in a manner that can be accepted.

Taking stock is one of the hardest tasks of old age. Doing this among one's peers is highly therapeutic. Often when a aged person has shared and freely expressed doubts and fears about past decisions or short comings, fellow group members can relate to these feelings. Ebersole (1978) relates that an older man cried in a group because of his lack of education only to find that others in the group felt similar shortcomings. The group members supported one another in their attainments in spite of this supposed deficiency.

Ebersole (1978) has found that sometimes there are wounds that will not heal. Relating these to the group and expressing the rage, hurt, or pain is cathartic and may relieve some of the suffering. It would seem that in such a therapeutic process as the life review a follow up might be needed. However, that rarely happens in this kind of group particularly if it is designed as a support group.

It is not necessary or even advisable to confront or interpret in a reminiscing group. Rather, sharing and listening are the major components to facilitate interaction. If a particular member seems to need more attention, then a referral to a psychotherapy group may be in order. Ebersole (1978) expresses the opinion that you tell persons who are having a lot of trouble that you recognize their discomfort and that after the session you meet and discuss it.

Several factors enter into establishment of a reminiscing group. Goals of the group determine techniques. The duration of the group must be established. Short term groups run for about ten weeks and generally focus on a particular group need and use a limited number of specific techniques. Long term groups run indefinitely with a periodic reassessment of goals. Group members should be involved in this process and in the selection of new members.

Selection of members is important for several reasons. Group members should be approached individually so that the purpose of the group can be explained and a verbal contract established. Personal choice and understanding of commitment add significantly to eventual involvement in the group. Aged persons seldom have choices about their companions or daily ac-. tivities so every opportunity must be made to promote autonomy. It is important to help each group member know who other members are so that the group will feel comfortable in relating precious memories. In institutionalized settings, elderly persons rarely have any say in choice of companions at meals or choice of roommates. Because of this, offering them a choice in selecting group members is very important.

Keeping the group to a manageable size of between six and nine members is important and is stressed by Burnside (1969). One reason for stressing small group size is transportation. Often it is advantageous to plan outings to movies or band concerts in the park. The group should have a permanent time and place set for meetings. The group then becomes an anticipated event that adds structure to uneventful lives (Ebersole, 1978).

It would seem to be advisable to have a near-equal number of men and women because this balance confirms the belief in the importance of sexuality in our interactions throughout the life span (Butler, 1976). Having male and female cotherapists adds another dimension. Research is limited on the effects of a male or female therapist on the group but it would seem that the sex of the leader may evoke different interactions and content. The effects of having all male or all female reminiscing groups as yet have not been researched.

Contrary to reality orientation and remotivation therapy groups, reminiscing groups usually begin in a more relaxed manner since everyone has a lot to share about life. As the group moves into a work phase, difficulties may arise. People can become grief stricken as they relate disappointments or failures. Another problem is that group members may have a tendency toward focusing on their present concerns. When this occurs, the group counselor must skillfully guide the group back to reminiscing. Also, reminiscing can be anxiety producing. The group leader must be prepared to deal with this and be capable of moving back to reminiscing at the appropriate time. Sometimes, because of the nature of the facility or the lack of social support staff, this is the only place in which the aged person can express concerns or fears and be heard. The decision to set aside reminiscing in a given session and follow the direction of the group is based on several factors. Do group members have time to work on these concerns at other times? Is this group the only vehicle available in which these elderly have the opportunity to collectively express daily problems?

Leaders of reminiscing groups need formal and sufficient training to be effective group leaders. Courses in group procedures and techniques and supervised clinical practice with groups of elderly are mandatory. Perspective group leaders need to have had the experience of being in a reminiscing group with their peers to realize the depth of awareness and the deep consciousness that these groups can evoke. Before assuming responsibility for such a group, an internship as a co-leader should have been completed. In a reminiscing group, group dynamics play a very important role. Knowledge of group process is imperative and it seems doubtful that anyone without proper credentials as a group leader should be allowed to conduct such groups.

Group Psychotherapy With Elderly Persons

Group methods that have been reviewed thus far call for varying group dynamics skill levels. As we move into the area of group psychotherapy, one must be aware that the group counselor needs to be fully grounded in theories of group dynamics and must have considerable supervised experience in group psychotherapy. This section of the chapter will draw very heavily on Yalom's (1975) *The theory and practice of group psychotherapy*, which is considered by many to be the most complete and authorative work available in the field. It will also draw from Burnside's (1978) *Working with the elderly: Group processes and techniques*, in which Burnside has adopted many of Yalom's concepts as they apply to group psychotherapy with the elderly.

What is group psychotherapy with the elderly? Berger (1968) has described it thusly:

> Group psychotherapy refers to regularly scheduled voluntarily attended meetings of acknowledged clients with an acknowledged trained leader for the purpose of expressing, eliciting, accepting, and working through various aspects of the client's functioning, and developing the client's healthier and more satisfying potentials.

Thus, the clients who are referred for group psychotherapy are very often highly depressed or highly agitated and disruptive or lack the ability to do reality testing. Hopefully, a group experience will provide a "beneficial, controlled life experience within a group setting by the establishment of relationship with the leader, or interaction with group members or both, together with some clarification of one's motives and those of others in the interaction" (Goldfarb, 1972, p. 114).

Since the group leader who is offering psychotherapy to the aged will be faced with a tough assignment, that leader must be very skilled in creating what Yalom (1975) calls the curative factors in group therapy. These are:

1. Altruism
2. Group cohesiveness
3. Universality
4. Interpersonal learning—"input"
5. Interpersonal learning—"output"
6. Guidance
7. Catharsis
8. Identification
9. Family enactment
10. Insight
11. Installation of hope
12. Existential factors

Burnside (1978) has extrapolated from this list the curative factors that are most germane to group therapy with the elderly. Group cohesiveness develops over time and makes the group a meaningful experience. On-going relationships are very important to the aged who have slowly lost many meaningful relationships. Universality refers to the commonness that sharing demonstrates. It is very reassuring to older persons that others have shared similar feelings and can understand them.

Catharsis is the ability and license to freely express feelings, even hostile ones. This provides the elderly with a means to vent, whereas they usually have to bury many of their feelings. When they realize there will be no retribution, the elderly quickly learn to use the group as a sounding board. Identification increases self esteem in older persons because they can identify with others in the group or even admire and behave like the leader. Becoming more articulate is one recognizable result of an older person's identification with the leader. To instill hope in the elderly is a very humanistic curative factor. Many of the elderly have begun to give up, but the group teaches them that they can still learn and can have power over their own lives.

Group therapy is mostly unstructured with focus on here and now data presented by members, usually a predetermined set of exercises are not planned. Rather, emphasis in group psychotherapy is on the leader's technical skills, personal qualities, and ability to provide core facilitative conditions.

Selection of members for a therapy group with the elderly is a key design issue to insure a successful experience. Certain physical problems bear on selection of members since these problems may interfere with their participation. Persons with severe hearing problems or who can not talk because of impairment or disease probably should be excluded. Altholz (1978) states that the most common reason for excluding someone is an inability to communicate. This refers not just to the ability to talk but also to the ability to verbalize thoughts and feelings. Although some persons could benefit just from attending, therapeutic value lies in one's interaction with others in the group.

The psychiatric diagnosis could be an important criteria for selection. If all potential members are withdrawn depressives, the group may never become active due to members' inability to initiate anything or due to their lack of energy to verbalize. On the other hand, a group composed of agitated persons may create a chaotic situation that the leader can not overcome and control. Altholz (1978) cautions against mixing brain impaired with non-impaired. Many older persons are afraid of becoming "senile" and their participation in a group of "senile" persons, represented by those impaired members, could be very threatening.

Because of the severity of problems usually present in therapy groups, the group counselor must be well prepared for this task. The counselor certainly needs a thorough knowledge and understanding of the biological, psychological and sociological aspects of aging. Other chapters in this book addressed some of these issues.

TRAINING

Yalom (1975) discusses four major components that he considers essential to a comprehensive training program. It would seem that Yalom had in mind persons who were trained at the doctoral level. His four components are: (1) observation of experiencing group therapists at work, (2) close clinical supervision, (3) a personal group experience, and (4) personal psychotherapy or self exploratory work. A brief commentary on these four components will be given now and more will be said about them later in the section on implications for counselor training programs.

Students can derive great benefit from observing a group therapist who has acquired clinical experience in groups with the elderly. A two-way mirror is an excellent way to provide students with a first hand view of therapy in action. Video taping can also provide some of the same experiences, but it can create discomfort among the elderly and be distractive to them. If only one or two persons are to observe, they may sit in the room but outside the circle of participants.

To find suitable group observation opportunities is not easy in the area of gerontology. It is helpful if professors teaching courses are engaged in clinical work with the elderly. Given the nature of many academic appointments in counselor education or counseling pyschology, this is not often possible.

Counselor training programs have long realized the need for supervision. Practicum courses in individual counseling have long been standard offerings in counselor education/-psychology programs. Fewer programs have offered specific courses in group practicum. Yalom (1975) feels that clinical supervision is the *sine quo non* in the training of a group therapist. The beginning group therapist's first group can be a threatening experience; without proper supervision it can be a disaster. Group supervision is more difficult than individual supervision. Just to remember the cast of characters from several groups at once can be a forbidding task. The elderly present many developmental, psychological, and biological problems. This further underlines the need for inexperienced therapists to receive ongoing supervision.

Personal group experiences, according to Yalom (1975), have become widely accepted as an integral part of training programs. He notes that the American Group Psychotherapy Association recommends a minimum requirement of sixty hours as a participant in a group. As of this writing, the American Personnel and Guidance Association, the Association of Counselor Education and Supervision and the Association of Specialists in Group Work have all shied away from formulating standards concerning participation in group counseling. Group therapy is a powerful intervention modality and all potential leaders need to experience the feelings of vulnerability, hostility, and tenderness that can be present in a group. In addition, they need professionally developed standards to guide their preparation.

The last of Yalom's (1975) suggestions for training of group therapists, that of personal psychotherapy, has not been included in many counselor training programs. Yalom (1975) admits that so individualized a process would be hard to regulate.

> The therapist who lacks insight into his own motivations may, for example, avoid conflict in the group because of his proclivity to mute his feelings; or he may unduly encourage confrontation in a search for aliveness in himself. He may be overeager to prove himself or to make insistently brilliant interpretations and thereby emasculate the group (p. 517).

In working in groups with elderly clients, one needs to have done personal values clarification and exploratory work about one's feeling and attitudes about aging and the aged. Personal therapy may be a very valuable way to do this. Increasingly, this author has noticed that many graduate counseling students are now, or have been, in personal therapy. The value and importance of personal therapy for future as well as present counselors is being recognized as a valuable adjunct to the training experience. If this therapy is in the group setting, it gives the future group counselor additional exposure to experienced group counselors.

GROUP WORK WITH FAMILIES OF THE ELDERLY

There seems to be two approaches that emerge in the literature on group work with families of the elderly. The first of these approaches is discussed in detail by Herr and Weakland (1978). This approach involves working with one family as a group. Most of the work reported has been concerned with counseling the family in a crisis situation. The second approach involves working with members of several families as a group. This has usually involved working with families of the institutionalized elderly (Brody & Spark, 1966) or working with families concerning issues of death and loss. Recently, articles are appearing which report group work with families of the elderly which are facing decision making about institutionalization (Hausman, 1979; York & Caslyn, 1977).

An interesting phenomenon that has emerged, as life expectancy of Americans lengthens, is that older adult children who are facing retirement and aging must make decisions about their still older parents. It is often very difficult for an older person who is approximately 65 to deal with parents who could be in the 85+ range. It is sometimes physically impossible for someone who is 65 or older to handle a very elderly parent; or it may be that psychologically the older adult child is going through a traumatic time and can't handle the extra burden of providing support for very old parents.

Working With The Entire Family

The first type of family group counseling with the elderly is usually crises orientated. The identified patient (IP), in this instance an elderly member of the family, may be having difficulty and consequently the whole family may be having problems. However, to get an entire family involved is very difficult. While all the family may be feeling the pain involved with a grandmother's acting out behavior, often family members want the counselor to treat the grandmother and remove the problem. Family counselors would view the above as a problem in the family system and would treat the entire system or as much of it as possible (Minuchin, 1974). Difficulties are defined in terms of family difficulties rather than in terms of the elderly person having a problem. Herr and Weakland (1978) warn the counselor not to be discouraged if one can not get all the family members involved. Rather, work with those who can be reached and demonstrate that this is a family problem and not just the problem of the identified patient.

There are several problems that the family counselor needs to anticipate. The counselor may be verbally attacked by family members who are feeling stress. According to Herr and Weakland (1978), this is a good sign because the family is ready to challenge the counselor rather than accept totally what is offered. The counselor is advised to be open and frank with the family dealing directly with their concerns.

In counseling families, the gerontological counselor must realize that there are some families which cannot be helped. To increase chances of success counselors should avoid certain behaviors such as unjustified optimism. For families who are very pessimistic about a resolution of the problem, a counselor's optimism could invalidate their feelings. Also unabated optimism may set the stage for failure. If the counselor predicts that next week will be better and it isn't, the family may lose confidence in the process.

A counselor undertaking group work with families of the elderly should have a thorough understanding of the family systems approach to family therapy. Salvador Minuchin's *Families and family therapy* (1974) and Kantor and Lehr's *Inside the family* (1976) offer adequate basic knowledge of family counseling. Some of the basic concepts that the counselor should consider are family rules, boundaries, the identified patient, and power.

Each family has rules usually unspoken that define how members will function. For instance, "mother is the only person who is allowed to get irrational in this family" could be a family rule. Rules are the *shoulds* in family interactions.

Boundaries are the mechanisms by which families establish and maintain their territory within the larger community space by regulating both incoming and outgoing traffic. Traffic means people, objects, events, and ideas (Kantor & Lehr, 1976).

A question that the counselor should always ask is: "Who is the identified patient?" In working with families of the elderly, most likely it will be the elderly person who has the problem. The IP will have a combination of physical and psychological symptoms. These serve to distract from the personal and interactional problems of other family members. Other questions are "What would happen if the IP got better?" and "How would the IP get what one wants if cured?" An IP serves a very important function within a family system. Counselors should be aware of this fact.

Another consideration in working with a family system is the question of who has the power in the family. Different family members may have or use their personal power differently. For some their power may be in the bankbook, for others it may be the ability to psychologically intimidate or manipulate. Others exercise power by being sick of becoming disabled. The counselor needs to identify what each family member does to get what they want from the system.

A second type of group work with families of the elderly involves working with some members of the family to provide information, helping them learn to cope with situations, or in relieving anxiety and guilt involved in the institutionalization of a family member. Corey and Corey (1977) mention that there is a pressing need for therapy groups for people with aged relatives in institutional settings. Very often feelings of guilt, anger, failure or helplessness keep family members away. Groups for family members could allow families to share their experiences with other families and thus relieve much of the stress involved in trying to care for the elderly.

Hausman (1979) conducted short term counseling groups for people with elderly parents. The groups had three major goals (a) to find a balance between responsibility to one's self, one's nuclear family and one's parents; (b) to make specific decisions about the extent of the member's obligations to their parents; and (c) to learn to deal with one's parents in a mature way leaving behind unresolved issues from childhood and adolescence that so often interfere with objective evaluation of needs and provisions for real help. These groups met weekly for eight sessions. The atmosphere was informal and permissive. Interventions were mainly limited to reminders to stay with the group's task, clarifications of misunderstandings, preventing monopolizing, interpretations, and summarizations. Didactic material was used occasionally to correct family misconceptions about disability and disease, and to offer information on community resources.

Hausman (1979) found that short-termed, time limited, task oriented groups were effective in helping people who had concerns about their elderly parents. Many other types of groups for family members could be designed. Hopefully, counselors can begin to use a more preventative educational approach and work with groups of concerned family members before institutionalization of the elderly member is warranted.

Counselors who wish to work in groups, wherein the family including the elderly person is involved, will need to be trained in family counseling. Family counseling is a special kind of counseling and involves an understanding of the growing body of theory and research that has emerged in the last ten years. The American Association of Marriage and Family Therapists have been developing standards for preparation of family counselors. If counselors were to adopt a systems approach as was suggested earlier, graduate course work or workshop experience in family systems would be needed. For the second type of group work discussed, that of groups with family members, skills gained from involvement in graduate courses in groups may be sufficient.

NEWER TYPES OF GROUP WORK

Several newer approaches to group work with the elderly have emerged. While counselors have not been involved heavily in other forms of group work that have been discussed thus far, the counseling literature has pointed to several outpatient educative-preventative forms of group work with older persons. Lombana (1976) has outlined several. She states, "If it were possible to help our citizens more thoughtfully to direct the course of their lives, prepare in advance for retirement, maintain appropriate health habits, develop satisfying avocational interests, and maintain a healthy self-esteem, the despair of millions of Americans could be drastically reduced" (p.144).

Preretirement Counseling

Retirement is viewed by many persons as the first "insult" of aging. Retirement is tangible proof that a person is publicly recognized as an "older" person, a "senior" citizen (Manion, 1976). In a youth orientated society, this can be a frightening realization which can have psychological ramifications.

Recently, this has been recognized in both the private and the public sector, and preretirement programs have been developed. Some industries and businesses offer preretirement programs. In doing so, they share responsibility to provide for the welfare of their employees who are about to retire. The public sector seems to be more conscientious in its quest to provide adequate opportunities for preretirement planning. Many preretirement programs concentrate on factual information provided by lawyers, physicians, accountants, and so on. Very few programs are concerned with issues of changing interpersonal relationships, altered relationships within families, shifts in patterns of decision making, and subtle changes in self concept (Ullmann, 1976).

Manion (1976) has categorized preretirement programs into four types: coping, prescriptive, educative, and T-group approaches. The coping approach suggests how one might cope between retirement and death with money and health problems. The prescriptive approach is usually problem orientated and offers suggestions on how to avoid disaster by using the correct formula. Specialists from various fields provide interesting general information in the educational model, usually to large audiences with little time for individualization. The fourth catagory, the T-group approach, is a highly subjective method designed to allow discussion of one's needs, resources, problems and aspirations in retirement.

Manion (1976) suggests that a more integrative approach toward preretirement counseling is necessary. He suggests and outlines components of a program using a small group interaction model. This approach is of interest because it advocates a group counseling approach that most graduate level counselors are familiar with and are trained to deliver. It allows counselors to become involved with no additional training.

Growth Group for the Elderly

Many of the group experiences described in this chapter have a remediation or rehabilitation theme. However, many older persons continue to grow spiritually and mentally. Growth groups for older persons are emerging. Older adults are being exposed to new ways of relating to their inner beings, their environment, and the past and future as part of their present.

The Senior Actualization and Growth Explorations (SAGE) project on the West Coast (Newman & Newman, 1979) is designed to work toward improvement and growth with men and women 65 years and older. By viewing aging as the creative interplay of life forces rather than as a deterioration process, older persons have learned to grow, change, and develop in a manner similar to younger persons. There has been considerable improvement in the overall health and well being of participants as well as renewed interest in life and self responsibility.

SUMMARY

Youngsters in schools are being exposed to new methods for growth and development. Why shouldn't elderly citizens have a right to an equivalent opportunity? Transpersonal psychology has begun to be integrated into our school systems. Educators are studying ways in which imagination, dreams, fantasy, concentration, biofeedback, and meditation may be included in a student's experiences. It is pointed out that the development of several realms of human consciousness are important educational areas for children. So, too, through growth experiences these techniques should be used with the elderly.

REFERENCES

Altholz, J.A.S. Group psychotherapy with the elderly. In I.M. Burnside, (Ed.), *Working with the elderly: Group processes and techniques.* North Scituate, Massachusetts: Duxbury Press, 1978.

Barnes, E.K.; Sack, A.; & Shore, H. Guidelines to treatment approaches. *Gerontologist*, 1973, 13, 517-519.

Blackman, A. Over 65 set growing by 1600 a day in U.S. In H. Cox (Ed.), *Focus: Aging.* Guilford, Connecticut: Dushkin Publishing Group, 1978.

Blake, R. Counseling in gerontology. *Personnel and Guidance Journal*, 1975, 53, 733-738.

Berger, M. Similarities and differences between group psychotherapy and short-term group process experiences— clinical impressions. *Journal of Psychoanalysis and Process*, 1968, 1, 11-29.

Brody, E., & Spark, G.M. Institutionalization of the elderly: A family crisis. *Family Process*, 1976, 5, 76-90.

Burnside, I.M. *Working with the elderly: Group processes and techniques.* North Scituate, Massachusetts: Duxbury Press, 1978.

Burnside, I.M. Group work among the aged. *Nursing Outlook*, 1969, 17. 68-72.

Butler, R. The life review: An interpretation of reminiscence in the aged. *Psychiatry*, 1963, 26, 65-76.

Butler, R. *Sex after sixty.* New York: Harper and Row, 1976.

Cohen, S., & Spence, D.L. *Special program for older citizens.* (Final Report) University of Rhode Island, 1976, (mimeo).

Corey, J., & Corey, M. Groups with the edlerly. In J. Corey & M. Corey (Eds.), *Groups: Process and practice.* Monterey, California: Brooks/Cole, 1977.

Dennis, H. Remotivation therapy for the elderly: A surprising outcome. *Journal of Gerontological Nursing,* 1976, 2, 28-30.

Dennis, H. Remotivation therapy group. In I.M. Burnside (Ed.), *Working with the elderly: Group processes and techniques.* North Scituate, Massachusetts: Duxbury Press, 1978.

Ebersole. P.P. Establishing reminiscing groups. In I.M. Burnside (Ed.), *Working with the elderly: Group processes and techniques.* North Sictuate, Massachusetts: Duxbury Press, 1978.

Goldfarb, A. Group therapy with the old and aged. In H. Kaplan & B. Sadock (Eds.), *Group treatment of mental illness.* New York: Aronson, 1972.

Hausman, C.P. Short term counseling groups for people with elderly parents. *Gerontologist,* 1979, 19, 102-107.

Herr. J.H., & Weakland, J.H. The family as a group. In I.M. Burnside (Ed.), *Working with the elderly: Group processes and techniques.* North Scituate, Massachusetts: Duxbury Press, 1978.

Johnson, D.W., & Johnson, F.P. *Joining together: Group therapy and group skills.* Englewood Cliffs, New Jersey: Prentice-Hall, 1975.

Kantor, D., & Lehr, W. *Inside the family.* San Francisco: Jossey-Bass Publishers, 1976.

Konopka, G. *Social group work: A helping process.* New York: Prentice-Hall, 1963.

Lombana, J. Counseling the elderly: Remediation plus prevention. *Personnel and Guidance Journal,* 1976, 55, 143-144.

Long, R.S. Remotivation-factor artifact. *Mental Hospital Service,* 1962, 151, 1-8.

Manion, U.V. Pre-retirement counseling: The need for a new approach. *Personnel and Guidance Journal,* 1976, 55, 119-121.

Maynard, P.E.; Warner, R.W.; & Lazzaro, J.A. Group counseling with emotionally disturbed students in a school setting. *Journal of Secondary Education,* 1969, 44, 358-365.

Minuchin, S. *Families and family therapy.* Cambridge, Massachusetts: Harvard University Press, 1974.

O'Brien, C.R.; Johnson, J.; & Miller, B. Counseling the aging: Some practical considerations. *Personnel and Guidance Journal,* 1979, 288-291.

Newman, B., & Newman, P. *Developmeht through life:A psychosocial approach*. Homewood, Illinois: Dorsey Press, 1979.

Patterson, C.H. *Relationship counseling and psychotherapy*. New York: Harper & Row, 1974.

Rogers, C. *Carl Rogers on encounter groups*. New York: Harper & Row, 1970.

Rotenburg, S.E. *Use of social group work in fostering social roles of institutionalized aged*. Paper presented at Annual Scientific Meeting of the Gerontological Society, New York: October, 1976.

Super, D.E. Transition: From vocational guidance to counseling psychology. *Journal of Counseling Psychology*, 1955, 2, 3-9.

Taulbee, L.R. *The a-b-c's of reality orientations: An instruction manual for rehabilitation of confused elderly persons*. New Port Richey, Florida: Author, 1976.

Taulbee, L.R. Reality orientation. A therapeutic group activity for elderly persons. In I.M. Burnside (Ed.), *Working with the elderly: Group processes and techniques*. North Scituate, Massachusetts: Duxbury Press, 1978.

Taulbee, L.R., & Folsom, J.C. Reality orientation for geriatric patients. *Hospital and Community Psychiatry*. 1966, 133-135.

Verwoerdt, A. *Clinical geropsychiatry*. Baltimore, Maryland: Williams & Wilkins, 1976.

Warner, R.W., Jr.; Niland, T.M.; & Maynard, P.E. Model reinforcement group counseling with elementary school children. *Elementary School Guidance and Counseling,* 1971, 5, 248-255.

Yalom, I.D. *The theory and practice of group psychotherapy* (2nd edition). New York: Basic Books, Inc., 1975.

York, J., & Caslyn, R. Family involvement in nursing homes. *Gerontologist*, 1977, 17, 500-505.

Modes of Counseling with Elderly Clients

Nikki Smith

ABSTRACT

This chapter reviews a number of models for counselor intervention, e.g., analytic therapy, brief therapy, supportive therapy, applications of learning theory, milieu therapy, eclectic action, and group intervention strategies. Applications for counseling the elderly are discussed for all models. Cautions are outlined for each. Research that is needed is suggested.

INTRODUCTION

Counseling the aged requires recognition that practical, theoretical, and technical aspects for therapy, and consequently for the therapist, may be significantly different when one works with aged clients than when one works with younger clients.

Older people are unlikely to seek help for normal developmental problems. This may be due to lack of understanding of therapy, lack of resources to support therapy, cultural background that values stoicism and privacy, and fear of loss of control and manipulation. Whatever the cause, the elderly who finally seek help are apt to be in what Zinberg (1965) calls a "chronic state of emergency."

A number of problems may exist when one considers using therapy with the elderly. Families may have to be involved in scheduling. Frequent consultations may be required with physicians and social agencies. Problems of financing therapy may increase dependency in elderly clients. Finally, elderly clients may be less "psychologically oriented" and, therefore, require different therapeutic approaches.

It is apparent that special problems exist, but successful therapy is possible with elderly clients, and aging may be the positive factor in motivation toward help (Butler, 1975; Gruen, 1957). This chapter addresses forms that this *help* usually takes.

Analytic Therapy

The first question in discussing analytic therapy with the elderly is — can it be successful? Most of the literature refers to Freud's (1924) view that the age precludes flexibility necessary to restructure character. (It is necessary to recall that Freud's views of personality were flexible and growing; that he made this assertion at a time when life expectancy was considerably less than it is today.)

As early as 1919, Abraham (Bryan & Strachey, 1954), after successfully treating older neurotics, concluded "the age of the neurosis is more important than the age of the patient." Insight therapy, Abraham asserts, can be effective with the elderly who have experienced some years of normal sexual and social usefulness. Although he reports both success and failure with older patients, Abraham (1966) warns "we should not overestimate fixity of character even in later years."

In the analytically oriented literature reviewed here, some report treatment of the elderly as next to impossible or dangerous with psychoanalysis (Cath, 1965, Hollender, 1952); others use the approach (Abraham, 1966; Berezin, 1965; Birren, 1965; Levin, 1965; Michaels, 1965); while others, some modification of it (Goldfarb, 1955, 1963; Wolff, 1957, 1971). An obvious disadvantage of analytic psychotherapy is that it is aimed at the minority of elderly who have the financial and intellectual resources to accept it (Stotsky, 1972).

Therapy with elderly people should, according to Cath (1965), recognize established ego incapacity, excessive neurotic anxiety, life-long symptom complexes, and external changes in anchorages that threaten previously erected defenses. Variables which affect the elderly individual's adjustment include the structure of the id and ego, sublimitations, the physical body, the external world, and the social environment.

Using the Jungian model, Cutner (1950) views the task of the last half of life as individuation, as integration of personality accomplished by introversion of libido. This discovery of previously unconscious personality parts allows wholeness in the individual.

In Wayne's model (1953), the counselor is active, providing environmental manipulations as well as analysis and interpretations. Although Wayne agrees with the assertion (Rochlin, 1965; Zinberg, 1965) that a stressful current problem often brings the elderly to therapy, he adds that the crisis should be used as a nucleus in counseling to maintain client interest in developing insight into unconscious dynamics. It is his belief that painful interpretations may be accepted with less resistance by the old than by the young.

This position, that the elderly are capable of insight and that it is most beneficial, has many adherents. In this view, the struggle of life is good preparation for therapy: it loosens the ground and shatters character defenses (Grotjahn, 1955) and allows the gain of distance, a vantage point from which to view the self and to view human weaknesses (Zinberg, 1963).

The weakening of some defenses leads to better contact with the unconscious (Meerloo, 1961), and so the elderly may be better able to accept unpleasant insight interpretations that would be resisted in the young (Zinberg, 1963; Gotjahn, 1955; Butler, 1960).

Insight is also therapeutic in old age when it is turned to retrospection and used as a basis for therapy (Butler, 1960; Grotjahn, 1955) and it offers greater relief to the elderly by allowing them to face past conflicts (Meerloo, 1961).

With elderly clients, the past becomes a therapeutic tool. Zinberg reminds us that in the dynamic view, the elderly must detach libido in order to learn something new, and warns us that it is best to allow automatic responses to remain automatic.

Brief Therapy

Brief, goal-directed psychotherapy is one approach to the life situation of the elderly. Rooted in traditional psychoanalytic theory, brief therapy is accomplished in one to six sessions of 45 to 50 minutes. The goal is to help the patient return to a premorbid condition. Not only is this mode practical for the elderly, it also allows examination of the patient's environment and intervention when necessary.

One of the proponents of brief therapy is Safirstein (1972), who points out that the elderly, more than any other age group, are likely to become dependent on the counselor: a dependency which could become iatrogenic and last for the patient's lifetime.

A very personalized version of brief therapy is used by Goldfarb (1955) to alleviate anxiety, improve the elderly client's relationship with one's social world, and increase self-regard through mastery. Goldfarb's operational theory views all behavior as motivated to secure help. He posits that, if the elderly individual is able to believe help and hope are possible, anger and anxiety will decrease. Along with this need for help, Goldfarb explains that the elderly individual's feeling of worthlessness is the basis of a need to dominate and manipulate; although it may be consciously denied.

Feelings of power and mastery need to be retried, although real domination is not necessary; the client's conviction that one can dominate the therapist is enough (Goldfarb, 1955). To this end, the client is seen for two 15-minute sessions the first week, and as seldom as possible after that. It is essential that the result, ownership of strength, be achieved in the first few sessions. The counselor attempts to increase the client's self-esteem by providing emotional gratification. An illusion of mastery or power over the therapist is encouraged. Later, Goldfarb asserts, the counselor is seen as a powerful ally.

Goldfarb reports that this form of brief therapy leads to increased self-esteem, improved functioning, and realization of goals. After each session, the client should leave with feelings of strength. These protective feelings can alleviate panic and helplessness; fear and rage should decrease. Basic limitations should still exist, but inhibiting psychological elaboration should be diminished.

Goldfarb finds his method of brief therapy successful for the elderly with psychoneurotic disorders and for those with acute brain syndromes. He does not, however, find it effective with psychotics.

Wolff (1957, 1971) reports success using Goldfarb's therapy with elderly patients in several psychiatric institutions. He described therapy with 54 patients, "burned out schizophrenics" and psychoneurotics, all of whom displayed some degree of choronic brain syndrome with degrees of disorientation and impaired memory; but all able to communicate (1971). They were seen for 50 minutes for three to nine months. Improvement was noted, Wolff (1971) asserts, after 12 sessions. Of the 54, 34 were improved and 22 were released after four months. Although 44 of the patients gained partial insight through therapy, the original goal of helping them gain insight to strengthen the ego was replaced by one of ego support.

The focus of ego support was on improving self-esteem, a direct attack on patients' feelings of being "old and "second-class citizens." This technique, Wolff (1971) reports, pointed out the individual's assets, the importance of life experience, and emotional maturity. The suggestive technique was often "preferable" according the Wolff. Patients also were encouraged to verbalize hostility against authority figures and resentment against their children.

Wolff is one of the few counselors who emphasizes religion: a belief in God and life in heaven after death as a technique which he asserts help elderly patients overcome fear of death.

Obderleder (1970) believes "brief" or "crisis" therapy is the best therapeutic answer to disorganization produced by loss, change and threat so common in the experience of the aged.

She describes crisis therapy with twelve hospitalized elderly patients diagnosed as having senile psychosis or arteriosclerosis with psychosis who recovered after six months. They met as a group, with an active counselor. Focus was on the self in the present, utilizing one interesting technique, reported by Butler (1967), in which the elderly were asked to describe their mirror images.

Repeatedly, Oberleder stresses alternative interpretations of symptoms usually associated with organic decrements. The "crucial determinants" of the senility crisis, she reports, are unresolved conflicts of middle age.

Brief therapy, then, appears to be a realistic therapeutic answer for the elderly client who may come to counseling in crisis, without psychologic orientation or financial resources, and in need of environmental intervention. It appears to be workable with individuals and groups, and within a variety of therapeutic frameworks.

Supportive Therapy

Hollender (1952) asserts that defenses should not be challenged unless substitutes can be provided and that deep personality changes should not be attempted. If elderly individuals do not understand the counselor's interpretations of their emotional problems, the counselor should attempt to reduce stress and bolster defenses through reassurance, environmental manipulation, and direction.

Cath (1965) suggests therapy aimed at alleviation of depression or depletion to help the restitutive attempts of the ego. Rather, than a focus on neurotic traits and defenses, Cath believes therapy with the elderly should treat the individual's reaction to stress or the causative factor in depression and stress.

Most important in therapy with the elderly, Cath believes, is a significant relationship that will assist the patient's restorative potential. Support, reassurance, and clarification are more necessary with the elderly because decrements may interfere with memory, and because tolerance for insight varies.

The interpersonal relationship offered through supportive therapy may be more important to the elderly client than to any other group (Cath, 1965; Wolff, 1971).

Wolff (1971) believes healthy adjustment by the elderly depends on the strength of their belief that life is worthwhile. In therapy he emphasizes the idea that "good productive lives deserve gratitude." He adds that the counselor's task is to help elderly clients recognize that physical decline may be compensated for by placing more value on the cognitive and emotional aspects of life.

For Stotsky (1972), individual therapy with the aged must be supportive, and may be directive and issue-oriented. Major personality reconstructions are less important than aiding the client to cope with real life situations.

Accordingly, Zetzel (1965) posits that adjustment first requires mature, passive acceptance and resignation "of that which is both painful and inevitable." The adjustment that is not smooth cannot be alleviated by substitute activity (Reisman, 1954; Zetzel, 1965) and depends on the strength of inner resources that can be mustered.

Transference and Countertransference

Transference, like other phenomena in the psychological life of the elderly, appears to take on unique characteristics when the relationship involves an elderly member.

Older people tend to identify the counselor with a familiar other in order to better relate (Abraham, 1954; Butler, 1960; Kauf, 1955; and Zinberg, 1963). The counselor may represent images of both parent and child, although the elderly client's sensitive pride about one's own parental authority must be considered.

Safirstein (1972), who believes independent functioning is the best way to promote increased self-esteem, sees transference as a threat to functioning which should be prevented. However, transference is necessary to allow development of what Grotjahn (1955) calls the "revised oedipal constellation." In this transference neurosis, strong in the elderly, patients feel hostile toward the counselor, who represents the younger generation, and the future which has excluded them. Grotjahn suggests therapy may help patients realize that their lives may be continued in their progenies.

If, as Safirstein suggests, transference with a dependent elderly client may be "sticky," even stickier is the threat of countertransference. Negative countertransference is influenced by the counselor's repressed conflicts with parents (Meerloo, 1955); unresolved Oedipus complex (Wolff, 1971), negative stereotype of old age (Wolff, 1971)—and even doubt that successful treatment is possible.

Obviously, counselors should assess their own stereotypes and resolve relations to their parents before accepting elderly clients (Grotjahn, 1955; Wayne, 1953).

Learning Approach

Labouvie (1963) applies learning theory to gerontology with a firm hand. Relegating biological decrement to a minor role, she proposes a counseling model that identifies interaction of environment, experience, and behavior change in aging. This model recognizes individual cognitive differences in access to training; performance deficits as environmental deficits; and age deficiences as environmental deficiencies.

The model is easy to accept. But then what? It is difficult to understand how environmental manipulation can work outside an institutional setting. For "normal" people, environmental manipulation is beyond the purview of psychology, dipping into political and social power outside the realm of this paper.

It is hard to believe that Labouvie would accept the other realistic possibility, occupational therapy or programmed leisure.

Another view of the interaction between the elderly individual and the environment is expressed by Hoyer (1973), who agrees that behavioral deficits can be viewed as modifiable environmental deficiencies. Hoyer offers an answer: operant conditioning. This approach offers the promise of establishing desired behavior, eliminating destructive behavior, and suggests immediate change. However, it does not offer depth. In his discussion of behavior change through modification of environmental contingencies, Hoyer admits uses of the operant approach with the elderly have been in institutions, offering the familiar example of token economy.

Although the concept is academically sound, Hoyer simply does not present a convincing method of operationalizing it. Instead, we are reduced to suggestions for self-reinforcement: a band-aid on the wound of self-esteem. Hoyer is probably closer to the mark when he suggests the use of an operant approach earlier in life to assure successful aging. Or, better yet, application of an operant approach to focus on the younger generation who control the status of the aged.

Milieu Therapy

When attempts are made to change behavior of the elderly by altering institutional environments, results have been successful (Bluestein, 1960; Williams, et al., 1970; and Wolff, 1971). Milieu therapy is based on the theory that maladaptive behavior is a direct response to opportunities in expectations from the environment, and that individuals will be unequally affected by environmental changes (Wolff, 1971). The goal of milieu therapy is to help each patient to an optimal level of physical, social and psychological usefulness.

This approach, which can be criticized by professionals as too simplistic, should not be entirely dismissed. Its "psychological usefulness" has been documented (Wolff, 1957). Reported results include gains in self-esteem, ego-strength, acceptable expression of aggressive drives, socialization, memory, and concentration (Gottesman, 1973; Mason, 1965; and Wolff, 1971).

In some instances (Bluestein, 1960; Mason, 1965; Winick, 1967; and Gottesman, 1973), patients have been trained to be productively useful and to accept responsibility for money management. This reportedly leads to increased self-confidence, security, and responsibility.

This mode is directed to institutionalized aged and is limited by the control needed to alter environments. It may be limited by its own artificial nature. Wolff (1971) reports a control group treated by milieu relapsed after treatment terminated. At this time, this modality appears suitable for enlightened institutions.

Eclectic Action

We have seen that therapy with elderly clients is generally brief and calls for a more active counselor, whether its theoretical basis is toward insight or action. Some forms of action therapy are difficult to categorize because they use multi-disciplinary team approaches, incorporating group and individual therapy.

Modified behavior therapy with hospitalized elderly patients using team approaches with recreation, occupational, physical, and psychological therapy is reported by Bluestein (1960) and

Donahue, et al. (1960). Reported results show the elderly can be helped back to higher levels of physical and personal independence.

Another team approach, "psychiatric management," is particularly well-suited for the elderly who deny the need for help. The focus here is on reality, rather than insight; on promoting the ability to function in the real world, and is based on the premise that most disturbances of the elderly are transitory. Partial regression produced by drugs or electroshock therapy may be used to protect against anxiety. With a goal of providing massive reassurance while restoring the patient's defenses, this model may require the counselor to visit the elderly at home, often bringing small gifts to fortify dependency needs. The counselor is required to be continuously available.

One manipulative therapy attempts to change the elderly individual's environment by changing attitudes of the family (Sheps, 1959). This model recognizes alterations in social roles that take place in the family as the elderly individual becomes sick and helpless, and posits that fear in the elderly results when they are not relieved of responsibility by their children.

The counselor encourages children to admit helplessness of their parents, to give up the illusion of parents as magical and powerful, and to accept role reversal; thereby gratifying dependency needs of elderly parents without guilt or anger.

This model appears practical for families of helpless, dependent elderly individuals, but at the same time relegates the elderly to a powerless role, ignoring their needs for power as identified by Ginzberg (1955) and Goldfarb (1955). Its use appears to be limited to families of the institutionalized elderly who are severely incapacitated.

Peterson (1973) also suggests work in family therapy with the elderly, but Stotsky (1972) warns that this modality as a therapeutic device can produce disorganization and pain by dredging up family problems and conflicts, inviting "three-generational acting out" as well as unresolved parental hostility on the part of the counselor.

Attitude therapy (Ginzberg, 1955) includes elements of reality therapy and milieu therapy in its goal of manipulating factors in the elderly individual's environment which influences behavior to satisfy emotional needs. It uses the individual's adaptive abilities and assumes the elderly have a need to manage.

This model is based on the belief that many elderly individuals face the greatest threat of their lives when they recognize the effect of physical and mental decrement on their behavior. As they unsuccessfully seek help from the environment, they lose contact with reality. As a result, they experience anxiety, panic and finally psychosis.

Group Modality

Group therapy may be the preferred modality for elderly patients (Green, 1965; Liederman, 1965; Stotsky, 1972; Wolff, 1957). The group itself offers resocialization, an important step out of the terrifying isolation of old age (Liederman & Green, 1965; Wolff, 1957). Being with others in the group stimulates thinking (Wolff, 1957) and keeps the elderly alert to current events (Stotsky, 1972).

In a group, variety of choice makes transference and interpersonal relationships easier, curbs dependency and promotes conversation (Wolff, 1957). The group can serve both as an outlet for aggression and as an aid in impulse control. Intragroup criticism decreases hostility and delusional ideation (Wolff, 1957). Talk in the group may focus on the past, religion, politics, physical symptoms, and narcissisitic preoccupations (Wolff, 1957; Stotsky, 1972).

Group therapy for elderly psychotic patients is effective if, rather than personal restructure, "realistic" goals such as improved communication and remotivation are set (Yalom & Terrazas, 1968; Wolff, 1971). In addition to realistic goals, Yalom and Terrazas suggest reducing patient isolation and focusing on ego enhancing aspects and patient similarities. Group cohesiveness should be encouraged to help patients reduce dependency and assume responsibility.

Success and practicality of group approaches have been repeated in the literature with a variety of populations of elderly subjects. Yet, one question has not been answered: how will group identity, proven to be a successful component in ameliorating detachment and depression, carry over into the elderly individual's usually disadvantaged and lonely life after one leaves the group? It seems possible that the stress of coping with existence as an elderly person may threaten improvements which follow group counseling.

Perhaps one answer may be peer counseling. In one program (Waters, Fink & White, 1975), the modeling effect of elderly leaders for increasing effectiveness outside— as well as within—the group is reported.

SUMMARY

The literature suggests that therapy with the elderly may be most successful if sessions are brief, the counselor is active, home visits are included, and a group modality is used. It may be that variables such as sex, education, ethnicity, and life patterns of socialization are important considerations in therapy. Research has not been done to verify the point.

In general, counselors with elderly clients may expect to be met with a crisis situation and a client who is unfamiliar with therapy. The client may have to deal with agencies and other professionals, as well as family members. Counselors should be alert to physical decrements, both as they affect clients, and as they mask and precede psychological problems. Counselors must be aware of the importance the interpersonal relationship represents to lonely clients, as well as the positive and negative aspects of transference and countertransference.

In addition to reviewing models used in counseling the elderly, this chapter has attempted to mention some techniques which may be effective: home visits, the importance of body contact, the need to be active and suggestive, and the possibility that counseling sessions should be shortened.

It seems important to note some things that were *not* mentioned in the literature. Although the literature in therapy with minorities stresses the importance of understanding clients in a historical and cultural context, the literature on therapy with elderly clients does not. This author considers this a serious omission, and posits that understanding should not be assumed on the basis of ethnic or socioeconomic similarity. Values, attitudes, and norms vary among age cohorts. It is important for counselors to understand and respect the background that helped form their clients, and behavioral expressions of that background.

REFERENCES

Abraham, K. *On character and libido development*. D. Bryan & A. Strachey (Eds. & Trans.). New York: W.W. Norton & Company, Inc., 1966.

Abraham, K. The applicability of psycho-analytic treatment of patients at an advanced age. In B. Bryan & M. Stratchey (Eds. and Trans.), *Selected papers of Carl Abraham*. New York: Basic Books, Inc., 1954.

Bellak, L., & Small, L. *Emergency psychotherapy and brief psychotherapy*. New York: Grune and Stratten, 1965.

Berezin, M.A. Introduction. In M.A. Berezin & S.H. Cath (Eds.), *Geriatric Psychiatry*. New York: International Universities Press, Inc., 1965.

Berezin, M.A. Some intrapsychic aspects of aging. In N.E. Zimberg & I. Kaufman (Eds.), *Normal psychology of the aging process*. New York: International Universities Press, Inc., 1963.

Birren, J. Reactions to loss and the process of aging: Interrelations of environmental changes, psychological capacities, and physiological status. In M.A. Berezin & S.H. Cath (Eds.), *Geriatric psychiatry*. New York: International Universities Press, Inc., 1965.

Blustein, H. A rehabilitation program for geriatric patients. *Journal of the American Geriatrics Society*, , 1960, 8, 204-209.

Busse, E.W.; Barnes, R.H.; Silverman, A.J.; Thaler, M.; & Frost, L.L. Studies of the processes of aging: The strengths and weaknesses of psychic functioning in the aged. *American Journal of Psychiatry*, 1955, 111, 896-903.

Butler, R.N. Psychiatry and the elderly: An overview. *American Journal of Psychiatry*, 1975, 132, 893-898.

Butler, R.N. Research and clinical observations on the psychologic reactions to physical changes with age. *Mayo Clinic Proceedings*, 1967, 42, 596-619.

Cath, S.H. Some dynamics of middle and later years: A study in depletion and restitution and discussion. In M.A. Berezin & S.H. Cath (Eds.), *Geriatric psychiatry*. New York: International Universities Press, Inc., 1965.

Cutner, M. Analysis in later life. *British Journal of Medical Psychology*, 1950, 23, 75-86.

Donahue, W.; Hunter, W.W.; Coons, D.; & Maurice, H. Rehabilitation of geriatric patients in county hospitals. *Geriatrics*, 1960, 15, 263-274.

Freud, S. On psychotherapy. *Collected papers: Volume I.* London: Hograth Press, Ltd., 1924.

Ginzberg, R. Attitude therapy in geriatric ward psychiatry. *Journal of the American Geriatric Society*, 1955, 3, 455-462.

Goldfarb, A.I. A psychosocial and sociophysiological approach to aging. In N.E. Zimberg & I. Kaufman (Eds.), *Normal psychology of the aging process.* New York: International Universities Press, Inc., 1963.

Goldfarb, A.I. Psychotherapy of aged persons. *Psychoanalytic Psychotherapy Review*, 1955, 42, 180-187.

Grotjahn, M. Analytic psychotherapy with the elderly. *Psychoanalytic Psychotherapy Review*, 1955, 42, 419-427.

Gruen, A. Old age as a factor in motivation for therapy. *International Journal of Social Psychiatry*, 1957, 3, 61-66.

Hollender, M.H. Individualizing the aged. *Social Casework*, 1952, 33, 337-342.

Hoyer, W.J. Application of operant techniques to the modification of elderly behavior. *Gerontologist,* 1973, 13, 18-22.

Labouvie, G. Implications of geropsychological theories for intervention: The challenge of the seventies. *Gerontologist*, 1973, 13, 10-14.

Levin, S. Depression in the aged. In M.A. Berezin & S.A. Cath (Eds.), *Geriatric psychiatry.* New York: International Universities Press, Inc., 1965.

Liederman, P.C., & Green, R. Geriatric outpatient group therapy. *Comprehensive Psychiatry*, 1965, 6, 51-60.

Looft, W.R. Reflections on intervention in old age: Motives, goals and assumptions. *Gerontologist,* 1973, 13, 6-10.

Mason, A.S. The hospital service clinic: A work modality for the geriatric mental patient. *Journal of the American Geriatric Society*, 1965, 13, 545-549.

Meerloo, J.A.M. Psychotherapy in elderly people. *Geriatrics*, 1955, 10, 583-587.

Meerloo, J.A.M. Transference and resistance in geriatric psychotherapy. *Psychoanalytic Review,* 1955, 42, 78-82.

Meerloo, J.A.M. Modes of psychotherapy in the aged. *Journal of the American Geriatric Society*, 1961, 9, 225-234.

Oberleder, M. Crisis therapy in mental breakdown of the aging. *Gerontologist*, 1970, 10, 111-114.

Peterson, J.A. Marital and family therapy involving the aged. *Gerontologist*, 1973, 13, 27-31.

Reisman, D. Some clinical and cultural aspects of aging. *American Journal of Sociology*, 1954, 59, 379-383.

Rochlin, G. Discussions. In M.A. Berezin & S.H. Cath (Eds.), *Geriatric psychiatry*. New York: International Universities Press, Inc., 1965.

Safirstein, S.L. Psychotherapy of geriatric patients. *New York State Journal of Medicine*, 1972, November 15, 2743-2748.

Sheps, J. New developments in family diagnosis in emotional disorders of old age. *Geriatrics*, 1959, 14, 443-449.

Stotsky, B.A. Social and clinical issues in geriatric psychiatry. *American Journal of Psychiatry,* 1972, 129, 31-40.

Wallen, V. Motivation therapy with the aging geriatric veteran patient. *Military Medicine,* 1970, 135, 1007-1010.

Waters, E.; Fink, S.; & White, B. *Peer group counseling for older people.* Paper presented at the 83rd Annual Convention of the American Psychological Association, Chicago: September 3, 1975.

Wayne, G.J. Modified psychoanalytic therapy in senescence. *Psychiatric Review*, 1953, 40, 99-116.

Weinburg, J. Environment, its language and the aging. *Journal of the American Geriatrics Society*, 1970, 18, 681-686.

Williams, J.R.; Kriauciunas, R.; & Rodriguez, A. Physical, mental, and social rehabilitation for elderly and infirm patients. *Hospital and Community Psychiatry,* 1970, April 42-44.

Winick, W. *Industry in the hospital: Mental rehabilitation through work*. Springfield, Illinois: Charles C. Thomas, 1967.

Wolff, K. Group psychotherapy with geriatric patients of a mental hospital. *Journal of the American Geriatrics Society*, 1957, 5, 13-19.

Wolff, K. Rehabilitating geriatric patients. *Hospital and Community Psychiatry*, 1971, January, 24-27.

Wolff, K. Individual psychotherapy with geriatric patients. *Psychosomatics*, 1971, 12, 89-93.

Yalom, I.D., & Terrazas, F. Group therapy for psychotic elderly patients. *American Journal of Nursing*, 1968, 68, 1690-1694.

Zetzel, E.R. Dynamics of the metapsychology of the aging process. In M.A. Berezin & S.H. Cath (Eds.), *Geriatric psychiatry*. New York: International Universities Press, Inc., 1965.

Zimberg, S. The psychiatrist and medical home care. *American Journal of Psychiatry,* 1971, 127, 102-106.

Zinberg, N.E. Introduction, and, Special problems of gerontological psychiatry. In M.A. Berezin & S.H. Cath (Eds.), *Geriatric psychiatry.* New York: International Universities Press, Inc., 1965.

Zinberg, N.E., & Kaufman, I. Cultural and personality factors associated with aging: An introduction. In N.E. Zinberg & I. Kaufman (Eds.), *Normal psychology of the aging process.* New York: International Universities Press, Inc., 1963.

Working with Minority Elderly: A Training Program

Judy H. Katz
Kristin Sheridan Libbee

ABSTRACT

Volunteers and paraprofessionals are an important part of agencies providing services to the elderly. Like all personnel, however, these persons must be trained to meet the special needs of their clientele. This chapter outlines a three-hour workshop designed to train volunteers and paraprofessionals to better meet the needs of minority elderly. The workshop goes beyond raising awareness to incorporating cognitive, affective, and behavioral strategies which enable participants to focus on cultural differences and the need for personal and institutional change.

INTRODUCTION

Twenty-two million Americans donate their time, energy, and talents to volunteer services. Many others provide important services for a minimal wage, finding part of their recompense in the satisfaction of making a vital contribution to others (Hestir, 1976). One area that has benefited from the use of such personnel is that of supplying services to the elderly. Volunteers, as well as paraprofessionals and full-time staff, perform in such capacities as outreach workers, senior citizen center staff, and service coordinators. The use of such personnel has many advantages. Properly trained volunteers are able to extend agency services, work as part of a service team, and perform many social services activities. The use of volunteers has also been found to be a dependable, cost effective, and efficient use of person-power (McCaslin, 1976).

Volunteers bring many skills to the community agency. Yet any agency has needs and knowledge unique to itself; it is essential that all personnel receive specialized training. The elderly community has a variety of specialized needs which are important for the volunteer to understand and respond to, particularly those pertaining to transportation, nutrition, housing, physical health, legal assistance, and feelings of separation, grief, and loneliness. Volunteers need information about where services are available through community, state, and federal programs. They can benefit as well from training in communication and listening skills which will help them disseminate information, act as effective advocates for the elderly, and provide counseling on a paraprofessional basis.

Volunteers also need training in addressing specialized concerns of particular subgroups of the elderly. One group of the elderly with specialized concerns are minority elderly (Mosley, 1977). Even more than their younger counterparts, minority elderly are often overlooked and ignored. Nor do dimensions of poverty that plague minorities in the U.S. cease as the minority population ages. Often isolated by virtue of their age, minority elderly are further isolated by virtue of their race.

Many of these elderly persons suffer triple jeopardy in that they are old, minority, and female. Yet often available agency services still do not filter into the minority community. Thus problems of poverty, malnutrition, substandard housing, high crime rates, and poor health affect a greater portion of the minority elderly population than of their white counterparts (Smith, Burlew, Mosley & Whitney, 1978). Moreover, when minority elderly do seek counseling or special services, they often encounter difficulties. Minority elderly persons seeking special services may find themselves dealing with a younger, white, middle class helper.

Many such helpers are not aware of important cultural differences: verbal and nonverbal communication, value systems, and world views (Vontress, 1976). In order to avoid misunderstanding and mistrust, particular attention must be paid to training helpers to work effectively with minority elderly. This article describes a training program designed to help volunteers and paraprofessionals work more effectively in meeting the needs of minority elderly in the state of Oklahoma.

Oklahoma has a special concern for the problems faced by the elderly: it is one of nine states in the U.S. with an especially high proportion of elderly citizens (U.S. Government, 1976). A substantial percentage of Oklahoma's elderly population are minority. Yet as is the case in most agencies, the majority of the people providing services to these minority elderly are white. The training program described here was implemented with largely white volunteers and paraprofessionals who work with Oklahoma's Areawide Agency on Aging. The authors facilitated this workshop on several occasions with about thirty participants in each session.

One constraint in training volunteers and paraprofessionals is that training time is generally limited. Given the broad range of areas that must be covered and the fact that most often volunteers are on the job, trainers are faced with very limited parameters. Although a 1 to 2 day workshop would be optimal, th reality is usually a 2 to 3 hour time frame. This training program was developed within that time frame.

THE TRAINING PROGRAM

Goals and Assumptions

A workshop designed under such severe time constraints immediately raises the question of what goals to choose. One vital goal is developing an awareness of issues concerning minority elderly. Yet without practical skills, raising awareness only produces what has been referred to as "more knowledgeable racists" (Katz, 1978). Therefore, an equally important goal is to develop some skills for responding to the needs of minority elderly. These are indeed ambitious goals, but the authors feel strongly that a meaningful training workshop deals with these goals in combination, not in isolation.

This workshop is also based on several assumptions. The primary assumption is that every person has cultural constructs which both shape that person's perspective and partially determine how that person sees the world and interacts with others. Secondly, it is assumed that these cultural constructs are implicit and largely out-of-awareness. To recognize them and make them explicit, thus introducing the possibility of reassessment and change, produces a more effective helper. A third important assumption is that most people have given little thought, time, or concern to the needs of minority elderly. Therefore, even a short workshop can have an impact. The final assumption forming the basis of this experience is that prejudice runs deep; it cannot be eradicated in a three-hour (or even 45-hour) workshop.

Content

The workshop utilizes a combination of mini-lectures, role plays, and small group work. The lectures are designed to present a conceptual base, the role play to relate that conceptual base to the participants' work experience, the small group work to generate alternative behaviors, and practical skills to apply to the work setting.

As a preface to the first mini-lecture, participants are asked to brainstorm as a large group some of the critical factors which influence one's world view and thus one's effectiveness in working with minority elderly. Some examples of elements often identified by participants are: family background, education, religion, significant others, experiences, ethnic heritage, stereotypes, and prejudices. This response is characteristic of workshops dealing with race: as soon as trainers begin to address differences and difficulties, white participants begin to deny them.

This denial process will continue with many participants throughout the workshop, and each step in the workshop process is designed to investigate it. However, the denial is not strongly confronted. The trainers assume that defenses are broken down slowly. Permitting participants some defenses allows them to continue to participate in a threatening experience. Hopefully the experience sows some seeds for future consideration and future training sessions.

The first mini-lecture addresses Denton Roberts' (1975) concept of cultural scripts. According to Roberts, an individual is comprised of seven boundaries: personal, sexual/gender, family, racial, provincial, socioeconomic, and cultural. The lecture stresses the importance of dealing with each of these areas in order to understand and work effectively with others.

For the purpose of this workshop, and also as a way of addressing the issue of denial, the lecture focuses particularly on the racial boundary and the importance of identifying the components of one's racial identity. Participants are invited to contribute some messages they may have internalized or some experiences they think resulted from their racial identities. It is the lecturer's task to integrate these contributions meaningfully. Nevertheless, it is important for participants to take as much ownership of their own racial identities as early as possible in the training session.

With this background, participants are then asked to individually brainstorm a list of factors in themselves, their environments, and their agencies which help and hinder their effectiveness in working with minority elderly. These individual lists are then shared in small groups. Common themes are identified and reported to the large group by a spokesperson chosen by each small group. A second brief lecture then synthesizes the findings of the small groups, identifies commonalities, and explores the implications for working with the minority elderly.

Participants are invited to become involved in the process of identifying common detrimental attitudes, examining possible effects of these attitudes, and generating more helpful attitudes. As a feedback device, trainers use results of this session to generate a chart which is later mailed to workshop participants or their agencies. The chart is intended to serve as a workshop follow-up, reminding participants of what they learned and of their own abilities to identify and make needed changes. An example of a chart that resulted from one workshop is presented in Figure 1.

Figure 1
WORKING WITH MINORITY ELDERLY

Attitudes that may not be helpful in working with minority elderly.	Possible effects of that attitude on your effectiveness.	Attitudes that are more likely to be effective in working with minority elderly.
1. Color is unimportant—we're all the same under the skin.	Disregards the important part of a person's identity and experiences.	Recognize and appreciate differences in culture and race.
2. A member of one ethnic group can understand what it means to be a member of another ethnic group. (Learning from school books, courses, television, religious teachings, etc. may be helpful in better understanding others but does not teach everything.)	Blinds people from seeing areas that they need to learn about other racial/ethnic groups.	Recognize that no matter what level of awareness you may have, there is still more to learn. Be open to learning. Don't wait to be told—ask!
3. Minority elderly have the same needs and preferences as white elderly (e.g., they like the same music, read the same magazines, are interested in the same activities).	Minority elderly would be reluctant to come to Senior Citizens' Centers.	Recognize that the needs of minority elderly may be different from white elderly. Solicit input from minority elderly in developing Senior Citizens' Center programs.
4. All people of an ethnic/racial group are alike in their attitudes and concerns.	Generalizes, stereotypes, and boxes minority elderly. Ignores individual differences.	Minorities are human—with individual needs, feelings, aspirations, and attitudes.
5. I know what is best for the elderly, including minority elderly (e.g., telling a black woman that it is not good for her to stay home and watch soap operas).	Makes minority elderly defensive and feel alienated. May induce anger. No one will accept help when told it is for their "own good" or decided upon by someone else.	Be a resource person to minority elderly persons—not a savior. See yourself as being there to help serve the person's needs. Mutually define what those needs are.
6. I'm perfectly trustworthy, sincere, and committed to my job. Minority elderly should recognize that.	This attitude has no effect on dissolving the distrust that may exist because of cultural conditioning. Puts distrust on a personal level rather than on a cultural level.	Awareness that distrust may not be personally directed. Recognize that distrust may be legitimate. Take risks to confront distrust and be committed to working on it with the other person.

Following a ten minute break, two volunteers perform a role play in front of a large group (See Figure 2). Participants are given an observation sheet prior to the role play to help them focus on items of concern. Specifically, the worksheet instructs participants to look for behaviors that help and hinder communication on the part of the outreach worker and to examine both spoken and unspoken concerns of the client. In small groups, participants consider dynamics they have observed and address alternative behaviors both for role play participants and for themselves in their own settings.

The purpose of this exercise is to move participants from examining theories and attitudes to examining concrete behavioral data and operationally defining alternative behaviors. This process provides a critical link between talking about the problem and moving toward action. After each group reports its findings, a brief wrap-up emphasizes the importance of implementing the behaviors outlined by individuals in their small groups.

Figure Two

ROLE PLAY

OUTREACH WORKER:

You are a white female outreach worker who is making a home visit to a Black female senior citizen, age 70. You would like her to get out more and come to the Senior Citizen Center. Your task is to encourage/persuade her to come down to the center. Approach this in the best way you know how.

SENIOR CITIZEN:

You are a Black female, age 70. You are leery and concerned about going down to the Senior Citizen Center, although you would like to get out of the house more. Some of your concerns include:

1. Whether other minorities are there.

2. What type of activities go on; are they all geared to the White Culture?

3. Attitude of white outreach; can I trust her?

4. Family pressure not to go to White Senior Citizen Center.

5. Transportation.

Evaluation

A standard evaluation tool has been administered following all workshops. The results of evaluations have indicated a positive response from participants. However, no behavioral measures have been utilized, and thus no conclusions can be drawn concerning the "back-home" effectiveness of the workshop. Nevertheless, it is important to examine the kinds of responses which have been elicited in participants and their implications for more effective helping of minority elderly.

Perhaps the most important accomplishment of this workshop is an acceptance by participants of color as a basic issue. While color has long been a political issue, many white people have been taught on the interpersonal level not to recognize racial differences. This workshop breaks the norm. It helps participants to recognize and view racial differences in a positive way.

Counseling for the Growing Years

Thus participants move from denial of the relevance of differing cultural perspectives to an initial understanding of the role and impact of race in individuals' lives.

Once this awareness occurs, participants are able to examine the ways their own behavior fails to reflect this recognition and to eventually change their behavior so that they act from a more culturally aware basis. Participants also become aware that they have limited ability, as non-minorities, to meet the needs of minority elderly. The need for volunteers of all racial groups then becomes apparent.

Conclusion and Implications

A workshop conducted in such a limited time frame can fall prey to two errors. The first is that because the issue of cultural differences is being addressed in such a short time, the workshop is only a token attempt and thus of little value. The second is that because so much must be addressed in dealing with cultural differences, it is hopeless to try to do anything in a three hour workshop. Yet what has been remarkable about this workshop is that such a brief experience stimulates much discussion, energy, and examination. examiniation. Obviously, it could be used as a foundation for a longer experience.

A longer time frame could address a wider variety of issues in greater depth, evaluate and provide feedback on back-home performance, and provide support for implementing changes within agencies. Yet, this workshop combines affective, cognitive, and behavioral goals and strategies to address fundamental issues in working with minority elderly. Its focus is awareness and action—both important components of meeting needs of minority elderly.

REFERENCES

Hestir, L. **Texas** Volunteer Workshop, Joe C. Thompson Center proceedings. Austin, Texas, 1976.

Katz, J. *White awareness: Handbook for anti-racism training.* Norman: University of Oklahoma, 1978.

McCaslin, R. *The older person as a mental health worker.* Texas Research Institute of Mental Sciences, Houston, Texas, 1976.

Mosley, J. **Problems** of the aged. *Journal of Nonwhite Concerns,* 1977, 6 (1), 11-16.

Roberts, D. The treatment of cultural scripts. *Transactional Analysis Journal,* 1975, 5 (1), 29, 31, 35.

Smith, W.; Burlew, A.; Mosley, M.; & Whitney, W. *Minority issues in mental health.* Reading, Massachusetts: Addison Wesley, 1978, pp. 57-64.

Vontress, C. Counseling middle-aged and aging cultural minorities. *Personnel and Guidance Journal,* 1976, 55 (3), 132-135.

U.S. Government. *Facts about older Americans.* Washington, D.C.: U.S. Government Printing Office, 1976. (pamphlet)

Appendix A

Bibliography: Aging

Compiled by:

Helen S. Panje

Books

Atchley, R.G. *The social forces in later life: An introduction to social gerontology* (2nd edition). Belmont, California: Wadsworth, 1977.

Bengtson, V.L. *Intergenerational relations and aging: A selected bibliography.* Los Angeles: E.P. Andrus Gerontological Center, 1975.

Birren, J.E., & Schaie, K.W. *Handbook of the psychology of aging.* New York: Van Nostrand Reinhold, 1977.

Daltan, N., & Ginsberg, L.H. (Eds.). *Life-span developmental psychology: Normative life crisis.* New York: Academic Press, 1975.

Fischer, D.H. *Growing old in America.* New York: Oxford University Press, 1977.

Harris, L., & Associates, Inc. *The myth and reality of aging in America.* Washington, D.C.: National Council on the Aging, 1975.

Kalish, R.A. *Late adulthood: Perspectives of human development.* Monterey, California: Brooks/Cole Publishing, 1975.

Kart, C.S., & Manard, B.B. *Aging in America.* Southern Oaks, California: Alfred Publishing Company, 1976.

Seltzer, M.; Corbett, S.; & Atchley, R. *Social problems of the aging.* Belmont, California: Wadsworth, 1978.

Journal Articles

Ansello, E.F. Ageism—the subtle stereotype. *Childhood Education,* 1978, 54, 118-122.

Back, E.W. Transition to aging and the self-image. *Aging and Human Development,* 1971, 2, 296-304.

Becker, H.S. Personal change in adult life. *Sociometry,* 1964, 27, 40-53.

Bengtson, V.L. Inter-age perceptions and the generation gap. *Gerontologist,* 1971, 11, 85-86.

Borges, M.A., & Dutton, L.J. Attitudes toward aging: Increasing optimism found with age. *Gerontology.* 1976, 16, 220-224.

Francher, J.S. It's the Pepsi generation. . . Accelerated aging and the television commercial. *International Journal of Aging and Human Development,* 1973, 4, 245-255.

Gubrium, J.F. Being single in old age. *International Journal of Aging and Human Development,* 1975, 6, 29-41.

Kilty, K.M., & Field, A. Attitudes towards the aging and toward the needs of older people. *Journal of Gerontology,* 1976, 31, 586-594.

Lawrence, J.H. The effect of perceived age on initial impressions and normative role expectations. *International Journal on Aging and Human Development,* 1975, 5, 369-391.

McTavish, D.G. Perceptions of older people: A review of research methodologies and findings. *Gerontologist,* 1971, 11, 90-101.

Schonfield, D. Family life education study: The later adult years. *Gerontologist,* 1970, 10, 115-118.

Seltzer, M.M. Differential impact of various experiences on breaking age stereotypes. *Educational Gerontology,* 1977, 2, 183-189.

Seltzer, M.M., & Atchley, R.C. The concept of old: Changing attitudes and stereotypes. *Gerontologist,* 1971, 11, 226-230.

Thomas, E.C., & Yamamoto, K. Attitudes towards age: An exploration in school age children. *International Journal of Aging and Human Development,* 1975, 6, 117-129.

Thorson, J.; Whatley, L.; & Hancock, K. Attitudes toward the aged as a funciton of age and education. *Gerontologist,* 1974, 14, 316-318.

Appendix B

Information for Educators on Aging

Compiled by:

Helen S. Panje

Community Sources

Senior Citizens Center, Senior Information and Referral Service and Senior Centers, both private and publicly sponsored.

Local offices of Social Security Administration, Retired Senior Volunteer Program, American Association of Retired Persons, Area Agency on Aging.

Retirement communities, retirement homes, convalescent hospitals.

Community Mental Health Association and Family Service Association.

Department of Gerontology studies in the local community colleges, four-year colleges and universities.

National Sources

Senate Special Committee on Aging, G-225 Senate Office Building, Washington, D.C. 20510.

ACTION (Coordinates volunteer programs involving older persons) 806 Connecticut Avenue, N.W., Washington, D.C. 20201.

Administration on Aging, Department of Health, Education and Welfare, Office of Human Development, Washington, D.C. 20201.

Social Security Administration, 6401 Security Building, Baltimore, Maryland 21235.

American Association of Retired Persons, 1909 "K" Street, N.W., Washington, D.C. 20006.

American Public Welfare Assocation, 1313 East 60th Street, Chicago, Illinois 60637.

Gerontological Society, One Dupont Circle, N.W., Washington, D.C. 20036.

Gray Panthers, 3700 Chestnut Street, Philadelphia, Pennsylvania 19104.

National Center for Voluntary Action, 1625 Massachusetts Avenue, N.W., Washington, D.C. 20006.

National Council of Senior Citizens, 1511 "K" Street, N.W., Washington, D.C. 20005.

National Council on the Aging, 1828 "L" Street, N.W., Washington, D.C. 20036.

Miscellaneous Resources

SERVE (Community Service Society of New York) Committee on Aging, 105 East 22nd Street, New York, New York 10010.

RSVP (Retired Senior Volunteer Program), 14 South Perry Street, Rockville, Maryland 20850.

National School Volunteer Program, 300 North Washington Street, Alexandria, Virgnia 22314.

NOW Task Force on Older Women, 6422 Telegraph Avenue, Oakland, California 95609.

International Senior Citizens Association, 11753 Wilshire Boulevard, Los Angeles, California 90025.

Ethel Percy Andrus Gerontology Center, University of Southern California, University Park, Los Angeles, California 90007.

Iowa Gerontology Project, Oakdale Hospital, University of Iowa, Oakdale, Iowa 52319.

New England Gerontology Center, New England Center for Continuing Education, 15 Garrison Avenue, Durham, New Hampshire 03824.